PUBLIC MONEY, PRIVATE AGENDA

A. Surya Prakash is an author, columnist and distinguished fellow at the Vivekananda International Foundation. He has held several important editorial positions in media organizations in India. He was Editor, Zee News; India Editor, *Asia Times*; and Executive Editor, *The Pioneer*. His columns appear in *The Pioneer, Dainik Jagran, Eenadu* and *Samyukta Karnataka*. He is also the author of *What Ails Indian Parliament*. He was awarded a D.Litt by Tumkur University for his work on parliamentary institutions, including this thesis on MPLADS. He lives in Gurgaon, Haryana, with his wife, Pushpa Girimaji, a consumer rights columnist. They have a son, Ujwal Arkalgud.

PUBLIC MONEY, PRIVATE AGENDA
THE USE AND ABUSE OF MPLADS

A. SURYA PRAKASH

RUPA

Published by
Rupa Publications India Pvt. Ltd 2013
7/16, Ansari Road, Daryaganj
New Delhi 110002

Sales centres:
Allahabad Bengaluru Chennai
Hyderabad Jaipur Kathmandu
Kolkata Mumbai

Copyright © A. Surya Prakash 2013

All rights reserved.
No part of this publication may be reproduced, transmitted,
or stored in a retrieval system, in any form or by any means, electronic,
mechanical, photocopying, recording or otherwise,
without the prior permission of the publisher.

ISBN: 978-81-291-2417-3

10 9 8 7 6 5 4 3 2 1

The moral right of the author has been asserted.

Printed at Parksons Graphics Pvt. Ltd, Mumbai.

This book is sold subject to the condition that it shall not, by way of
trade or otherwise, be lent, resold, hired out, or otherwise circulated,
without the publisher's prior consent, in any form of binding or cover
other than that in which it is published.

Contents

Preface		*vii*
Introduction		1
1.	The Origin of MPLADS	10
2.	MPs Want More	27
3.	MPs Want Their Names 'Permanently' and 'Prominently' Etched in Stone	49
4.	One Rule, Many Exceptions!	68
5.	MPLADS and the 'Trust' Deficit	95
6.	MPLADS Makes Strange Bedfellows—MPs and Bureaucrats	110
7.	In Sickness and Health	133
8.	Cyclones, Earthquakes, Tsunamis and MPs	147
9.	Lok Sabha Committee vs Rajya Sabha Committee	162
10.	MPLADS and Corruption	168
11.	The Supreme Court on MPLADS	190
12.	The Comptroller and Auditor General on MPLADS	202
13.	What Independent Surveys Say about MPLADS	251
14.	MPLADS and Accountability	260
Conclusion		276

Preface

The Members of Parliament Local Area Development Scheme (MPLADS) was launched twenty years ago in 1993. The scheme envisaged the creation of a fund which MPs could utilize for development projects in their constituencies. It began with an allocation of ₹1 crore per annum per MP. A few years later, the amount was increased to ₹2 crore and again in 2011 to ₹5 crore. Since its inception, MPLADS has been mired in controversy with many citizens questioning the rationale for such a scheme. The objections are many, ranging from the constitutional argument that it violates the principle of separation of powers between the legislature and the executive, to the argument that it has become yet another source of corruption. The scheme, however, has not only survived these protests, but has also seen a five-fold increase in its corpus. It has also got a stamp of approval from the Supreme Court. Since colossal sums of public money are spent every year on MPLADS, a need was felt for a comprehensive look at how the scheme had been implemented over the past two decades. This book is a modest attempt in this direction and it has been possible because of the Vivekananda International Foundation (VIF), New Delhi.

There are few institutions in India which fund research in the area of parliamentary studies; VIF is one of them and I am grateful to the foundation and its director, Mr Ajit Doval, for granting me a fellowship to undertake this study.

I also wish to thank Dr Makkhan Lal and Dr Anirban Ganguly of VIF and Mr R.C. Rajamani, Editorial Consultant, *The Statesman*, for their help at different stages of this project. Thanks are also due to Ms Elina Majumdar, Commissioning Editor, Rupa Publications India for her suggestions and patience; Mr S.K. Ray Chaudhuri, the copy editor whose sharp eye and experience has substantially enhanced the quality of the text; and Ms Kadambari Mishra, Senior Copy Editor, for transforming my manuscript into an elegant book. My niece, Choodie Shivaram, was of great help at the final stages of this project and I owe her a big thank you for setting aside her work to help me out.

Mr V. Kishore Chandra Deo, the Union Minister for Tribal Affairs and Panchayati Raj and one of India's senior-most parliamentarians deserves a special mention for the interest he has evinced in my studies relating to democratic institutions. My conversations with him helped create the framework for my first book—*What Ails Indian Parliament*. The present book, too, is a result of his valuable insights into the working of Indian MPs. I sincerely thank him for his interest and support.

Finally, a word about my wife, Pushpa Girimaji. Much of the credit for my academic pursuits and research goes to her and her belief that one must go beyond journalism if one wishes to add some value to the discourse on institutions and processes. I thank her for her love and encouragement.

Introduction

In the initial years after Independence, many scholars and parliamentarians from thinly populated Western democracies found it difficult to appreciate the social and political complexities that confront people's representatives in a country like India, which was overpopulated and underdeveloped, yet liberal and democratic. Barring scholars like Granville Austin and W.H. Morris-Jones, both of whom devoted several decades to the understanding of the working of India's Constitution and democratic bodies, most others, who have seen Western democracies at work, sought to mechanically apply alien standards and models to Indian parliamentarians and thereby judge India's tryst with democracy with a degree of harshness. The sceptics were often baffled by the commitment of millions of poor and dispossessed people to the democratic process that enabled them to regularly 'punish' elected representatives and political parties which failed to deliver on promises, prop up new parties and formations, and change governments. Some Indian scholars, too, shared this cynicism and felt that representative democracy was, as Dr B.R. Ambedkar, the architect of India's Constitution, had feared, nothing more than a 'top dressing' on a soil that was essentially undemocratic.

It is true that the parliamentary system that the country had adopted was essentially a 'Western' or unfamiliar system and that ab initio it looked as if there was a mismatch between this alien system and the complex socio-political reality of Indian society. Those who saw this mismatch alongside poverty and acute social and economic inequalities felt that this unreal marriage would fall apart quickly and India would lapse into dictatorship and anarchy like many other nations in the Asian region. But those who predicted the early demise of parliamentary democracy failed to factor in the critical role that a peculiar Indian trait, often described as jugaad, would play in ensuring the survival of this system of representative democracy. Jugaad is a non-typical solution to a problem or even a patchwork solution that ends a predicament for the moment but may not offer a permanent solution. Jugaad can mean different things to different people but the core idea that it represents is a hybridization of ideas that comes from quick, out-of-the-box thinking which results in making something work. For example, fitting a four-wheel trailer to a Royal Enfield motorcycle so as to have a low-cost vehicle to transport agricultural products to the market.

Such out-of-the-box thinking permeates every aspect of life in India and the parliamentary system is no exception. Those who have watched the British House of Commons at work from the public galleries will vouch for the fact that the restrained, regulated, dull and monotonous debates that are on in that chamber put most visitors and members to sleep. This House springs to life for just an hour every week during the prime minister's Question Time. The German Bundestag, true to German tradition, works like clockwork with such precision that it virtually eliminates the chances of surprise or non-completion of business on any given day. The Indian Parliament, on the other hand, is a study in contrast. In its two Houses—the Lok Sabha and the Rajya Sabha—members proceed on the assumption that rules are meant to be bent or broken. While the day's agenda is circulated in advance to members, Members of Parliament (MPs) have their own plans. Whatever be the official agenda for the day, the presiding officers have to contend with a hundred individual agendas which tend to disrupt the day's business and make the two Houses dysfunctional. For example, there are disaffected social groups in some part of the country or the other at any given time. There are also regular political battles among competing political parties in different states. Many MPs march into Parliament angrily every day to take up the cause of such social groups or to give vent to their anger over the activities of a rival political party. All this leads to disruptions and the noise and chaos of the Indian marketplace is sometimes reflected within these chambers.

Citizens from some of the older democracies would see the proceedings in the Indian Parliament to be a bit too animated for comfort. While some element of vitality is welcome, frequent disruption of proceedings, shouting matches between members in the treasury and Opposition benches and regular bouts of pandemonium can hardly ensure purposeful debate and serious lawmaking. But, as if by agreement, the MPs and the presiding officers of the two Houses ensure the peaceful coexistence of the functional and the dysfunctional.

A good example of parliamentary jugaad is the 'Zero Hour' in the Indian Parliament and its legitimization by presiding officers. On a normal day, the proceedings of the Lok Sabha begin with the Question Hour at 11 a.m. After Question Hour, the Speaker calls upon ministers and chairpersons of committees to table notifications and reports. Thereafter, the House discusses Call Attention Motions and such other business. Legislative business is taken up after the lunch break. However, all these plans go haywire because dozens of members, without any previous notice, use the interregnum between Question Hour and the next item of business—called the Zero Hour—to raise issues which they claim to be of utmost public importance, without notice. Since dozens of MPs come to the House with the sole intention of monopolizing this brief interlude, they try to out-shout each other, and things become so chaotic that the Speaker is often obliged to adjourn the House abruptly and walk away. Many Speakers have tried in vain to dissuade members from violating the rules and raising issues in this manner without notice and without permission. Eventually, the presiding officers have come to the conclusion that the chaos of the Zero Hour is inevitable and have decided to regularize and regulate it. So, MPs are advised to give notice of their intention to 'disrupt' proceedings, so that they could be called by the Speaker, one at a time. This way, the interruptions would no longer be proceedings in violation of the rules; they would get legitimized. Even this arrangement can go off-tangent at times, but the fact is that the Zero Hour has acquired a certain degree of legitimacy in the day's proceedings. The emergence of the Zero Hour can certainly be counted as an Indian Parliamentary jugaad.

There are many other aspects of parliamentary work that would fall in the same category, but the most significant jugaad is MPLADS—Members of Parliament Local Area Development Scheme. This scheme offers MPs an opportunity to utilize a fund to build projects and create durable assets in their constituencies. The scheme opened with an allocation of ₹1 crore a year per MP in 1993–94. The corpus was raised to ₹2 crore a year in 1998 and has since been enhanced to ₹5 crore a year from the fiscal year 2011–12. MPs pressed for the creation of such a fund because they felt stifled by the local bureaucracy whenever they tried to address the needs of their constituents. They wanted a separate fund which they could dip into to build community projects.

The yearning for executive power among Indian MPs can be traced to three factors:

- Loss of anonymity consequent to the delinking of elections to the Lok Sabha and the state assemblies in 1971.
- The perception among MPs that the bureaucracy is haughty and insensitive and disconnected from the large mass of people living below or just above the poverty line.
- The general view among parliamentarians that their political clout is measured not in terms of their

contribution to lawmaking and pursuit of national goals but in terms of the tangibles that they deliver in their constituencies. In other words, they believe that their ratings depend on what they directly 'give' to individuals and communities at the micro, that is, the constituency level and not on what they do at the macro, national level.

Each of these points needs elaboration:

Prime Minister Indira Gandhi's decision in 1971 to advance the Lok Sabha election ended the tradition of a general election held at five-year intervals to elect a new Lok Sabha and new assemblies in all the states. The elections to the Lok Sabha and the state assemblies were held simultaneously in 1952 (when these democratic bodies were constituted for the first time after the adoption of the Constitution), 1957, 1962 and 1967. The next general election was due in 1972, but Indira Gandhi decided to advance the Lok Sabha election by a year, thereby ending the tradition of simultaneous elections to Parliament and the state assemblies.

The delinking of the Lok Sabha election and the elections to state assemblies meant a sudden loss of anonymity for MPs. Until 1967, Lok Sabha candidates nominated by major political parties enjoyed a great deal of anonymity because the people were more focused on candidates to the state assembly, who were their immediate local representatives. This gave Lok Sabha candidates the luxury of riding piggyback on the party's candidates for the state assembly election, who were sweating it out during the campaign. Since Delhi was too distant, in the first score of years after the Constitution was adopted, the voters had little interest in the election to Parliament. They also had no idea of what an MP could do for them and this was another reason for the prevailing disinterest. Further, since the Lok Sabha candidates of major political parties were banking on the success of their party's state assembly aspirants, little was known of the potential MP. Voters only knew that they should stamp on the same symbol on the two ballot papers—for both the 'upper vote' and the 'lower vote'. The MP was therefore nothing more than the man or woman who got the 'upper vote'! After the election, the MP would head off to Delhi and participate in parliamentary debates, which were reported rather extensively in newspapers, but hardly read by the people because a majority of them were illiterate. So, the MP remained an unknown commodity.

However, all this changed in 1971 when candidates contesting the Lok Sabha election, advanced by a year, were forced to fend for themselves. They had to present themselves before voters, spend their own funds (and not ride on the campaign funds of the Members of Legislative Assemblies (MLAs), go on padayatras (processions on foot) and cycle processions, touch the feet of senior voters etc., while begging for votes. Since then, the MP is under the keen glare of voters and the constant refrain in most Lok Sabha constituencies is that the MP is not seen enough and that he is not doing enough for those who supported him. This is so because parliamentary constituencies in India are huge, both in geographical and demographical terms. In many constituencies, the distance from end to end can be over 200 kilometres. Also, as against an MP in the United Kingdom who represents about fifty thousand voters, an Indian MP represents anywhere between one to two million voters and therefore, keeping in touch with electors is a Herculean task.

Loss of anonymity has meant that the MP is constantly in public glare. He has to be seen 'giving' something to an individual or a community all the time. Merely being a good politician who works towards social cohesion and harmony in a district and for the overall development of the region is not enough. Such service is invaluable, yet in many ways intangible. People want deliverables that they can see and use—like a bus stand, a bridge, a computer centre or a school.

The pressure from 'down under'—the constituency—which began building up post-1971 was passed on to the government by MPs, forcing the former to make available concessions to them which they could palm off to their constituents. This began with the quota of domestic gas connections given to MPs. Since the waiting period for a domestic gas connection was anywhere up to five years, this became a valuable 'quota', specially when the government offered MPs one hundred gas coupons per year for distribution within their constituencies. Side by side, other quotas and concessions were established, including ten priority telephone connections per year to be recommended by each MP. This quota came into being during the socialist phase of our economic development when the telecommunications sector was a government monopoly. The government was not only the sole service-provider but also the sole manufacturer of telephone instruments. Given the lethargy of the government sector, the waiting period for a telephone connection in the 1970s and '80s was anywhere between five to eight years. MPs were also given the power to nominate two candidates for admission to central schools. Apart from these quotas, their recommendations worked in many other areas. This may sound laughable in this day and age, but MPs were given priority in allotment of cars and scooters during the licence-permit era when the waiting period for a car (the Ambassador or the Fiat) or scooter (Bajaj) was five years. Even more absurd was the shortage of wristwatches, of all things, and MPs had the priority to buy wristwatches made by the state-owned HMT. Readers who have grown up in an India which opened up its economy, may find it funny that one needed sifarish (a recommendation) to buy a wristwatch, but that is what the economic policies of the government did to the simple aspirations of the people! In addition, there were some other peculiar perks. For example, constituents could go to the office of the Reserve Bank of India and exchange old currency notes for new on an MP's recommendation.[1]

However, despite this basket of goodies, MPs felt that it did not amount to much. They needed something more substantial in their hands to satisfy their constituents. It was in this environment that the idea of MPLADS germinated. As stated earlier, MPLADS is a purely Indian innovation. It is a scheme that in many ways symbolizes the Indian mind, which is often capable of out-of-the-box thinking and novel solutions that may not occur to minds which are strictly conditioned to structured, linear thinking. Until MPLADS came on the scene, no one in the democratic world had found a way by which parliamentarians could breach the Lakshman rekha that strictly separates the legislature and the executive in the Westminster model. A constitutional thinker groomed in the Westminster tradition of separation of powers would find this development abhorrent and see this jugaad only in a pejorative sense. That may well be, but now that MPLADS is a reality, one need not be surprised if it were to be replicated in other democracies in the developing world.

The distrust of the civil servant is another major factor. Even though reservations for socially disadvantaged groups in higher education and in government jobs has enabled candidates from the underprivileged classes to make it to the central and state services, politicians as a class perceive the bureaucracy as a bunch of uncaring file pushers, which has frustrated all governmental efforts to tackle poverty and underdevelopment, especially in the countryside. They do not see a bureaucrat's class or caste as making any major difference to his approach to the problems of the less privileged. The common refrain is that they (the bureaucrats) are all the same.

Before the introduction of MPLADS, all that an MP could do if he saw merit in a project proposed by his constituents, was to dutifully endorse it to the district collector and hope that the official would agree with him and allocate some funds for the same. However, the chances of this happening were bleak because in India an MP and a district collector do not get along because one invariably thinks rather poorly of the other. Often district collectors see MPs as a bunch of corrupt and selfish persons who promote nepotism and favouritism and are ever ready to break rules and conventions in order to feather their own political nests. MPs reciprocate this sentiment because they often view district collectors as arrogant, selfish and conceited citizens and who, despite the anti-corruption façade, are as corrupt as politicians and the others in the administrative wings of the government. MPs say district collectors are so consumed by their sense of self-importance that they have no idea about people's aspirations. Therefore, MPs and district collectors certainly see one another as interlopers and constantly look over their shoulders to guard their turfs. MPLADS must be seen in the context of this hate–hate relationship between the parliamentarian and the district administration. Parliamentarians are thrilled because this scheme gives them the power, for the first time, to choose projects for execution within their political domain and to even make financial provision for the same.

NOTE

For a more detailed account of the special privileges that Indian MPs enjoyed until the mid-1990s, please see the chapter titled 'The Quota Raj' in A. Surya Prakash's *What Ails Indian Parliament?* (Indus, an imprint of HarperCollins Publishers India Pvt. Ltd, New Delhi, 1995), beginning on p. 233.

1

The Origin of MPLADS

Where and how did this idea of an elected representative having a separate fund at his disposal to build community infrastructure projects in his constituency originate? The origin of the Members of Parliament Local Area Development Scheme (MPLADS) makes interesting reading. The idea that some money must be placed at the disposal of a public representative to enable him to prioritize the needs of his voters was first launched by the Bombay Municipal Corporation (as it was known then) in the 1970s. The municipal body decided to set apart a fund of a paltry ₹50,000 a year for each corporator and allow him or her to decide on the municipal works on which it could be spent. The corporation executed these works alongside the works it had planned on its own. Over a period of time, the fund available to corporators has risen to over ₹10 lakh a year.

Once the municipal corporators acquired the power to dispense patronage, members of the Maharashtra Legislative Assembly could not have been far behind. They got on to the idea rather quickly and pressured the state government to introduce an MLA Local Area Development Fund. The state government created such a fund in the mid-1980s with every member of the legislative assembly having the power to sanction projects worth ₹10 lakh a year. Over the years this fund has also swelled. Legislators in other states cited the example of Maharashtra and pressed for similar schemes in their states, and representatives in Uttar Pradesh and Bihar assemblies soon joined the ranks of MLAs in Maharashtra.

These developments gave MLAs a distinct advantage over MPs in these states because the MLA fund allowed them to 'give' something to their constituents whereas all that MPs could offer were promises. MPs found that people were flocking to MLAs for this reason and felt that they, too, ought to have the facility to dip into a fund and execute community projects. The demand was raised by members of the ninth and tenth Lok Sabhas. They wanted a scheme for MPs which would apply uniformly across the country, but the man who put together a cogent case for an MPLADS fund and doggedly pursued it until it was launched was Mr Ram Naik, a Bharatiya Janata Party (BJP) MP from Maharashtra.

Naik launched the campaign in January 1990 by writing to the then finance minister, Mr Madhu Dandavate, seeking a 'constituency fund' of ₹2 crore for every MP. Since Mr Dandavate also hailed from Maharashtra, he was conversant with the fund created for MLAs in the state. Naik followed this up with a memorandum to the prime minister bearing the signatures of a hundred MPs and by raising the issue during the debate on the Appropriations Bill in the Lok Sabha in April 1992 and May 1993. The Union government, which was headed by Prime Minister P.V. Narasimha Rao could sense that the idea had become very popular among MPs across the political spectrum because of the enthusiastic support it received from all sections of the House when it was raised by Mr Naik and a few others in the Lok Sabha. The prime minister was also aware that although a member of the Opposition had mooted the proposal, it was backed by a majority of the ruling Congress MPs. He, therefore, decided to extract maximum political mileage within his party and outside by announcing at a meeting of the Congress Parliamentary Party that the government proposed to launch a scheme that would make available ₹1 crore per annum for every MP to spend in his constituency.[1]

The matter came up for discussion at a meeting of the Business Advisory Committee (BAC) of the Lok Sabha on 23 July 1993. This meeting, which was attended by senior representatives of all major political parties, considered the main features of the scheme and the parameters within which it would be implemented. The government informed the BAC that it would allocate ₹1 crore per MP per year to enable parliamentarians to identify developmental projects for immediate execution in their constituencies. From the projects suggested by the government, it was clear from the very beginning that it wanted MPs to utilize the fund to create tangible assets that would improve the physical infrastructure and also promote the delivery of social sector programmes in their constituencies. It said MPs could suggest execution of public works like construction of school buildings; provision of drinking water through sinking of wells, etc.; construction or repair of village roads, bridges, shelters for the aged and handicapped, hospitals and irrigation canals and afforestation schemes. MPs would have to write to the district collector and list out the projects that they wanted.

Even at this stage, when the scheme was yet to be formally launched, the government was wary of the manner in which the scheme would be implemented. It was also keen to limit the role of MPs to identifying works for execution but to keep them away from the decision-making process in the implementation of a project, lest it lead to unethical conduct and allegations of corruption. It therefore told the BAC that 'MPs should not enter into contracts for the execution of these works with contractors or agencies'. The district administration would be responsible for the execution of these works and MPs should not be involved in making payments to contractors. The district administration would accept the suggestions made by MPs unless the work was not feasible or 'inexecutable'. Payment for the work done would be made by the district collector or the officials deputed by him.[2]

The government's initial assessment of the budgetary implications of this scheme was that it would cost the exchequer about ₹900 crore a year if members of both Houses of Parliament were given this facility. However, it claimed that this would not be a financial burden on the government because the government was already spending ₹6000 crore annually on employment-generation schemes in rural areas. The money required for this scheme would be drawn from this sum earmarked for employment generation, it said.

Finally, the note said the scheme would make MPs 'more responsive and effective' and 'strengthen the system of parliamentary democracy'.[3]

Justifying the launch of MPLADS, the Union government said in its very first report on the scheme that in a democratic polity, 'elected representatives not only reflect the hopes and aspirations of the people but also have an understanding of the developmental and felt needs of the communities'. Further, MPs are often approached by their constituents 'for capital intensive works that create durable assets needed in the constituencies'. Consequently, there was a demand by MPs that 'they should be able to recommend such works for execution in their areas'.[4]

The scheme took effect soon after it was announced by Prime Minister P.V. Narasimha Rao during the winter session of Parliament in 1993, but the immediate public reaction was adverse. Since this scheme was not modelled on anything that existed in other democracies, there was little understanding of how it worked. While it was true that the scheme had given MPs a toehold in the administrative process at the district level, the execution of projects remained firmly within the realm of the bureaucracy. But the story that went out via first reports in the media was that the Union government had announced a bonanza of ₹1 crore per year for every parliamentarian and given each MP the right to operate this fund according to his whim. These reports caused immense damage not only to the proposed scheme but to the image of MPs as well.

The government made a modest allocation of ₹5 lakh per MP for 1993–94 since only one quarter of the fiscal year was available for implementing the scheme and since the guidelines were yet to be formulated. The allocation was enhanced to ₹1 crore per MP from 1994–95 to 1997–98. It was then doubled to ₹2 crore per MP from the fiscal year 1998–99 onwards. But this was only to be expected because on the very day the prime minister announced the scheme in Parliament, the Joint Parliamentary Committee for facilities and remuneration of members submitted an interim report recommending an allocation of ₹2 crore per annum per MP for development work in each constituency.[5]

Once the scheme got going, MPs realized that it gave them greater visibility in their constituencies. Those who utilized these funds well found that their constituents were less critical of them and their work. MPs, therefore, began mounting pressure on the government to enhance the corpus to ₹5 crore per annum. The government finally succumbed to this demand and declared that the enhancement would take effect from 1 April 2011.

Following the launch of the scheme in December 1993, the Ministry of Rural Development issued a set of guidelines in February 1994. The scheme was transferred to the Ministry of Statistics and Programme Implementation (MS&PI) and this ministry revised the guidelines in December 1994. Thereafter, the guidelines were revised in February 1997, September 1999 and April 2002 but, the process of revision continued; it was 'comprehensively revised' yet again on 16 November 2005.[6]

The revision of guidelines has been a continuous process because the committees on MPLADS in the Lok Sabha and the Rajya Sabha have been constantly bombarded with requests from MPs to either amend the guidelines or permit a one-time waiver of a particular rule so that a particular proposal, which is otherwise prohibited, can be pushed through. As will be seen in later chapters, the committees initially resisted the temptation to permit a deviation from the guidelines. But if an MP has enough 'pull' within the committee or held an office which gave him enough political weight, the committees hummed and hawed for a while and eventually okayed a proposal that actually violated the guidelines and said that this must be treated as 'a special case'. However, if groups of MPs challenged a particular rule and kept up the pressure, either or both of the committees would give in and direct the government to amend the guidelines in order to accommodate the views of the MPs. There have also been situations where the committees have had to helplessly give ex-post-facto 'approval' to some projects that have already been approved by the district authorities in gross violation of the guidelines because large sums of money had already been spent on them.[7]

While at the Centre, the MS&PI is responsible for policy formulation, release of funds, and for working out the methodology for monitoring the scheme, one department in every state or Union Territory (UT) is designated as the nodal department to supervise and monitor the implementation of the scheme. This department has the responsibility to coordinate with the districts and other departments of the government. This nodal ministry is informed by the Union government whenever funds are released to the districts. The districts in turn keep both the nodal ministry and the Union government informed of the status of every project.

As regards implementation of projects, several agencies come into play. The district authorities are responsible for supervision and for determining the agency that will execute the project. Sometimes, this is done through local self-governments, government agencies or Non-Government Organizations (NGOs).

Key Features of the Scheme

Some of the key features of MPLADS are as follows: It is fully funded by the Union government and the funds are directly released to the district authorities; MPs are expected to recommend developmental works based on locally felt needs and preference is given to works relating to national priorities like drinking water schemes, public health, education, sanitation and roads; and the district authority has the power to examine the eligibility of the work, sanction funds and select the agency to execute the work and monitor the projects. The guidelines, as revised in November 2005, state that Lok Sabha members can recommend works in their respective constituencies whereas Rajya Sabha members can recommend works anywhere in the state from which they are elected. Nominated members of the two Houses, on the other hand, are allowed to select works for implementation in any part of the country. This was initially not the case but the government saw merit in the argument that it would be incorrect to put nominated members in a straitjacket because they often represented a much wider constituency that cut across the geographical boundaries of states. Among those who argued this were two members of the Anglo-Indian community nominated to the Lok Sabha. Since this is a tiny community spread across many states, they said it would be unfair to insist that they spend MPLADS funds in just one state.

Even with regard to elected Lok Sabha and Rajya Sabha members, there are some exceptions. While all Lok Sabha members are expected to spend their funds within their constituencies, they are allowed to spend up to ₹10 lakh in an area outside their constituency but within their state if that area is hit by a natural calamity. Further, in the case of a 'natural calamity of a severe nature' (so declared by the Union government), an MP can recommend works up to ₹50 lakh in the affected area, wherever it may be in the country. In such cases the funds are transferred by the MP's nodal district to the authorities in the district hit by the calamity.

As regards district authorities, the guidelines stipulate that in the event of rejection of a proposal, they must inform the MP within forty-five days; all recommendations received in the office of the district authority till the last date of the term of the MP are to be executed, provided they are within the guidelines and funds are available, and the agency hired for implementing a project must be given a time-frame to complete the work and this should not normally exceed one year.[8]

The two Houses also set up committees on MPLADS. Since strict enforcement of guidelines invariably results in some friction between MPs and the bureaucracy, the committees serve as a listening post and as a complaint cell for MPs and also render valuable service as arbitrators between MPs and the MS&PI. Sometimes the committees uphold the MPs' point of view and direct the government to amend the guidelines or direct that a 'one-time exception' be made in a particular case, but more often than not, the committees reject the proposals put forward by MPs whenever they are in conflict with the rules.

The role of the Union government and the governments in the states and UTs are well defined. The nodal ministry at the Centre is the MS&PI. It has the task of monitoring the release of funds, cost of works sanctioned, funds spent, etc., and bringing out an annual report on MPLADS. It has to monitor the receipt of completion reports, utilization certificates and audit certificates from the district authorities; hold annual meetings at the national level to review implementation and also to review the scheme state-wise; review implementation of the scheme by district authorities in areas which have a predominantly Scheduled Caste (SC) and Scheduled Tribe (ST) population; and address issues arising out of audit objections.[9]

In the states and UTs, a department is designated as the nodal department to ensure supervision of the projects. The states are expected to have a committee headed by the chief secretary/ additional chief secretary/development commissioner to review MPLADS with district officials and MPs once a year; train district officials in MPLADS; engage auditors to audit MPLADS accounts in every district; and place data on implementation of the scheme on their websites.

District authorities, too, have their task cut out. They are responsible for overall coordination and supervision of works and inspection of at least ten per cent of the works; monitor implementation in areas dominated by SC and ST citizens; maintain work registers and furnish details to the nodal ministries at the Centre and in the states and inspect works executed by societies and trusts. As regards the implementing agencies, they are expected to furnish reports on the physical and financial progress of each project to the district authority every month with a copy marked to the nodal ministry in the state; provide utilization and completion certificates within one month of completion of a work; and refund to the district authority any unspent funds along with interest that may have accrued on the amount within a month of completion of a project and close the bank account opened for the purpose.[10]

Does MPLADS Violate the Doctrine of Separation of Powers?

The year 1993 constitutes a watershed in the history of the Parliament in India because, with the launch of MPLADS, Indian parliamentarians had successfully breached the wall that had effectively separated them from the Executive and from taking executive decisions. It constituted a significant deviation from the Westminster model that sanctified the doctrine of separation of powers—something that would be repugnant to constitutional experts cast in the traditional mould. This is best explained by Mr Edward Fellowes, a former clerk of the British House of Commons. He says, 'The House of Commons does not control the Executive in the sense that the driver of a motor car controls the vehicle. That would be to substitute the House of Commons for the Executive and rob the latter of all initiative, create confusion and delay, and would probably finish by bringing parliamentary democracy to an end.'[11]

This argument that MPLADS constitutes a deviation from the standard Parliament–Executive equation has been emphasized by several people, some of whom are ex-MPs. Among the scheme's prominent critics are Mr Era Sezhiyan, a former MP and a parliamentarian given to research and scholarship and Mr J.M. Lyngdoh, former chief election commissioner. Both of them have hit out at the scheme and have challenged its constitutional validity and efficacy and demanded that it be scrapped.

The opponents of the scheme argue that MPLADS goes against the tenets and philosophy of the Constitution; the parliamentary system; the demarcation of powers in the federal system; democratic decentralization; and finally, against the principles of responsibility and accountability for money drawn from the public exchequer. In India, apart from the argument that it disturbs the principle of separation of powers between the Legislature and the Executive, opponents of the scheme also object to it on the ground that it violates the principle of federalism and devolution of powers enshrined in the Constitution.

Mr Sezhiyan authored a study titled 'MPLADS—Concept, Confusion and Contradictions' under the aegis of the Institute of Social Sciences, New Delhi, in which he vehemently opposed the scheme on the ground that conceptually it was against both the parliamentary system and the federal system.

Mr Sezhiyan's view is that although the scheme was launched to facilitate MPs, in practice it has proved to be detrimental to the prime role of MPs. 'By giving the annual grants individually to the MPs, the scheme distorted the collective responsibility of the members. As the MPs became part of the administration in implementation of the scheme, they have taken on themselves enormous workload which not only distorted their supervisory role over the executive but diverted their attention from the more important parliamentary work which cannot be delegated to anybody else. In the midst of the heavy schedule of work, it is not humanly possible for an MP to pay adequate attention and to involve himself administratively to plan, to supervise and to successfully implement numerous works recommended solely under his discretion. Lack of time and pressures from the electorate make the MP to hurriedly make the choice of works and send recommendation to the concerned district authority.'[12]

The Sezhiyan charge sheet against MPLADS also spoke of the general perception about this scheme. 'There is widespread impression that the MPs have been misuing the funds under the scheme for their own benefit,' he said and quoted Mr P.R. Kumaramangalam, a former minister; Mr Indrajit Gupta, former home minister and one of India's best-known parliamentarians; Mr Kuldip Nayyar, MP, Rajya Sabha; and Mr S.S. Ahluwalia and Mr Sanjay Nirupam, MPs, regarding the misuse of the scheme and on the need to scrap it for this reason. In his view, the scheme lacked accountability in the absence of a monitoring mechanism and this was best explained by the government's inaction on audit reports and the Planning Commission's evaluation reports.

Yet another charge levelled by Mr Sezhiyan against the scheme was that though ostensibly the scheme was drafted to promote synergy between MPs and their constituents, it had been hijacked by bureaucrats and was under their 'mismanagement'.

'The names and involvement of the MPs in the scheme had been fully exploited by the bureaucracy, with the result that the MPs got a bad name and the bureaucracy got away scot-free for all the irregularities and waste of public funds.' Regarding the role of the MS&PI, he says once the funds are released, this ministry washes its hands off and does not take any responsibility for the same. At the district level, once the works are sanctioned, the district collector does not take any further interest in the progress of the work.

According to him, the bureaucracy's acts of omission and commission are as follows:

The district heads give sanctions in excess of the amount released; unspent balance is shown as 'expenditure booked' but not expended; the district collectors and the Implementing Agencies (IAs) do not refund unspent balances; district heads allow some works without technical and administrative sanctions; district heads sanction and execute works which are not permissible under the scheme and neither the nodal ministry nor the district heads maintain assets registers in respect of most of the works which are completed. Mr Sezhiyan's report says that the basic problem in the concept of the scheme is 'the series of defects, distortions, irregularities, misuse, mismanagement, denigration and final degradation of the scheme'. It said that in the name of MPs, officialdom at the Centre and in the districts did everything without control or responsibility and, therefore, it was 'absolutely necessary' to have a thorough inquiry into the audit findings and irregularities raised in the media and to fix responsibility. Such an inquiry was needed 'to redeem the credibility of the MPs and Parliament'.[13]

Speaking on behalf of the 'India Rejuvenation Initiative', Mr Lyngdoh, who has an intricate knowledge of India's election law by virtue of his tenure as election commissioner and later as head of the Election Commission of India, declared that MPLADS and MLALADS (a similar scheme in operation in the states to give members of legislative assemblies the power to identify development-related projects within their legislative constituencies) 'must be immediately abolished'. Mr Lyngdoh said these schemes undermined the constitutional notion of separation of powers and distorted the role of elected representatives. In his view, if the underlying rationale for these schemes is accepted, a question mark is placed over all other government spending and 'norms give way to personal discretion and feudal notion of patronage occupies centrestage'. Eventually, they tend to weaken the democratic structure of the country. He said these schemes should be abolished and the funds allocated for them should be transferred to urban local bodies and Panchayati Raj institutions. This would increase the cash transfers to Panchayati Raj institutions and strengthen democracy at the grassroots as envisaged by the Constitution. The abolition of these schemes would also substantially reduce the heartburn among constituents and restore the focus of representatives in the state legislature and Parliament 'besides removing the taint of corruption from the fair faces of legislators'.[14]

The government however did not see any merit in the argument that the scheme violated the constitutional arrangement. Responding to this charge, the MS & PI said, 'The MPLAD Scheme has the authority of law as prescribed in the Constitution and is implemented in accordance with the constitutional provisions.'

The Lok Sabha Committee on MPLADS, which has been putting up a spirited defence of the scheme, disagreed with those who saw it as an unnecessary digression from Parliament's primary responsibilities. In a rather elaborate response to criticism from various quarters, the committee said in its fifteenth report by way of a preamble that legislators are the architects of the destiny of the people and, therefore, they 'orient' governance 'towards the welfare of the people'. As legislators are intrinsically involved with the people, it is but natural for constituents to approach their representatives to execute development projects and community infrastructure. It is in this context that MPLADS came into being. The objective of the scheme is to create 'durable assets' while meeting 'locally felt needs' of the people.

The committee opposed the view that MPLADS went against the parliamentary system and that it drew away funds from rural and urban local bodies and increased conflict between the district administration and local bodies in rural areas. It said the scheme did not interfere with the planning process at the district level. On the other hand, all that it did was to supplement development efforts at the district level. The scheme is sponsored by the Union government, but the funds are directly sent to the district authorities and the MPs merely have a recommendatory role. The sanction, execution and monitoring of the scheme is done by the district authorities. Further, the scheme is only supplementary to other central and state schemes. 'The role of MPs in this scheme thus cannot be categorized as against the parliamentary system and encroachment of the powers and functions of the executive by the legislators.' As MPs are not given grants or funds, 'mere recommendation of works of locally felt needs by them cannot be termed as substitution of important parliamentary work…'

On the other hand, it said the scheme 'seems to meet' the felt need of constituents 'which otherwise may not find a place in ordinary planning'.[15]

Although Sezhiyan and others seemed to have a strong case when they sought the scrapping of MPLADS, such arguments, advanced by a set of petitioners, did not impress the Supreme Court when a constitutional bench heard a clutch of writ petitions which challenged the scheme. The five-judge bench which heard these petitions in a case titled *Bhim Singh* v. *Union of India & Ors*, declared in its unanimous judgement of 6 May 2010, that MPLADS did not violate the principle of separation of powers. The court said that while the concept of separation of powers was visible in the Constitution, there was no strict separation of powers in the Indian Constitution as in the American or Australian Constitutions. In India, the court said, 'the Constitution does not prohibit overlap of functions, but in fact provides for some overlap as a parliamentary democracy. But what it prohibits is such exercise of function of the other branch which results in wrestling away of the regime of constitutional accountability.'[16]

The bench declared that some overlap of functions of different branches of the state was okay but 'a law would violate the principle of separation of powers if it takes over the essential function of the other branch leading to lapse of constitutional accountability. It is through this test that we must analyse the present system.'

Therefore, in the court's view, MPLADS did not violate the concept of separation of powers as MPs were 'only seeking to advance public interest and public purpose' through the scheme and it was 'quite logical' for an MP to carry out developmental activities in his constituency. The court also held that there were adequate safeguards in the guidelines and it had no reason to believe that the scheme would not be effectively controlled and implemented. Further, since the MP only proposed schemes and left the implementation to local bodies, there was no real breach of the separation of powers principle.[17]

The court was not impressed by several other arguments put forth by the opponents of the scheme. For example, it did not see the scheme as violating the constitutional provisions empowering Panchayati Raj institutions and municipal bodies. Nor was it swayed by the argument that these funds were being misused. The guidelines were adequate and so was the monitoring mechanism, it said.[18]

While Mr Sezhiyan, Mr Lyngdoh and a few others wanted the scheme scrapped, there were others who felt that major changes were needed in the operation of the scheme in order to overcome the adverse publicity that the scheme had attracted ever since its launch. But, sometimes the remedy can be worse than the disease. For example, Mr Bhanu Prakash Singh, former governor and Union minister wrote to the Speaker of the Lok Sabha in January 2006 and suggested measures to improve the MPLAD Scheme 'in the wake of adverse publicity'. He felt that MPLADS 'was an innocuous scheme' which had been introduced to take care of local needs of people without going through the rigmarole of administrative delays. Yet there was an adverse reaction to the scheme from different sections of society and people cast aspersions on MPs even though the latter had no role except to suggest schemes that could be implemented. He therefore suggested the constitution of a Joint Parliamentary Committee (JPC) on MPLADS, submission of proposals by MPs to the JPC and enhancement of allocation under the scheme.

The Lok Sabha Committee on MPLADS said the idea of having a JPC on MPLADS had been considered and rejected in the past and there was no rethinking on this score. Secondly, since a JPC was ruled out, the suggestion that all MPLADS proposals be vetted by a JPC did not warrant consideration. It, however, endorsed Mr Singh's suggestion that the corpus be enhanced and reiterated the demand that it be raised at least to ₹5 crore a year.[19]

The attitude of the Lok Sabha Committee to criticism of the scheme and the conduct of MPs is typical of the response of most parliamentary committees. MPs are so touchy about their privileges that they have lost the ability to introspect and review the overall conduct of members and its impact on the image of Parliament. Here too, while the committee virtually dismissed the idea of a JPC to monitor MPLADS, it was more than willing to grab the suggestion that the corpus be enhanced to ₹5 crore. The relentless pressure put by MPs on the government to increase the fund has been discussed in the next chapter.

NOTES

1 This chronology is based on a file maintained by Mr Ram Naik on MPLADS, which he shared with the author.
2 See Annexure I for the first set of Guidelines for the MPLAD Scheme issued by the Ministry of Rural Development, Government of India in February 1994.
3 Based on a note circulated by the government at a meeting of the Business Advisory Committee of the Lok Sabha on 23 July 1993.
4 First Report, Member of Parliament Local Area Development Scheme (MPLADS), Ministry of Statistics and Programme Implementation, Government of India, New Delhi, December 2006, p. 3.
5 Interim Report, Joint Parliamentary Committee to Suggest Facilities and Remuneration for Members of Parliament, presented to the Lok Sabha, 23 December 1993, Lok Sabha Secretariat.
6 First Report, Member of Parliament Local Area Development Scheme (MPLADS), Ministry of Statistics and Programme Implementation, Government of India, New Delhi, December 2006, p. 3.
7 See Annexure II for the latest edition of the guidelines as they stood on 1 August 2011. This can be accessed on the website www.mplads.gov.in.
8 First Report, Member of Parliament Local Area Development Scheme (MPLADS), Ministry of Statistics and Programme Implementation, Government of India, New Delhi, December 2006, pp. 4–5.
9 Ibid., p. 11.
10 Ibid., pp. 11–14.
11 L. M. Singhvi (ed.), *Parliament and Administration in India*, The

Institute of Constitutional and Parliamentary Studies, 1972, p. 2.
12. Fifteenth Report, Committee on MPLADS 2008–2009, presented to the Lok Sabha, 23 March, 2001, Lok Sabha Secretariat, New Delhi, p. 3.
13. Ibid., pp. 5–7.
14. Ibid., p. 8.
15. Ibid., p. 10.
16. *Bhim Singh* v. *Union of India & Others*, (2010) 5 Supreme Court Case, 572.
17. Ibid., pp. 575.
18. For a more detailed discussion of the verdict of the Supreme Court on the efficacy of the scheme, please see Chapter 11, titled 'The Supreme Court on MPLADS'.
19. Thirteenth Report, Committee on MPLADS 2006–2007, presented to the Lok Sabha, 7 December 2006, Lok Sabha Secretariat, New Delhi, pp. 34–35.

2

MPs Want More

Until the advent of MPLADS, most MPs had to cut a sorry figure when their constituents wanted sanction of projects to improve local infrastructure, as they had no funds to disburse, even to implement minor works. All development had to be funded by either the central or the state governments or local bodies like zila parishads and village panchayats. All that an MP could do was plead on behalf of his constituents with the government or local body concerned. If the MP's equations with the state or local governments were not good, most of his requests would end up in wastebaskets in these offices. This seemed a distinct possibility because by the time MPLADS was introduced, India's political map had begun to look like a kaleidoscope with people in different states preferring political parties of various hues to run governments at the state level. They also sent some representatives of these regional parties to represent them in Parliament. Further, there could be a kind of zig-zagging of parties with one party ruling at the federal level, another in the state and possibly a third at the municipal or district level. Sometimes this would get even more complicated when these parties entered into coalitions to secure power at any of these levels. This bewildering mishmash of parties in power added to the woes of MPs because whenever the district or state administration was in the hands of a rival party, they would invariably cold-shoulder an MP's proposal.

On the other hand, if an MP was on the right side of the political fence and his equations with the chief minister of the state and other ministers and with those who man the elected bodies at the district and village levels were good, there was always the problem of shortage of funds and many of the schemes proposed by him were put on hold for want of resources.

Even if an MP happened to overcome all these hurdles, his re-election would be in doubt because Indian voters are notorious for turning against incumbents, whether at the constituency, the state or the national level. The oft-repeated complaint of an Indian voter about his or her MP is that the latter was 'never seen' after his election to Parliament and that he had done 'nothing' for the constituency.

Therefore, a large number of MPs launched a campaign in the early 1990s for creating a separate development fund which would be utilized according to the wishes of parliamentarians. MPs felt that if they had some funds at their disposal every year, they would have 'something to show' by way of work, to their constituents. Their wishes were granted when the Union government headed by Prime Minister P.V. Narasimha Rao decided to launch MPLADS in 1993 after consultations with the Speaker of the Lok Sabha, Mr Shivraj Patil. The scheme took off primarily because the Speaker, Mr Patil, put his weight behind it. Aware of the humongous pressure that constituents put on their MPs in India, the Speaker felt that MPLADS was a novel idea. The scheme was initially launched with an allocation of ₹1 crore per annum per MP and a set of guidelines was drawn up. The money would be sent to the district administration and spent according to the schemes proposed by each MP.

However, within a couple of years, MPs began demanding that there be more money in the kitty. Eventually, the government gave in to the demand and doubled the allocation in December 1998 to

₹2 crore per year per MP, but even this is considered too meagre by parliamentarians. Meanwhile, seventy-six MPs led by Mr Prakash Paranjpe signed a petition addressed to the Speaker in December 1999 asking for a proportionate increase in the funds available to an MP depending on the size of the electorate. In their letter, they sought a substantial increase in the fund. Mr Paranjpe said he had 2.75 million voters in his constituency (Thane in Maharashtra) and ₹2 crore per year was inadequate to implement development schemes. There were many more MPs who, like him, represented huge constituencies. These MPs suggested that the fund be raised to ₹3 crore for all constituencies with one million electors, ₹5 crore for constituencies with 2.5 million electors, and so on.[1]

The Speaker forwarded this representation to the government and Mr Arun Shourie, the Minister of State for Statistics and Programme Implementation came up with the following response to the proposal in his letter to the minister in-charge of parliamentary affairs: 'MPLADS allocation per year per MP was doubled on 23 December 1998. Funds are being released from the year 1998–99 in accordance with this enhancement. The unutilized balance—on which the government is paying interest—is over ₹1500 crores. Out of the allocation of ₹1580 crores for the current year, 1999–2000, we have been able to release only ₹268 crores pertaining to this year up to 31.1.2000. That works out to just 17% of the total allocation. In view of the low rate of utilization and in view of the dire conditions of governmental finances, there really is no justification to seek enhancement of the allocations for MPLADS.'[2]

The Lok Sabha Committee on MPLADS found no merit in Mr Paranjpe's argument that there must be a proportionate increase in allocation under the scheme based on the population in each constituency. However, it disagreed with the minister and said there was a case for uniform enhancement of the fund. It noted that the fund was doubled to ₹2 crore per year per constituency from 1998–99, but said this was 'just not sufficient' to implement development schemes in constituencies. It, therefore, recommended that the allocation be further raised from ₹2 crore to ₹4 crore.[3]

However, strange as it may seem, within three months the committee had begun to waver on this question. Mr Ummareddy Venkateswarlu wrote to the committee asking that the funds available in the scheme be enhanced to ₹3 crore per annum. The ministry once again said that the allocation cannot be enhanced. The committee, however, recommended that the allocation should be increased to ₹3 crore per annum, possibly forgetting that it had recommended a revision to ₹4 crore only three months ago![4]

The matter, however, continued to agitate MPs and the Lok Sabha Committee and the committee returned to this issue at its meeting on 22 February 2001. At this meeting, the question of enhancement of the MPLADS fund from ₹2 crore to ₹4 crore was discussed yet again. The committee was also apprised of what transpired at a meeting called by the Speaker on 13 December 2000. In that meeting, which was attended by leaders of political parties and some ministers, including the finance minister, the latter is reported to have said that it would be difficult to enhance the fund in that fiscal year because the supplementary budget for the year had been presented by him to Parliament that very day. The committee took note of the deliberations at that meeting and said in view of the increasing demand made by constituents on MPs for development schemes, MPLADS funds should be increased from ₹2 crore to ₹4 crore per annum. It hoped the government would act on this recommendation at least in the next fiscal year, namely, 2001–2002.[5]

The Lok Sabha Committee returned to this issue in its ninth report which dealt with the action taken by the government on the committee's second report which had been presented to the Lok Sabha on 22 August 2000. It recalled that even at that time, the MS&PI had taken the stand that the funds available to each MP could not be enhanced. However, the committee had said that the allocation should be increased to ₹3 crore per member. The ministry responded by saying that it could not accept this recommendation.

In the ninth report, the committee said it noted 'with concern' the ministry's response to its recommendation. It said a variety of works based on locally felt needs were being executed under MPLADS as also many welfare programmes like drinking water facilities, ambulances, community halls, hospital buildings, etc., for the benefit of the people. However, despite innumerable requests from MPs since 1998, the government has not enhanced the allocation although there was all-round price escalation. In such a scenario, it was difficult for MPs to keep pace with the demands of their constituents. In view of these facts the committee said that it would reiterate and 'strongly recommend' that if not more, the government must enhance the allocation per MP per year to ₹5 crore. It hoped the government would take 'prompt action' and implement this recommendation.[6]

The demand for increasing the fund not only persisted throughout the decade but grew bigger with the passage of time. The issue cropped up once again at the fag end of the fourteenth Lok Sabha when the Lok Sabha Committee undertook a review of the MPLAD Scheme. The committee said that in its earlier reports, it had taken note of the growing demand for developmental works in constituencies and observed that the existing allocation of ₹2 crore per annum was inadequate. A sum of ₹2 crore was too meagre to meet the aspirations of the people. It had, therefore, recommended that the annual allocation under MPLADS be raised to ₹10 crore from the fiscal year 2009–10.

The matter was examined by the MS & PI and a memo was sent to the Department of Expenditure, Ministry of Finance, and to the Planning Commission for appraisal in August 2008. The Department of Expenditure informed the ministry in January 2009 that the proposal had not yet been appraised by the Planning Commission and their input was necessary to take a decision. Subsequently, the Planning Commission replied to the ministry and said that 'given the scarcity of resources', it was not in favour of increasing the annual allocation under this scheme.

The Planning Commission, however, hedged its bets because the validity of the MPLAD Scheme had been challenged before the Supreme Court. It said that it would undertake a fresh appraisal of the scheme only after the Supreme Court delivered its judgement 'and also when there is clarity on availability of additional funds'.[7]

The committee was most distressed to get this response from the government. It said the annual allocation for the scheme, fixed at ₹2 crore in 1998, 'is grossly inadequate' to fulfil the developmental needs of the people, particularly when the prices of construction materials have risen manifold and the value of the rupee has eroded by 50 per cent. 'The need for a suitable enhancement was therefore emphasized by the committee time and again in the past' and that is why it had recommended that the allocation be raised to ₹10 crore from the fiscal year 2009–10. It noted that the MS&PI had sought the opinion of the Planning Commission and the latter had said that it would express a view after the Supreme Court pronounced its judgement. Further, it has been given to understand that the Department of Expenditure in the Union government would examine the proposal for enhancement only after the opinion of the Planning Commission was known. 'The Committee does not approve of the stance taken by the Planning Commission in view of the fact that the scheme is an ongoing scheme and no formal court order has so far been issued forbidding its execution.' The committee said it was 'appalling' to note that the administrative ministry continued to dither on the question of increasing the outlay under the scheme and advanced the same plea (lack of resources) 'in utter disregard' of the committee's opinion. It said it was 'high time' the government did a realistic appraisal of the proposal and cut out the 'unsound arguments' advanced thus far by the ministries. It directed the MS&PI to convey its 'unhappiness' to the Department of Expenditure and the Planning Commission and emphasize the urgent need to increase the outlay.[8]

Following the Supreme Court's verdict upholding MPLADS,

the Planning Commission, as promised, took a call on the demand for increasing the annual allocation per MP under this scheme and once again rejected it. The commission's decision was conveyed to the Rajya Sabha Committee on MPLADS by Mr Montek Singh Ahluwalia, deputy chairman of the Planning Commission. This was in consonance with the opinion given by the commission to the MS&PI earlier. The Rajya Sabha Committee, however, was 'not amused'. It asked the secretary of the Planning Commission 'to consider pruning the outlays of a number of big ticket schemes to make available resources for MPLADS.'[9]

However, at the end of the day, the government succumbed to the collective pressure of 790 MPs and decided to hike the allocation under MPLADS to ₹5 crore per MP per year with effect from 1 April 2011. Finance Minister Mr Pranab Mukherjee announced the government's intention to increase the corpus for this scheme in the Lok Sabha while replying to the debate on the Finance Bill, 2011. Thereafter, the decision was formalized at a meeting of the Union Cabinet on 7 July 2011. This increase raised the annual spending under MPLADS by ₹2370 crore—from ₹1580 crore to ₹3950 crore. The Union Cabinet also agreed to the allocation of 2 per cent of the funds to districts or states 'for proper implementation and monitoring of the scheme'.[10]

The Indian Express also quoted Ms Ambika Soni, the information and broadcasting minister, as saying that 'this augmentation in the allocation to ₹5 crore will result in better fulfilment of the needs of the people and creation of durable community assets based on locally felt needs.' She also said that inflation had adversely affected projects under this scheme, thereby hinting that a higher allocation was inevitable. Among other things announced that day it was also said that the Cabinet had decided to provide an additional ₹5 crore to the MS&PI to monitor MPLADS through independent agencies. The government also took the opportunity to give the people an overview of what had been achieved under the scheme since its inception in 1993–94. It said that until 31 March 2011, MPs had recommended 13.87 lakh works. The district authorities had sanctioned 12.30 lakh works, of which 11.34 lakh works had been completed. Further, since the year of inception, the government had released ₹22,490 crore under MPLADS, of which ₹20,454 crore had been spent.[11]

An Additional Two Crore Rupees to Build Rural Roads

Despite this constant pressure from MPs, the government was in no mood to give in to the demand that the fund be doubled. The government was obviously worried about the budgetary implications of enhancing the corpus of the fund. Meanwhile, some MPs came up with a new stratagem to have more funds at their disposal. They sought additional funds, not under MPLADS but under a central programme to build rural roads.

In identical letters addressed to the chairman of the Lok Sabha Committee in March 2001, eleven members of the House from Andhra Pradesh urged the committee to direct the government to allocate an additional ₹2 crore to them for construction of rural roads. The MPs told the committee that their constituents wanted roads linking the rural hinterland to highways. A separate provision for construction of rural roads was, therefore, necessary.

The Lok Sabha Committee considered the demand and 'unanimously' resolved that every member of the Lok Sabha should be entitled to recommend construction of rural roads to the tune of ₹2 crore per annum in their constituencies under the programme titled the Pradhan Mantri Gram Sadak Yojana in addition to the ₹2 crore available to them under the MPLAD Scheme. The committee did not think that this facility ought to be extended to members of the Rajya Sabha, who come through an indirect election via state assemblies to the Upper House.[12]

Rajya Sabha Members Want to Extend Influence to Many States

Nominated members of the Rajya Sabha and Lok Sabha have

been demanding that they be permitted to utilize MPLADS funds in more than one state. While the Rajya Sabha has twelve nominated members, the Lok Sabha has two. The two nominated seats in the Lok Sabha are reserved for members of the Anglo-Indian community. Initially, the Anglo-Indian members of the Lok Sabha raised this issue. They said that since the community they represented was scattered all over the country, they should be permitted to use these funds across the country without any geographical restriction. Later, nominated members of the Rajya Sabha also joined in. The guidelines permit nominated members of both Houses to select schemes for implementation in one or more districts within a state of their choice.

Although the MS & PI had initially turned down the proposal on the ground that it would lead to coordination hassles, it finally gave in. It officially communicated its readiness in June 1999 to change the guidelines to accommodate the demand of nominated MPs. While doing so, it said nominated MPs had been writing repeatedly that they be allowed to recommend MPLADS works throughout the country on the plea that they are nominated to Parliament by the President and that they represent the entire country. The Anglo-Indian MPs, in particular, argued that their community was scattered all over the country. The ministry said it had not acceded to this request earlier because of the problem of coordination. 'Experience has shown that there are already problems in coordination by one nodal district with other districts even within the state and the problems are likely to be complicated if the coordination is to be done across the state boundary.' However, keeping in view the repeated requests made by members, the ministry had decided to recommend an amendment to the guidelines. It said 'since there are a total of only 14 nominated MPs, the coordination problems arising from the above proposal can be taken care of at the central level.'

It therefore suggested that para 1.2 of the guidelines may be amended to read as follows: 'Nominated members of the Lok Sabha and Rajya Sabha may also select works in one or more districts anywhere in the country'.[13]

The Rajya Sabha Committee on MPLADS pitched in strongly on behalf of nominated MPs and said that the concurrence of the Speaker of the Lok Sabha should be obtained 'as quickly as possible' so that the guidelines could be suitably amended.[14]

The Lok Sabha committee accorded its concurrence to the amendment of para 1.2 of the guidelines for the scheme as suggested by the ministry.[15]

The government accepted this recommendation and amended the provision relating to nominated members in para 1.2 of the guidelines as suggested by the Lok Sabha Committee.[16]

But the matter did not end here. Some time later, two members of the Rajya Sabha wrote to Mr Arun Shourie, the minister of state in the nodal ministry, in early 2000, seeking permission for funding projects outside their states. Mr V.N. Gadgil, ex-MP, said in his letter of January 2000 that he wanted to take up MPLADS works in Pune district in Maharashtra and Mandsaur district in Madhya Pradesh. He said members of the Rajya Sabha need to have some flexibility regarding choice of projects under this scheme and the guidelines should be amended to permit them to fund projects outside the state from which they are elected.[17]

Dr L.M. Singhvi, elected from Rajasthan, wrote to say that he had been a member of the Bar for more than forty-seven years and president of the Supreme Court Bar Association for several terms. 'This is the community to which I belong in a primary sense.' During the golden jubilee of the Constitution and the Supreme Court he said he wanted to contribute up to the maximum permissible limits for construction of halls and auditoria for the Bar outside Rajasthan. Since an exception had already been made in respect of the Anglo-Indian community, 'I hope the principle can be extended generally with a ceiling of 25 per cent for development outside the state (from which a member is elected),' he said.[18]

In its response to these letters, the ministry said that since the guidelines do not permit MPs to spend these funds outside the state from which they are elected, the matter would have to be considered by the Lok Sabha and Rajya Sabha committees. As regards Dr Singhvi's request that he be permitted to fund halls and auditoria for the Bar Associations, the ministry said the guidelines do not permit construction of such buildings because construction of buildings of trusts, societies and associations are prohibited as also buildings which are used by a particular group and not by the public in general.[19]

The Lok Sabha Committee opted for the easy way out. It agreed with the ministry that the guidelines do not permit Rajya Sabha MPs to use this fund outside their state. Therefore, it wanted the Rajya Sabha Committee to first take a call on this issue as this was a matter that primarily concerned the Upper House.

As regards Dr Singhvi's request that he be permitted to fund the construction of Bar Association buildings, the committee noted the opinion of the ministry that the guidelines do not permit construction of buildings for private associations, trusts and societies and that only buildings used by the general public can be financed under this scheme. However, it disagreed with this view and said such buildings should be financed. It, therefore, said a new item 26 (i) should be added to the Illustrative List of Works which would read as follows: '26 (i) Construction of Halls/Auditorium/Library Building for Bar Association'.

Dr Singhvi's proposal also became the cue for the chairman of the Lok Sabha Committee, Dr B.B. Ramaiah, to propose that the guidelines be further amended to permit funding of buildings of the Lions Club and Rotary Club. The committee approved this proposal and suggested the addition of the following item to the Illustrative List of Works: '26 (ii) Construction of Lions Clubs/Rotary Clubs subject to a ceiling of ₹10 lakh.'[20]

Nominated Members Wish to Operate across States

The definition of 'constituency' and 'constituency pressure' varies, depending on whether one is a member of the Lok Sabha or the Rajya Sabha. No member of any Parliament in any part of the world is subject to constituency pressure like an elected member of the Lok Sabha in India. On an average, every Lok Sabha member represents about 2 million people, of whom around 1.4 million are electors. Their constituencies are geographically well defined and they are directly elected by the people. When the MP is in his constituency, he is besieged by constituents who hang around his residence or office for long hours in the hope of meeting him and securing his help. These MPs have over a hundred visitors a day and they spend around ten to twelve hours meeting their constituents. While a majority of the visitors seek personal favours, there are a few who come to the MP with community-related problems. As against this, the members of the Rajya Sabha are better placed. They are elected by MLAs in each state and, therefore, do not represent a specific, geographically defined constituency like their counterparts in the Lok Sabha. Thus, they view the entire state as their constituency. However, since they are not directly elected, they face less pressure from constituents. But apart from these two categories, there is one other category of MPs, namely, the nominated members. The Rajya Sabha has twelve nominated members drawn from varied fields such as literature, science, art and social service. These members do not represent any identifiable constituency. The Constitution provides for the nomination of two members of the Anglo-Indian community to the Lok Sabha. These members do not represent any state, but represent a 'constituency' (the Anglo-Indians) that is dispersed across the country.

Ever since MPLADS came into being, there have been issues pertaining to establishing a locus for nominated members vis-à-vis spending of MPLADS funds. Nominated members of the Rajya Sabha have been demanding that they be permitted to spend their funds in more than one state in view of the special nature of their membership. Ms Shabana Azmi, an accomplished film actor and social activist, who was nominated to the Rajya

Sabha wanted the guidelines to be amended to permit nominated members to fund welfare projects in different states 'as nominated members did not belong to any particular constituency'.[21]

The Rajya Sabha Committee saw reason in this argument and said a nominated MP could allocate funds to different states in different financial years. This, however, would pose logistical problems in the absence of a nodal agency to monitor the MP's spending. The committee urged the MS&PI to obtain the Speaker's consent for such an arrangement for nominated MPs. The ministry agreed to the suggestion and amended the guidelines as follows: 'Nominated Members of Lok Sabha and Rajya Sabha may also select works for implementation in one or more districts anywhere in the country.'[22]

The case of the two nominated members of the Lok Sabha is also peculiar. They represent the Anglo-Indian community that is thinly spread across several states, including Karnataka, Tamil Nadu, Maharashtra and West Bengal. If the guidelines pin them down to one state, they cannot do justice to their 'constituency'. Hence, the amended rule enables them to direct MPLADS funds to schemes that may help their community or the region where this community lives in different states.

This brings us to yet another issue relating to nominated members. Since nominated members do not generally come from the political class, they do not experience the pressure of constituents as politicians do. As a result, many nominated members fail to utilize the funds available to them under MPLADS, resulting in the accumulation of unspent amounts. Taking note of this problem at its meeting held on 7 March 2002, the Rajya Sabha Committee agreed with the suggestion of the MS&PI that the unspent balances of nominated members should be distributed equally among their successors in the House. The ministry accordingly amended para 3.10 of the guidelines as follows: 'In respect of elected members of the Rajya Sabha, the unspent balance left by the predecessor members of the Rajya Sabha in a particular state will be equally distributed among the successor Rajya Sabha members in that particular state. The unspent balance left by the nominated members of the Rajya Sabha/Lok Sabha will be equally distributed amongst the successor Nominated Members of Rajya Sabha/Lok Sabha respectively.'[23]

Apart from nominated members, the committees of the Rajya Sabha and Lok Sabha also pressed for similar flexibility in allocation of MPLADS funds by the presiding officers of the two Houses. At its meeting held on 7 December 2001, the Rajya Sabha Committee recommended that the deputy chairman of the House be allowed to undertake developmental works anywhere in the country 'owing to the special position' that the occupant of this office held. The proposal was referred by the MS&PI to the Lok Sabha Committee, which approved it with a rider that the same facility should be extended to the Speaker and the Deputy Speaker of the Lok Sabha. The issue was tossed back to the Rajya Sabha Committee, which approved the same as per the revised proposal of the committee of the other House. However, despite these recommendations, the MS&PI was not in favour of extending this facility to the presiding officers. It said the government had considered the recommendation 'carefully' and decided 'to maintain status quo in the matter.'

The government obviously turned down the proposal initially because of the logistical problems that would follow if this recommendation was implemented. If presiding officers allocate funds in a piecemeal fashion in various states across the country, the government would find it difficult to keep track of funds and to monitor the works recommended.

The Rajya Sabha Committee, however, was in no mood to let this pass. Following the government's decision, the committee revisited the issue at its meeting on 9 August 2002. At this meeting, the chairperson informed the members that she had discussed this issue with the minister of state in the MS&PI and the minister had 'agreed to the proposal'. However, she said, she would be writing to the ministry yet again 'in order to have the matter sorted out'.[24]

Rajya Sabha MPs Want Predecessors' Funds to be Bequeathed to Successors

MPs just do not leave any stone unturned to extract as much money as possible from the exchequer for sanctioning public projects. The popularity of the MPLADS programme has prompted many MPs to demand a higher allocation of funds. While this demand is still pending, Rajya Sabha members have realized that there are unspent amounts in the names of retiring members and are anxious to ensure that these funds do not revert to the Consolidated Fund of India. They feel that these funds should be bequeathed to the successor MPs in each state. This demand arose within years of the launch of the scheme, so much so that the Union government took a decision in December 1998 that unspent balances in each Rajya Sabha member's account should be transferred to successor MPs. Thereafter, in April 2000, the MS&PI wrote to the chief secretaries of all states and said information on unspent funds must be collated and communicated to them.

Mr B.P. Singhal renewed the demand when he wrote to the nodal ministry in July 2000 and said unspent MPLADS funds of ex-MPs of the Rajya Sabha should be passed on to their successors. He said whenever there were unspent balances of Rajya Sabha members, 10 per cent of the amount could be left with district collectors and the remaining 90 per cent distributed among the successor MPs. The MS&PI responded by saying it had already advised state governments on 25 April 2000 to issue instructions to nodal departments dealing with MPLADS to coordinate with districts and get information on the unspent funds of retiring MPs and the funds available for distribution among their successors. All this needed to be worked out, the ministry said. It, however, did not approve of the idea of leaving just 10 per cent of the amount with the district collectors to cover expenses for the unfinished part of the sanctioned works of ex-MPs. If more needed to be spent on these projects, it would be difficult to ask the successor MPs to refund the amounts already distributed to them.

In its letter to all chief secretaries, the MS&PI said that in accordance with the government's decision announced in Parliament on 23 December 1998, the unspent balance left by the predecessor Rajya Sabha MPs in a particular state would be equally distributed among the successors in that state. It enclosed a list of predecessor and successor Rajya Sabha MPs representing each state or UT from 1993 to 1998 and said the nodal department in the state government dealing with MPLADS should get information on balances remaining in the accounts of every ex-MP and work out the share of funds to be passed on to the successors. It said the state should provide a table showing total funds released under the scheme for each MP; the cost of all works completed till the date of retirement; further sums needed for completion of ongoing projects; funds needed to execute projects sanctioned before the MP's date of retirement; and finally, funds needed for projects recommended by the MP forty-five days prior to his date of retirement. The balance that remained after deduction of all these sums in respect of each MP could be totalled up and passed on to the successor MPs from the state. It said the aggregate amount in respect of one batch of retiring MPs for a particular year should be added and equally divided among the MPs elected against the vacancies caused by the said batch of retiring MPs. For example, if a total balance of ₹100 lakh is calculated in respect of a batch of five retired MPs, the share of the next five MPs elected against these vacancies would be ₹20 lakh each. The re-elected MPs from the same state should be excluded from this process. The interest accrued on these funds remaining in the accounts of retiring MPs should also be divided equally among the successors.[25]

The Lok Sabha Committee took the view that since the question related to Rajya Sabha members, it would be appropriate for the Rajya Sabha Committee to consider it first.[26]

MPs Want Matching Contribution from States

Members of Parliament have been relentless in pressing for implementation of MPLADS. The campaign was sustained over several years until the Union government relented and announced the scheme in 1993. Thereafter, MPs have persistently been arguing for enlarging the corpus of the fund. MPs have also been looking at other ways to augment the funds at their disposal to propose projects in their constituencies. One such proposal was the demand that state governments be directed to provide matching grants for all projects proposed under MPLADS. This was a clever ploy by MPs to double the fund without any fresh burden on the Union government.

Mr Y.S. Vivekananda Reddy, a member of the Lok Sabha, wrote to Mr Arun Shourie, the minister of state in MS&PI in May 2000 suggesting that state governments chip in with a matching grant for all projects proposed by parliamentarians under MPLADS. Mr Reddy made this suggestion after the minister rejected his request for raising the funds available to each MP every year. He urged the minister to convince state governments to underwrite 50 per cent of the cost of all projects proposed by MPs. If the states accepted this idea, the funds available to each MP every year would automatically double to ₹4 crore, he said.

The minister said he would put the matter before the MPLADS committees in the two Houses of Parliament. While doing so, he told the MP, '...as you know, the finances of the State Governments are in even worse shape than those of the Centre.'[27]

The Lok Sabha Committee considered the issue and said it shared the opinion of the MS&PI that the financial condition of the state governments was not very sound. Yet, it felt that if state governments chipped in with a matching contribution, the reach of MPLADS would be doubled. However, it made it clear that the contribution of state governments 'should not be made mandatory'.[28]

The Rajya Sabha Committee made this recommendation in its very first report when it said state governments should be 'requested' to sanction matching grants for MPLADS projects. This recommendation, however, did not find favour with the MS&PI. The ministry said MPLADS was an independent centrally sponsored scheme under which the choice of the MP was 'supreme'. It said 'state governments cannot be impressed upon to provide matching grants in each and every case and no mandatory provision can be formulated exclusively for this.' The ministry said the guidelines already provided for sharing of funds from other sources and these provisions could be utilized 'whenever an occasion arises'.[29]

The Rajya Sabha Committee said it 'fails to understand' the ministry's opinion that state governments cannot be impressed upon to provide a matching grant and that, in any case, this cannot be made mandatory. Matching grants from states will give 'a meaningful dimension' to MPLADS projects and it will also ensure timely completion of projects.

The ministry should therefore 'give a serious thought' to this recommendation and urge state governments to come up with matching grants, it said.

The MS&PI decided to duck the issue. It said it had received a similar request from an MP and had decided to refer this matter to the MPLADS committees of both Houses.

Following this response, the Rajya Sabha Committee said the ministry should act on its decision 'immediately'.[30]

Thereafter, the Rajya Sabha Committee concurred with the opinion of the Lok Sabha Committee. It said that if state governments could contribute 50 per cent of the cost of each project, it would double the impact of the scheme. However, it felt that the contribution of state governments should not be made mandatory.[31]

Where Should MPLADS' Funds Be Parked?

Yet another issue that this particular MP was exercised about was the bank in which the fund meant for his constituency would be lodged. The government and the Lok Sabha Committee had made it clear that the MPLADS funds should be deposited in public sector banks only. This ensured that an unhealthy rivalry would not ensue among private banks to bag these deposits in the districts. Such rivalry would result in some unscrupulous banks trying to corrupt either the MP or the district collector in order to get the deposits. Yet, it transpires that there is some healthy rivalry among nationalized banks as well to get these deposits. It would be the effort of every bank manager in the district to get the MP or the district collector to park these funds in his bank. Since this is MPLADS, the MP believes that it should be his prerogative to decide where the funds will be parked. Since the wheels of government move slowly, the sum of ₹2 crore that is allotted to an MP annually begins to accumulate and earn a decent amount of interest. The MP is keen to keep this deposit in a bank which has been helpful to him in the past or whose manager is his supporter or his party's sympathizer. The district collector, on the other hand, has his own plans regarding where to park these funds. He would like to oblige a bank manager who has been helpful to him or who is supportive of some governmental programmes launched in the area.

Mr Venkateswarlu said these funds should be deposited in nationlized banks 'in consultation with the MP'.[32]

The MS&PI, however, was far from pleased to note this suggestion. It said, as regarding prior consultation with the MP, 'it may please be noted that in this regarding (sic) the DCs have to exercise their discretion'.[33]

The committee considered this suggestion and said that first of all, MPs should be provided photocopies of bank passbooks and a bimonthly update so that they know the pace of utilization of funds. As regards consultation on where to park the funds, the committee felt that 'there is no harm in agreeing to the suggestion' that the deposit be made in a bank in consultation with the MP. 'The committee desires that the existing instructions should be reiterated to all DCs for compliance.'[34]

Apart from where the funds are parked, MPs are often unsure of the pace at which these funds are utilized. Mr C. Kuppuswami wrote to the Lok Sabha Committee in March 2000 stating that there is a need for a uniform procedure to maintain accounts. The committee said district collectors must open separate books of accounts in nationalized banks for each MP and photocopies of updated passbooks should be given to MPs on a bimonthly basis.[35]

Clubbing of Funds by Several MPs for a Single Project

As in the case of the proposal by four MPs to allocate funds to buy equipment for the Rotary Blood Bank in Delhi, there have been instances of groups of MPs coming together to fund a single project. The Rajya Sabha Committee considered the issue when four MPs from Kerala (three from the Rajya Sabha and one from the Lok Sabha) got together to fund the construction of a building for a government college at Chavara, Kerala. The committee approved the proposal and said that MPs could club their funds to execute projects. Acting on the recommendation of the committee, the MS & PI issued instructions to the government of Kerala that the funds of these four MPs could be clubbed to construct the building of the Government College.[36]

Another instance of such clubbing related to the proposal of Mr Karnendu Bhattacharjee, member of the Rajya Sabha and Mr Santosh Mohan Dev, member of the Lok Sabha, to jointly fund the construction of a community-hall-cum-auditorium at Silchar at an estimated cost of ₹3 crore. Since the cost of the project was huge, it was a case that warranted the clubbing of funds by MPs as also relaxation of guidelines which stipulate expenditure with an upper limit of ₹25 lakh per project. The Rajya

PUBLIC MONEY, PRIVATE AGENDA | 47

Sabha Committee approved it and the government conveyed its approval for relaxation of the guidelines in regard to the project cost to the district collector of Silchar.[37]

NOTES

1   First Report, Committee on MPLADS 1999–2000, presented to the Lok Sabha, 12 May 2000 Lok Sabha Secretariat, New Delhi, p. 17.
2   Ibid., pp. 17–18.
3   Ibid., p. 18.
4   Second Report, Committee on MPLADS 1999–2000, presented to the Lok Sabha, 22 August, 2000, Lok Sabha Secretariat, New Delhi, pp. 14–15.
5   Fourth Report, Committee on MPLADS 2000–2001, presented to the Lok Sabha, 23 March 2001, Lok Sabha Secretariat, New Delhi, p. 9.
6   Ninth Report, Committee on MPLADS 2000–2001, presented to the Lok Sabha, 20 December 2001, Lok Sabha Secretariat, New Delhi, pp. 2–3.
7   First Report, Committee on MPLADS 2009–2010, Fifteenth Lok Sabha, presented to the Lok Sabha on 24 February 2010, Lok Sabha Secretariat, New Delhi, p. 3.
8   Ibid., p. 4.
9   'Plan Panel's No to Calls for MPLADS Corpus Hike', p. 1, *The Indian Express*, New Delhi, 13 September 2010.
10 *The Indian Express*, New Delhi, 8 July 2011, p. 5.
11 Ibid.
12 Fifth Report, Committee on MPLADS 2000–2001, presented to the Lok Sabha, 24 April 2001, Lok Sabha Secretariat, New Delhi, pp. 10–11.
13 First Report, Committee on MPLADS 1999–2000, presented to the Lok Sabha, 12 May 2000, Lok Sabha Secretariat, New Delhi, p. 3.
14 Ibid., p. 7.
15 Ibid., p. 8.
16 Sixth Report, Committee on MPLADS 2000–2001, presented to the Lok Sabha, 31 July 2001, Lok Sabha Secretariat, New Delhi, p. 5.
17 Second Report, Committee on MPLADS 1999–2000, presented to the Lok Sabha, 22 August 2000, Lok Sabha Secretariat, New Delhi,

p. 25.
18 Ibid., pp. 25–26.
19 Ibid., p. 26.
20 Ibid., p. 27.
21 Second Report, Committee on MPLADS, presented to the Rajya Sabha, 11 December 2001, Rajya Sabha Secretariat, New Delhi, p. 48.
22 Ibid., p. 40.
23 Fourth Report, Committee on MPLADS, presented to the Rajya Sabha, 17 December 2002, Rajya Sabha Secretariat, New Delhi, p. 22.
24 Ibid., pp. 4–5.
25 Second Report, Committee on MPLADS 1999–2000, presented to the Lok Sabha, 22 August 2000, Lok Sabha Secretariat, New Delhi, pp. 30–31.
26 Ibid., pp. 28–29.
27 Third Report, Committee on MPLADS 2000–2001, presented to the Lok Sabha, 21 December 2000, Lok Sabha Secretariat, New Delhi, p. 27.
28 Ibid., p.27.
29 Second Report, Committee on MPLADS, presented to the Rajya Sabha, 11 December 2001, Rajya Sabha Secretariat, New Delhi, pp. 4–5.
30 Ibid., p. 5.
31 Fourth Report, Committee on MPLADS, presented to the Rajya Sabha, 17 December 2002, Rajya Sabha Secretariat, New Delhi, p. 42.
32 Second Report, Committee on MPLADS 1999–2000, presented to the Lok Sabha, 22 August 2000, Lok Sabha Secretariat, New Delhi, p. 11.
33 Ibid., p. 12.
34 Ibid., p. 14.
35 Ibid., p. 20.
36 Fourth Report, Committee on MPLADS, presented to the Rajya Sabha, 17 December 2002, Rajya Sabha Secretariat, New Delhi, p. 36.
37 Ibid., p. 44.

3

MPs Want Their Names 'Permanently' and 'Prominently' Etched in Stone

The anxiety of MPs to 'show' that they care for their constituents was largely behind the proposal that some funds be kept at their disposal for sanctioning some development schemes in their constituencies. Having achieved this in 1993, they wanted two more things done. The first was to enhance the fund so that they could do more. The second was to ensure that their contributions via this programme were permanently etched in stone. Clause 6.1 of the guidelines drawn up when the scheme was initially launched said that 'the name of the MP may be prominently erected at the site.' Many MPs felt that this was not enough because 'prominence' did not necessarily mean 'permanence'. Given the harsh climatic conditions in large parts of the country, it is common knowledge that signboards, though prominently erected, would be affected by the weather and the names of the benefactors behind all the 'noble' initiatives would wither away within a few years. Further, given the anti-incumbency trends in the Indian elections, many MPs would lose their seats in the next round and political rivals who trounce them would be only too happy to see the signboards extolling the work of their predecessors wiped out. Professor R.R. Pramanik was, therefore, speaking for most of his colleagues when he wrote to the committee in March 2000 seeking an amendment to Clause 6.1 of the guidelines. He said this clause should read '...the name of the MP shall permanently and prominently be erected at the site.'[1]

The MS&PI however, disagreed. It said there was no need to amend the guidelines because 'the existing provisions already mean to provide the fixation of permanent signboards and not temporary signboards. Therefore, there does not appear to be any need to amend the existing provisions.'[2]

The Lok Sabha committee however saw merit in the MP's proposal. It said Clause 6.1 should be amended to say that the name of the MP shall be 'permanently and prominently' erected at the sites.[3]

The committee's suggestion was accepted and Clause 6.1 of the guidelines was amended to read as follows: 'In order that people become aware that particular works have been executed with MPLADS funds, signboards carrying the inscription "MPLADS work" with the name of the MP, may be permanently and prominently erected at the sites.'[4]

MPs as Benefactors: They Want to Distribute the Cheques

The desire of every MP to be seen as a benefactor via MPLADS within his/her constituency is so great that he/she not only wants to be around when a project initiated under this scheme is inaugurated but also be there to hand over cheques to the agencies or contractors who execute the projects. This craving for local recognition of the MP's 'munificence', albeit at public cost, is so great that even the Lok Sabha Committee is supportive of it. The committee deliberated on this issue at its sitting on 26 July 2000 when a member, Mr Balbir Singh, raised it. Mr Singh told the committee that district collectors were not handing over cheques to the MPs because they viewed them as 'private persons'. This was the position even when the cheques were to be handed over to panchayats which had executed the works. Another MP who complained to the committee in this regard was Mr R.L. Bhatia. He said the collector of Amritsar refused to involve him in the distribution of cheques on the ground that it violated the instructions of the Punjab government. 'I shall be grateful if you send immediate instructions to the deputy commissioner, Amritsar to involve me in the distribution of MPLAD cheques to the beneficiaries,' he said.[5]

The committee considered these representations favourably and said, 'In the opinion of the committee the concerned District Collector/Magistrate should write to the MP informing him about the time of inauguration of the completed projects under MPLADS so that he could be present on the occasion. The committee recommends that the concerned MP, if he so desires, might be asked to distribute the cheques to the beneficiary/implementing agency under the MPLADS.'[6]

The government in its response said that instructions had been issued to all the district heads to inform the MP concerned about the time and venue of the inaugural function, if any, to be held for projects completed under MPLADS. As regards distribution of cheques to the beneficiaries or implementing agencies, the government said that it had decided that it would be better 'to leave the matters like handling cheques' to the implementing agencies/officers.[7]

These instructions notwithstanding, there have been instances when the district authorities have ignored the sitting MP during an inaugural ceremony. The Lok Sabha Committee had to deal with one such complaint from Mr A.P. Abdullakutty, the MP representing the Kannur parliamentary constituency in Kerala regarding the inauguration of the Vanchiyam–Adampara bridge. The MP wrote to the Speaker of the Lok Sabha on 21 May 2002 stating that the bridge in question, built with MPLADS funds, was scheduled to be inaugurated on 23 May but the district authorities had neither informed him nor obtained his consent. Local media reports indicated that the bridge would be inaugurated by a minister in the Kerala government in the presence of the local MLA and a former MP. He said this was unethical and constituted a clear violation of the existing rules. When contacted, the district collector told him that the inaugural function would go ahead as scheduled. The MP then urged the Speaker to stop the inauguration ceremony and also issue instructions to the district authorities to follow protocol in such matters. The MS&PI said instructions had gone out to all district heads that they should inform local MPs about the time and venue of inauguration of projects and schemes implemented under MPLADS.

The ministry said that the collector of Kannur had reported that the project was implemented with the funds provided by the former MP, Mr Mullapalli Ramachandran. However, strangely, though the ministry has the information in respect of all MPLADS projects, it chose not to settle this issue. It said a question had arisen as to whether the sitting MP or the former MP had sponsored this project and referred the matter to the Lok Sabha Committee to determine protocol in such situations.

Although Mr Abdullakutty's indignation appeared to indicate that he, too, had made some contribution to the bridge project, the Lok Sabha Committee did not answer the central question as to whether he had contributed to the project or not. While maintaining an ambiguity on this question, it recommended that 'both the MPs...former and the present who have contributed from their quota of MPLADS funds should be invited at the time of inauguration of a work...' The committee also recommended that in such situations the signboards at the project site must carry the names of both MPs.[8]

MPs Want to Choose the Agency Which Executes the Work

Ever since MPLADS was launched, there has been an ongoing conflict between MPs and district collectors on the choice of agencies/contractors to execute the projects cleared under this scheme. MPs feel that they ought to have a say in the choice of the agency which would execute each project because it is their fund and, therefore, their responsibility to ensure that the work is carried out in a proper way. The district collectors, on the other hand, are not willing to forego the right to choose the agency because, under the guidelines, they have the responsibility to implement the projects. Also, there is the lurking suspicion among district officials that if the MPs are given the right to choose the agency, they would knock off a fat commission from the contractor. The MPs counter this by saying that they have a responsibility to see that every work is executed well. Further, they point out that district collectors are no angels. Whatever be the merits of the arguments advanced on both sides, the fact is that the guidelines put the onus on the district collector.

This was emphasized by representatives of the MS & PI in the course of evidence they tendered before the Lok Sabha Committee on 26 July 2000. They drew the attention of the committee to para 2.1 of the guidelines, which reads as follows:

> Each MP will give a choice of works to the concerned head of the District who will get them implemented by following the established procedures, that is, he may be guided by the procedure laid down by the State Government subject to these Guidelines. In regard to works in urban areas, their implementation can be done through Commissioners/Chief Executive Officers of Corporations, Municipalities etc., or through the heads of districts concerned as per the option of the MPs. Implementation agencies can be either government or Panchayati Raj institutions or any other reputed non-governmental organisation who may be considered by the district head as capable of implementing the works satisfactorily. Engagement of private contractors is prohibited, wherever extant guidelines do not permit such engagement. For purposes of execution of works through Public Works Department (PWD), wings not

necessarily exclusively dealing with civil construction, but having competence in civil construction can be engaged—like for example, Public Health Engineering, Rural Housing Departments/Wings, Housing Boards, Electricity Boards, Urban Development Authorities etc. The head of the district shall identify the agency through which a particular work recommended by the MP should be executed.

As can be seen, the very opening sentence in para 2.1 of the guidelines states that 'Each MP will give a choice of works to the concerned head of the District who will get them implemented...' Again, the guidelines conclude on a similar note when it says, 'The head of the district shall identify the agency through which a particular work recommended by the MP should be executed.' From this it should be obvious to all concerned that the district collector has the final say in the selection of the agencies or contractors for executing these projects.

The wording of para 2.1, however, is not to the liking of either the Lok Sabha Committee or the MPs. As a result, they detect ambiguities where none exists. Even though the guidelines emphatically state that the district collector will have 'the final say', the Lok Sabha Committee perceived vagueness and said: 'The committee are of the opinion that Para 2.1 of the Guidelines on MPLADS was not clear as to who was the final authority—Member of Parliament or District Collector—to decide about the agency through which a particular work was to be executed under MPLADS.' The Committee, therefore recommended that the MS & PI 'should make it clear and issue necessary instructions in this regard without any delay'. It further said that since an MP was a representative of the people, he 'should have the discretion in the identification of agency through which a particular work was to be executed under MPLADS'. Also, giving the MP such discretion should not be a cause of worry because 'after all his discretion was limited to a government agency of the state government'.⁹

The Lok Sabha Committee revisited this issue in its ninth report which dealt with the action taken by the government on the recommendations made in the second report. This recommendation was placed under the category 'recommendations/observations in respect of which replies of government are still awaited', because the MS & PI diplomatically postponed a negative response to the proposal by saying that this recommendation had been forwarded to the Rajya Sabha Committee. 'Further action will be taken on receipt of recommendation of the Rajya Sabha Committee,' it said.¹⁰

Whatever the opinion of the government in this matter, this particular recommendation of the committee is full of flaws. First of all, it injects vagueness in para 2.1 of the guidelines where none exists. Secondly, it fails to see what is so obvious to anyone with basic language skills, namely, that there is no blanket prohibition of private contractors. Para 2.1 says that, 'Implementation agencies can be either government or Panchayati Raj institutions or any other reputed non-governmental organisation who may be considered by the district head as capable of implementing the works satisfactorily.' At another place, it states: 'Engagement of private contractors is prohibited, wherever extant guidelines do not permit such engagement.' Since the government often engages private contractors and prohibits their entry only in rare situations, it is obvious that a good portion of MPLADS projects is assigned to them.

Therefore, the committee's recommendation that MPs should have the discretion to choose the agency that executes the work because his discretion is 'limited' to a government agency, is wholly erroneous. It only shows the anxiety of the committee to see that MPs have the discretion to decide on the contractor for each project. That this was not a good idea became obvious when a television news channel did a sting operation on MPs and found many of them soliciting bribes and commissions from companies and contractors to clear projects under this scheme. The sting operation clearly established the fact that MPs were deciding the agencies or contractors who would execute the sanctioned works. The sting operation led to a furore in the Parliament, leading to the appointment of a parliamentary committee to probe the MPLADS payments scandal. As the parliamentary investigations began, the Speaker of the Lok Sabha suspended the MPs involved. The committee investigated all the cases that were highlighted by the television channel and came to the conclusion that the conduct of two MPs was 'improper and unethical' while that of two other MPs was 'irresponsible and negligent and clearly amounts to an act of impropriety'.[11]

The committee said that the conduct of none of the four MPs was above board and therefore, 'they need to be handed out appropriate punishment,' which was as follows: The period of abstention from the sittings of the House and the committees by all the four members would be deemed to be their suspension from the membership of the House and they may be reprimanded.[12]

MPs Want Final Say in Payments to Contractors

In its first report, the Rajya Sabha Committee asked the MS & PI to examine the suggestion of Dr B.B. Dutta, MP, regarding payments to executing agencies. The MP said that once a contract is awarded, 50 per cent of the project cost is given to the executing agency 'but the remaining amount is released only after protracted negotiations'. He, therefore, wanted the final payment to be made 'without delay' on the basis of a certificate issued by the MP concerned that the work had been completed. The ministry said it could not accept this recommendation because the MPLADS projects are executed under the supervision of district collectors and they have to follow the established procedure for making payments to executing agencies. Therefore, the suggestion that payments be made on the basis of certificates given by MPs 'cannot be acceded to'.

The committee rejected the opinion of the MS&PI and said if the executing authority displayed an 'element of distrust' in the completion certificates issued by MPs, the MPLAD Scheme would have 'no real meaning' and the basic objective of the scheme would be defeated. It said Dr Dutta's idea was good because it would prevent any delay in release of funds to the executing agency, which is what generally happens when the district collector has to certify the completion of a project.

The MS&PI, however, stood its ground. The power to certify the completion of projects and to disburse payments is central to the wielding authority and no bureaucrat worth his salt will ever give this up and surrender this authority to anybody else, even if it is the MPLAD Scheme. The ministry, therefore, said the district collector had to follow the established procedure while making payments. Since the onus for completing the work is on the district collector, the suggestion that the final payment due to the IA be made on the basis of certificates issued by MPs 'does not appear to be practicable as the concerned MP may not be able to visit the site...and certify its completion satisfactorily'. 'Moreover, in that case the collector cannot be held responsible if the work completion is not satisfactory.'

But the Rajya Sabha Committee rarely takes 'no' for an answer. Also, when the bureaucracy says anything which amounts to doubting the sincerity or commitment of MPs, it refuses to accept the government's point of view. This approach of the committee came to the fore in this case as well, resulting in a full-fledged tussle between MPs and the bureaucracy. Responding to the ministry's 'Action-taken Report', the Rajya Sabha Committee said it 'failed to understand' why the completion certificate given by an MP was not enough to disburse final payments. It said the district collector could inform the MP of the completion of the project and secure the MP's concurrence. It said the ministry was 'evasive' in its reply when it said the collector cannot be held responsible for the project if the MP issued the completion certificate. If this approach was accepted, there was every likelihood of the funds being misused and incomplete projects would be the order of the day.[13]

MPs Seek Mobility via MPLADS

Indian parliamentary constituencies are notoriously huge. With close to 1.2 billion people of whom 750 million are electors, the average Lok Sabha constituency has over 2 million people of whom 1.5 million are on the electoral rolls. Until the fresh delimitation of constituencies in 2007, the composition of parliamentary constituencies was rather haphazard. Even within a state, the disparity was obvious. Some were humongous like Outer Delhi with over 2.5 million electors and some were minuscule like Chandni Chowk with just 0.2 million electors in the heart of Old Delhi. The latest delimitation exercise has done much to ensure an equitable distribution of electors among all constituencies within a state. While that resolves the problem in so far as numerical disparity among constituencies is concerned, the geographical problem remains. Most rural Lok Sabha constituencies are spread over vast areas and can stretch to over 200 kilometres from end to end. This means an MP will have to spend a lot on travel to visit different parts of his constituency and this is certain to burn a hole in his pocket. MPs who find it difficult to cope with this situation keep pressing for transport facilities in their constituencies. It is always turned down by the Union government, though the governments in some states have directed deputy commissioners in the districts to provide cars to MPs for constituency tours. But, there is no uniformity in this, nor is there any guarantee that a car would be waiting at the MP's door on arrival even if a state has committed itself to offering such a facility for every MP.

The Rajya Sabha Committee, in its first report, raised the issue of providing vehicles to MPs to enable them to tour in their constituencies. It said that the interest accrued on MPLADS funds should be utilized to purchase vehicles for MPs because 'members do a lot of touring' to monitor development works in their constituencies. The MS & PI shot down this proposal ab initio but chose to rest its gun on the shoulders of the Rajya Sabha chairman. It said the chairman of the House had discussed this issue with leaders of political parties and 'he was not inclined to agree to the suggestion'. Once the ministry invoked the name of the chairman, the committee backed off. It said in its second report that 'since the Hon'ble Chairman, Rajya Sabha is not inclined to agree to the suggestion, the committee does not want to further pursue the matter'.

In order to ensure a credible and permanent transport arrangement for every MP within his constituency, Dr Lakshmi Narayan Pandeya, an MP from Madhya Pradesh, suggested that MPLADS funds be used to provide every MP with a car in his constituency. He said the maintenance of the vehicle could be done out of the interest that accrues on the MPLADS funds, which are deposited in banks.

The Lok Sabha Committee referred this representation to the minister of state for Statistics and Programme Implementation. The ministry responded by saying that these funds are to be utilized only for the creation of durable assets and that purchase of vehicles is just not covered under this scheme. The ministry pointed out that the only vehicle which can be purchased under the guidelines are ambulances. Further, the interest that accrues on the deposits can be utilized only for works permitted by the guidelines. The ministry said the guidelines do not permit incurring of revenue expenditure. Therefore, these funds cannot be used for maintenance of vehicles. Finally, it said this matter 'has already been considered by the Rajya Sabha Committee and the Chairman of the Rajya Sabha is not in favour of the same'.[14]

Another MP, Mr Suresh Pasi, asked the Lok Sabha Committee to permit the purchase of a jeep by MPs. But the matter did not end here because another parliamentary committee—the Joint Committee on Salaries and Allowances of Members of Parliament—had also considered this issue in one of its meetings in April 2000. The committee said that in response to the questionnaire circulated among MPs, 'a view had emerged that a vehicle should be made available to MPs whenever they visit their constituency.' It said one of the suggestions put forward was that the interest generated on MPLADS funds be utilized to provide a vehicle to the MP. The vehicle would be at the disposal of the district collector and provided to the MP, whenever the latter visited his constituency. The Joint Committee saw merit in this suggestion and decided to refer the same to the committee dealing with MPLADS.

The Lok Sabha Committee on MPLADS found this demand reasonable. It said banks offer 5 to 7 per cent interest on MPLADS funds. This money could be used to buy a vehicle. The vehicle would be in the custody of the district collector and made available to the MP when the latter visited the constituency. However, it felt that there should be a ceiling on maintenance expenditure. Justifying the proposal, the committee said the vehicle 'was not to be purchased every year and it would be a one time affair'.[15]

The government agreed to the suggestion and informed the committee that instructions had gone out to all district collectors to make available 'as far as possible' vehicles for MPs to enable them to inspect projects taken up under MPLADS.[16]

The desire to utilize these funds to buy cars for the use of MPs during visits to their constituencies was quite in contrast to the pious declarations made by MPs when the programme was launched. For example, the Rajya Sabha Committee on MPLADS said in its very first report that while it made sense to use the interest accrued on funds parked in banks for 'developmental' schemes, it was important to stress on the meaning of the term 'developmental'. It said the nodal ministry should adopt 'strict measures' to channelize resources for such projects which add to capital resources of a particular district and leads to augmentation of economic resources 'so that functional economic indicators like addition to increased per capita income, increased employment of labour etc. could be reflected in a more positive term after the project [...] is completed'.[17]

How all this squares up with the interest money being used to purchase vehicles for MPs is anybody's guess. Suffice it to say that the initial idealism evaporated a few years after the scheme got under way.

The MS&PI responded by saying that the purpose of the scheme was to create durable assets. Accordingly, the interest accrued would also be used for developmental work as approved under the guidelines. It hoped that works chosen by MPs would augment the economic resources of a district, leading to increased per capita income, employment generation, etc.[18]

In other words, the ministry, too, succumbed to pressure from MPs and gave in to the demand for purchase of vehicles, while offering superficial sympathy to the idea of using these funds only for 'developmental' works and for creation of 'durable assets'.

An Office for Our MP

In India, the government does not provide offices to MPs in their constituencies. In some states, the local governments allocate offices but there is no uniform national policy in this regard. As a result, most MPs have their offices within their homes in the constituency, but this is not a happy arrangement. Since several hundred constituents land up at the MP's residence to meet him when he is in the constituency, it results in a lack of privacy for the MP and members of his family. Once MPLADS got going, many MPs found that the number of visitors had only increased. Further, in India there is no tradition of calling and seeking an appointment when a constituent wishes to see his MP. Once it is known that the MP has returned from Delhi to spend the weekend with his family, constituents walk into his residence beginning from 8 a.m. and within an hour or so, the MP's drawing room is chock-a-block with visitors and, mind you, no one has come with an appointment. This has prompted many

MPs to demand a separate office in a prominent town in the constituency to meet visitors and monitor the progress of projects funded under this scheme and also to meet constituents who put forward proposals for various development projects. Among the MPs who pressed for utilization of this fund for this purpose was Professor R.R. Pramanik. In a letter to the chairman of the Lok Sabha Committee in March 2000 he said the fund should be used to build and maintain the MP's office in the constituency. The government, however, shot down the proposal.[19]

The matter was raised by a member of the Lok Sabha, Mr B. Venkateshwarlu, in a letter to the committee in February 2000. He sought the committee's permission to spend ₹10 lakh on the construction of an office for himself in his constituency as it would be useful to the people. The committee sent the request to the nodal ministry, which in its response said works of a capital nature leading to the creation of durable assets can be taken up under this scheme; however, these funds cannot be used to construct office buildings. Hence, these funds could not be used to construct MPs' offices, the ministry said. The committee concurred with the ministry on this issue and said the guidelines impose a specific restriction on the construction of office buildings.[20]

Who Will Bear the Administrative Expenses?

Once MPLADs got into operation, the question arose as to who would bear the administrative expenses at the district level. In the absence of a separate provision for meeting administrative costs and contingency expenses, the execution of projects depended wholly on the availability of staff and infrastructure in the nodal district for each MP. Given the tight budgets and limited human resources available to the district collector, sanction and monitoring of projects was invariably subject to delays. MPs sought to overcome this impediment by suggesting that a small percentage of the fund be set apart for administrative expenses.

The Rajya Sabha Committee discussed this issue at its meeting on 7 December 2001 and suggested that district authorities be allowed to deduct 0.5 per cent of the fund given to each MP every year as administrative costs. It said that the guidelines should be amended to provide for such deduction. It asked the MS&PI to work out the modalities and communicate the same to district authorities all over the country.

The ministry accepted the suggestion. It said this administrative cost should be mentioned separately while preparing estimates for a project. As regards what is permissible as contingency expenditure, it drew up an elaborate list, which included stationery, office equipment like computers, etc., payment of an honorarium/overtime to staff put on MPLADS work, and telephone and postal charges. It said the contingent expenses must not be used to purchase office furnishings, for office renovation, purchase of mobile phones and subscription charges for such phones, purchase of vehicles, fuel for vehicles and purchase of air-conditioners and refrigerators. It said a separate account would have to be maintained for contingent expenses and made available to auditors.[21]

The long negative list drawn up by the ministry has a reason. In many states, MPs are provided offices at the district headquarters and in the absence of such specific rules in regard to non-permissible expenses, there is every danger of this contingency allowance being used to furnish MPs' offices or to buy air-conditioners and refrigerators for them.

Guest Houses for Constituents

As stated earlier, Indian MPs are under tremendous constituency pressure. Electors make a lot of demands on MPs. They seek jobs, ration cards, school and college admissions and even financial assistance for marriages and other ceremonies. Apart from all this, they generally see the MP's house in New Delhi as some kind of a guest house for people from the constituency. Therefore, there is a steady flow of visitors, mostly unannounced, at the MP's house in the capital and most of them expect the MP to provide them board and lodging and logistical support for whatever they propose to do. Therefore, it is quite common to find dozens of people 'staying' at an MP's house in New Delhi. However, there are some MPs like those who represent Lakshadweep and the Andaman and Nicobar Islands, who come under added pressure because their electors want such guest house facilities at the mainland port they land in apart from the national capital. Giving in to such pressure, Mr P.M. Sayeed, Deputy Speaker of the Lok Sabha, who represented Lakshadweep, proposed that he wished to spend MPLADS funds to build guest houses for his constituents at Ernakulam and Kozhikode in Kerala and Mangalore in Karnataka. The proposal violated the guidelines because elected members of the Lok Sabha are barred from spending on projects outside their constituencies. Yet, the Lok Sabha Committee approved the same and the Rajya Sabha Committee followed suit, obviously in deference to the office that Mr Sayeed held in the other House.

The government, however, was not impressed. As usual, it said it had 'carefully' considered the recommendations of the two committees. However, it felt that construction of guest houses outside the constituency of the Deputy Speaker 'would create a bad precedent'. It said if the government relaxed the rule in Mr Sayeed's case, it 'would have widespread repercussions and should not be allowed'. Further, the guidelines also did not permit the construction of official or residential buildings. It conveyed its opinion to the two committees. After it heard from the government, the Rajya Sabha Committee decided not to pursue the matter.[22]

Transparency and Accountability in MPLADS

When MPs insisted that their names should be 'permanently and prominently' etched on the plaque put at every MPLADS project site, the government used the occasion to incorporate rules to promote public awareness of the scheme and to ensure transparency and accountability in the implementation of MPLADS. In order to achieve these purposes, the district authorities were instructed as follows: A plaque for each work executed under MPLADS should carry the inscription 'MPLADS Work', indicate the cost of the project, date of commencement, completion and inauguration and the name of the sponsoring MP; the plaque should be prominently erected at the workplace; a list of all completed and ongoing works with MPLADS funds should be displayed at the district authority office and posted on the website for information of the general public; information should be provided on all aspects of the MPLAD Scheme, such as works recommended by MPs, works sanctioned/not sanctioned, cost of work sanctioned, implementing agencies, quality of work completed, etc., to the general public as required under the Right to Information Act, 2005, as the implementation of the scheme had been brought under the purview of this Act. In addition, the district authorities were told that all work details should be uploaded to the MPLADS website (www.mplads.nic.in) where information on funds released and details of work completed or work under execution were available. The government made it to clear to all district heads that transparency must be ensured in regard to the execution of MPLADS by keeping data in the public domain. It informed them that the launch of the MPLADS website and updating of information on the progress of works on this website had been 'received well'.[23]

In its first report the government said 'strengthening financial discipline and enforcing transparency and accountability at the ground level have been of utmost importance under the MPLAD Scheme, particularly during the last two years'. In order to achieve this, the following measures were taken: Software for monitoring MPLADS works was launched in November 2004 to promote e-governance; the status regarding each project—physical and financial progress—is communicated to all MPs from time to time; district authorities were told that they are responsible for providing information to the people on all aspects of MPLADS under the Right to Information Act; a sum of ₹1 crore was automatically released for each MP soon after the constitution of the Lok Sabha or election to the Rajya Sabha; utilization certificates (UCs) for the previous financial year and audit certificate, for the funds released in the year prior to the previous year were made pre-requisites for the release of the next instalment; and district authorities were told it was important for the implementing agency to furnish work completion reports.[24]

Notes

1. Second Report, Committee on MPLADS 1999–2000, presented to the Lok Sabha, 22 August 2000, Lok Sabha Secretariat, New Delhi, p. 7.
2. Ibid., p. 9.
3. Ibid., p. 10.
4. Ninth Report, Committee on MPLADS 2000–2001, presented to the Lok Sabha, 20 December 2001, Lok Sabha Secretariat, New Delhi, p. 5.
5. Second Report, Committee on MPLADS 1999–2000, presented to the Lok Sabha, 22 August 2000, Lok Sabha Secretariat, New Delhi, p. 33.
6. Ibid.
7. Ninth Report, Committee on MPLADS 2000–2001, presented to the Lok Sabha, 20 December 2001, Lok Sabha Secretariat, New Delhi, p. 7.
8. Eleventh Report, Committee on MPLADS 2003–2004, presented to the Lok Sabha, 9 April 2003, Lok Sabha Secretariat, New Delhi, pp. 1–2.
9. Second Report, Committee on MPLADS 1999–2000, presented to the Lok Sabha, 22 August 2000, Lok Sabha Secretariat, New Delhi, p. 32.
10. Ninth Report, Committee on MPLADS 2000–2001, presented to the Lok Sabha, 20 December 2001, Lok Sabha Secretariat, New Delhi, p. 15.

11 Report of the Committee to Inquire into Allegations of Improper Conduct on the Part of Some Members in the Matter of Implementation of MPLAD Scheme, tabled in the Lok Sabha on 13 March 2006, Lok Sabha Secretariat, New Delhi, p. 40.
12 See ibid., p. 50, for a full discussion of the allegations against the MPs and the report of the committee. See also, 'MPLADS and Corruption', Chapter 10.
13 Second Report, Committee on MPLADS, presented to the Rajya Sabha, 11 December 2001, Rajya Sabha Secretariat, New Delhi, pp. 9–10.
14 Second Report, Committee on MPLADS 1999–2000, presented to the Lok Sabha, 22 August 2000, Lok Sabha Secretariat, New Delhi, p. 1.
15 Ibid., p. 2.
16 Ninth Report, Committee on MPLADS 2000–2001, presented to the Lok Sabha, 20 December 2001, Lok Sabha Secretariat, New Delhi, p. 4.
17 Second Report, Committee on MPLADS, presented to the Rajya Sabha, 11 December 2001, Rajya Sabha Secretariat, New Delhi, p. 2.
18 Ibid.
19 Second Report, Committee on MPLADS 1999–2000, presented to the Lok Sabha, 22 August 2000, Lok Sabha Secretariat, New Delhi, p. 8.
20 Ibid., p. 21.
21 Fourth Report, Committee on MPLADS, presented to the Rajya Sabha, 17 December 2002, Rajya Sabha Secretariat, New Delhi, p. 27–28.
22 Ibid., p. 50.
23 First Report, Member of Parliament Local Area Development Scheme (MPLADS), Ministry of Statistics and Programme Implementation, Government of India, New Delhi, December 2006, pp. 6–7.
24 Ibid., pp. 9–10.

4

One Rule, Many Exceptions!

People often complain that politicians in India have a natural inclination to violate the rules or to bend them to suit their needs. However much the political class may protest at such generalizations, the fact is that they are naturally inclined to flout the law.

If one looks for a sociological explanation for this trait among politicians, one could say that despite six decades of democracy, India is still a feudal society and the people have not got over the habit of putting persons who wield political power on a pedestal. Even if politicians initially object to the submissive attitude of the people and all the toadying and sycophancy that come their way, it eventually gets to them and they begin to see themselves as a class apart from the aam aadmi (common man). Consequently, everything the politician does is meant to retain and drive home this distinction and as everyone knows, this is best achieved when the politician signals that he is above the law that applies to the common man.

Thus, the basic instinct of politicians, barring some honourable exceptions, is to bend the rule and if this is not possible, to brazenly break the rule. If one wishes to study this special characteristic of the Indian politician, one must enter the world of MPLADS. One can see this trait in stark relief in the operation of this scheme, which began with the pious promise that it would create 'durable assets' and thus build the much-needed physical and social infrastructure across the country.

The scheme began with a set of guidelines to enable MPs to choose projects that would be in tune with the overall objective of the scheme. The guidelines were drawn up because everyone, including some well-meaning members of the political class, knew that the scheme would be skewed towards the self-aggrandizement of MPs without a clear list of dos and don'ts. Yet, within a few years of its launch, the government was under pressure from MPs to amend the guidelines or to stretch the meaning of words to such an extent that it completely negated the prohibition. However, there were many impatient MPs who were simply not willing to go through the rigmarole of getting the guidelines amended and decided to unilaterally bend the rules to fit in a project they had in mind. There were still others who unabashedly flouted the rule and left the government and the MPLADS committees in the two Houses to pick up the pieces. The authorities have, on occasion, been compelled to grant ex-post-facto clearance for a project which has been funded by an MP in gross violation of the guidelines.

The tendency among MPs to bend rules is so strong and compelling that even those who are vested with the responsibility to ensure compliance of MPs to the guidelines cannot withstand the temptation to flout them. That is why this chapter on flouting the rules must begin with the proposal of Mr B.B. Ramaiah, MP and chairman of the Lok Sabha Committee on MPLADS, which has the responsibility to ensure that the scheme functions within the defined parameters.

The MPLADS guidelines clearly prohibit the use of these funds for erection of memorials.

This rule is meant to prevent MPs from using public funds to promote their own families or political outfits. This prohibition is all the more relevant in the Indian context because in the absence of such a restriction, fawning MPs would seek to ingratiate themselves with party bosses by squandering away public money via MPLADS funds to build memorials for the forebears of their political masters. Yet, despite this strict rule prohibiting construction of memorials, Mr Ramaiah wrote to the committee on 20 March 2002 proposing erection of memorials for Mr G.M.C. Balayogi, former Speaker of the Lok Sabha, who died in a helicopter crash in Andhra Pradesh. Mr Balayogi, who died in harness, had been elected, like Mr Ramaiah, on a Telugu Desam ticket to the Lok Sabha. Mr Ramaiah wanted to construct the memorials at Kaikalur, Eluru and Tanuka in Andhra Pradesh. Mr Balayogi's helicopter had crashed at Kaikalur in the Krishna district, Andhra Pradesh. Mr Ramaiah said he wanted to spend ₹3 lakh for a memorial at Kaikalur and another ₹2 lakh for a memorial at Eluru, where Mr Balayogi attended his last public engagement. Since Mr Balayogi was the first Speaker to die in office, Mr Ramaiah felt that it would be appropriate to erect these memorials.

The Lok Sabha Committee was obviously in a bind. What choice does a committee have when the chairman himself proposes a deviation from the rules? The matter was considered at the committee's meeting on 9 April 2002 and promptly 'approved it as a special case' and forwarded it to the MS & PI for 'necessary action'.[1]

The matter went up to the Rajya Sabha Committee. This was a delicate issue for this committee as well because of two reasons. The proposed memorials were for a former Speaker of the Lok Sabha, who had died under tragic circumstances midway through his term. Secondly, it had been mooted by the chairman of the Lok Sabha Committee. The Rajya Sabha Committee approved it 'as a special case'. The MS & PI turned down the recommendation. It emphatically said that funding of memorials was prohibited 'in the light of the specific restriction of memorials or memorial buildings' in the guidelines. The government said 'there should not be any deviation from the Guidelines'.

The ministry's firm 'no' compelled the Lok Sabha Committee to revisit the proposal at its meeting on 16 May 2002. This time, the committee scaled down the number of memorials proposed and cleared the proposal for the erection of just one memorial at Kaikalur, the village where Mr Balayogi's helicopter had crashed, 'as a special case'.[2]

Even this was a violation of the guidelines, but the committee obviously did not have the heart or the gumption to knock down the proposal of its chairman and, therefore, came up with a recommendation that appeared to be a compromise. Meanwhile, the Rajya Sabha Committee had the government's opinion before it; yet, since the proposal had been scaled down, it approved the same at its meeting on 27 May 2002.

Thereafter, the committee's recommendation went to the MS&PI for action. The ministry, however, put its foot down and said construction of memorials was impermissible under MPLADS. The ministry said it had 'carefully' considered the proposal and decided that the erection of memorials 'is not a developmental activity, and therefore, no memorial should be allowed under MPLADS'. It reminded the committee of the guidelines and said 'the government is of the view that there should not be any deviation from the Guidelines in this case'. The Rajya Sabha Committee, however, was unhappy with the government's response. In the very first chapter of its fourth report it declared that it had not accepted the government's reply.[3]

Lord Denning's famous phrase, 'who will guard the guardians?' often comes to mind when one notices infringements by those who are supposed to enforce the rules.

However, the story of memorials is incomplete without a reference to two other proposals—by Mr Mahesh Chandra Sharma and the other by Mr A.C. Jose—for erecting memorials. Mr Sharma, a member of the Rajya Sabha wrote to the minister in charge of the MS&PI on 13 October 2000 and sought clearance for spending ₹3 lakh on a memorial community hall named after Pandit Deen Dayal Upadhyay in Bhansol Gram Panchayat in the

Udaipur district. The district magistrate of Udaipur, informed the MP that the proposal cannot be approved under the guidelines. The MP wanted the minister to intervene.

The ministry examined the request and reported that there is a specific restriction on construction of memorials and memorial buildings in the guidelines. It thereafter referred the issue to the committees of the two Houses. The Lok Sabha Committee considered the proposal at its meeting on 7 August 2001 and agreed with the ministry. It declined its approval and said there is a specific restriction on the construction of memorials and memorial buildings in the guidelines.[4]

What we see from this sequence of events is that the Lok Sabha Committee, which was headed by Mr B.B. Ramaiah rejected Mr Sharma's proposal in August 2001 on the ground that the construction of memorials was prohibited under the rules. Yet, seven months hence (on 20 March 2002), Mr Ramaiah himself moved the committee for the approval of three memorials for Mr Balayogi and the committee gave its consent a month thereafter.

Even more intriguing is the outcome of the proposal made by Mr A.C. Jose, an MP from Kerala. Mr Jose, a member of the Lok Sabha, proposed the erection of a statue of Mahatma Gandhi in a meditative pose, like the one in Parliament House, in front of the collectorate in Trissur. He said the statue would be 'an inspiration' for the people of Trissur and it would be funded from the interest accrued on his MPLADS fund. The Lok Sabha Committee approved the same 'as it relates to a pious action of extending a mark of respect to the Father of the Nation'. But the proposal was turned down by the MS&PI because it violated the guidelines. The member subsequently wrote to the committee and sought its intervention.[5]

The Rajya Sabha Committee considered this proposal on 9 April 2002, the very day it discussed the issue of memorials for Mr Balayogi, and approved it. However, this recommendation, like the one pertaining to the Balayogi memorial, did not find favour with the MS&PI. The government, as always, sugar-coated its negative response. It said it had 'carefully' considered the recommendations of the committees of the two Houses regarding the erection of the statue of Mahatma Gandhi and had decided 'not to allow any memorial'. The decision was conveyed to the secretariats of the two Houses in July 2002. The government said '...in view of the specific restriction under the Guidelines on MPLADS for construction of memorial buildings, it has been decided not to allow any memorial under the scheme'.[6]

However, here comes the twist. The MS&PI rejected the proposal for a Balayogi memorial but the Rajya Sabha Committee declared that it had not accepted the government's decision. But when the government rejected the proposal for a Mahatma Gandhi statue in Trissur, the Rajya Sabha Committee announced that it 'does not desire to pursue (it) in view of the reply of the government'! In other words, the committee applied one standard for Mr Balayogi and another for Mahatma Gandhi.

The exception made in prohibition the case of on memorials was only the first. Many more were to follow as MPs began proposing projects that did not conform to the guidelines. The fundamental rule that money must only be ploughed into projects that resulted in the creation of 'durable assets' was given a go-by as more and more proposals came in for funding purchase of books, furniture, television sets, refrigerators, etc.

If one is looking for an instance of gross violation of several clauses in the guidelines, there is no better example than the one from Sikkim.

The Rajya Sabha Committee considered the 'proposal' of Mr Bhim Dahal for an ex-post-facto approval of purchase of books at its meeting on 7 March 2002. Since it was faced with a fait accompli, the committee had no option but to approve the same 'as a special case'. Following the committee's decision, the MS&PI issued instructions to the district collector of Gangtok on 21 March 2002 for ex-post-facto relaxation in the guidelines for purchase of books costing ₹20 lakh.[7]

It is difficult to understand the 'instructions' given by

the ministry to the district collector of Gangtok to relax the guidelines, when the district authorities had themselves violated the guidelines to buy the books. Since the money had already been spent, the committees of the two Houses had no choice but to approve the purchase even though it violated several clauses in the guidelines. Equally surprising was the silence of the committees and the government on the conduct of the district authorities in this case.

Yet another case of ex-post-facto approval pertains to the construction of the Shri Aurobindo Institute of Indian Culture in Shillong. Two MPs—Mr B.B. Dutta and Mr O.L. Nongtdu—of the Rajya Sabha approached the House Committee for granting ex-post-facto approval for this project costing ₹1.52 crore. The committee approved the same and the MS&PI followed up the committee's decision by conveying the same to the district collector of East Khasi Hills district, Shillong.[8]

The Rajya Sabha Committee considered the proposal of Mr Anantray Devshanker Dave, a member of the House, regarding the purchase of books and furniture for the Pandit Shyamji Krishna Verma Public Memorial Trust, a public library at Mandvi. The committee cleared the proposal and said the district collector of Kutch should be appointed as a nodal officer for the procurement of books. The MS&PI promptly referred the matter to the Lok Sabha Committee while simultaneously asking the Rajya Sabha Secretariat to furnish details of the proposal.[9]

The Rajya Sabha Committee also cleared the proposal of Mr Dinsha J. Patel, a member of the Lok Sabha, for the purchase of storage refrigerators for blood banks. The committee also directed the authorities to appoint a government agency to purchase the refrigerator. The government responded by saying that it had asked the Ministry of Health and Family Welfare for information on items of public utility needed by government hospitals which can be included under the MPLAD Scheme, including storage refrigerators for blood banks. 'Further action will be taken on receipt of reply from them,' it said.[10]

How the Rules Bend Before Ministers

Mr Vijay Goel, a Lok Sabha MP, sought permission for the purchase of four buses or vans to ferry people through the Chandni Chowk area in his constituency in the heart of Old Delhi. Mr Goel said Chandni Chowk was a heritage city which attracted a large number of foreign and domestic tourists. The area, he said, truly represented the secular character of the nation. However, the area was overcrowded and traffic moved at a snail's pace. In order to streamline traffic, he wanted to introduce a free bus service to help tourists. The Lok Sabha Committee considered the matter at a meeting in March 2001 and put off a decision until the opinion of the MS&PI was obtained.

The MS&PI said that the guidelines do not permit the purchase of vehicles other than ambulances for government hospitals and reputed service organizations. The rules permit expenditure which leads to the creation of durable assets and there is a specific ban on revenue expenditure and procurement of inventory items or stock of any type.[11]

The Lok Sabha Committee declined permission for the purchase of buses on the ground that it was against the guidelines. It said the purchase of vehicles could create problems of maintenance and recurring expenditure.[12]

However, all the objections raised by the ministry and the committee vanished a year later. Around fifteen months after this report was submitted to Parliament, the committee reversed its decision on Mr Vijay Goel's proposal. This time, Mr Goel sought permission to purchase five battery-operated open buses (earlier he wanted to fund the purchase of four buses) to ferry tourists in the Chandni Chowk area in Delhi. The committee considered the proposal and without much ado approved the same at its meeting held on 5 December 2002. However, while doing so, the committee did not think it necessary to refer to its earlier decision and to provide reasons for reversing the same. Why did the committee do such a neat somersault? Further, the committee invariably refers such ticklish proposals to the MS&PI for its comments. However, it chose not to do so this time. Why? Thereby hangs a tale.

Between 7 August 2001, when Mr Goel's first proposal was rejected outright by the committee and the MS&PI and 5 December 2002, when the MP sent a fresh proposal to the committee, one major change had occurred: Mr Goel had not only become a minister but the minister of state in the MS&PI, the very ministry that supervises MPLADS and advises the committees of the two Houses!

In its eleventh report the committee said Mr Vijay Goel, the Minister of State for Statistics and Programme Implementation, had written to the chairman in November 2002 seeking permission for the purchase of five battery-operated open busus for the heritage city of Chandni Chowk. These buses would ferry tourists and would replace the large number of cycle rickshaws operating in the area. He said that Chandni Chowk represents the secular character of India because 'all religious places are on one road'. Chandni Chowk is always crowded and cycle rickshaws cause traffic jams. The congestion on this street could be overcome with the deployment of battery-operated buses. He proposed to buy such buses and hand them over to the Delhi government or any government agency.

Mr Goel made no reference to his earlier proposal or to the fact that the committee had rejected it. Instead, he said the purchase of such buses was not covered under the existing guidelines. He therefore wanted the committee to treat his request as a 'special case'.

He also said the proposal would foster 'national integration' and given the historical importance of the area, he hoped the committee would grant him permission.

The committee's report made a bland reference to its earlier decision, but did not state reasons for doing an about turn this time. It just concluded by saying it approved the minister's proposal on the condition that the state government or any other government agency to whom the buses would be handed over would have to 'bear the maintenance and recurring expenditure'.[13]

Bend It Like Goel: Part II

Around the time Mr Vijay Goel, Minister of State in the MS&PI, was bending the rules to buy buses to ferry tourists, he was also trying to use MPLADS funds to buy ambulances for a private hospital. He proposed in July 2002 that two mobile medical vans be purchased 'for the benefit of residents of Chandni Chowk Parliamentary Constituency of Delhi'.

According to the MS&PI, the ministry in which he is the minister of state, the minister wrote to the Municipal Corporation of Delhi (MCD) and said he had 'decided to release funds' from MPLADS for the benefit of his constituents. 'The vans can be attached to a major hospital and cater to the needs of the people.' He also said the authorities could contact Messrs Eicher Ltd or any other automobile company and obtain quotations to buy the vans. 'I hereby sanction ₹12 lakh for the purpose.' Though the minister's letter made no mention of the beneficiary institution and said the vans could be attached to 'any major hospital', the MCD wrote to Mr Goel's ministry on 16 October, 2002 to say that the vans were meant for Maharaja Agrasen Hospital, Punjabi Bagh, and sought the following clarifications: '(i) Whether purchase of mobile medical vans is allowed under MPLADS; (ii) And if so, can mobile van be attached to Maharaja Agrasen Hospital, Punjabi Bagh, being situated outside the parliamentary constituency of Hon'ble Minister.'

The MS&PI enclosed the letter of the MCD and wrote to the Lok Sabha Secretariat in November 2002 stating that the minister had recommended the purchase of two mobile medical vans 'for the benefit of his constituents'. Further, it said the vans were proposed to be given to Maharaja Agrasen Hospital, Punjabi Bagh, Delhi, 'a private hospital, not falling in the constituency of the Hon'ble Minister'.

It then went on to quote from the guidelines to say that they only permitted the purchase of ambulances for government hospitals or reputed service organizations and that the guidelines permit the purchase of mobile dispensaries in rural areas only by Panchayati Raj institutions. Finally, it noted the fact that a Lok Sabha member can recommend works only in his constituency. After reiterating the guidelines, it requested the Lok Sabha Secretariat to place this matter before the committees on MPLADS in the Lok Sabha and the Rajya Sabha for 'relaxation' of these conditions.

From the sequence of events detailed by the Lok Sabha Secretariat, it is clear that the minister did not initially declare that the mobile medical vans were meant for a private hospital. He also did not declare that the hospital in question was outside his parliamentary constituency. All that he said was that these vans had to be bought 'for the benefit of his constituents'. How could mobile medical vans purchased for a private hospital outside his constituency benefit his constituents? This question went completely unanswered. Also, there was no indication as to what these 'mobile medical vans' comprised and what they were meant to do. Were they mere ambulances or were they equipped to deal with medical emergencies or to conduct diagnostic tests? Little is known of the purpose of these vans.

Yet, the Lok Sabha Committee approved this proposal without a murmur. It said it considered the proposal of the minister for the purchase of medical vans for Maharaja Agrasen Hospital, Punjabi Bagh, under MPLADS 'for the benefit of residents of Chandni Chowk Parliamentary Constituency of Delhi' and approved it. The committee made no reference to the fact that the proposal was violative of the guidelines in many ways and that the guidelines do not permit the purchase of medical vans or mobile dispensaries, even for NGOs, let alone private hospitals. Nor did it refer to the fact that the hospital in question was a private hospital—an institution which cannot benefit from MPLADS under the guidelines. Finally, the committee was also surprisingly silent about the fact that the hospital was located outside the MP's constituency—yet another reason for declining consent for a proposal in normal circumstances. Yet, despite all these deviations, the proposal was cleared without laying down any conditions whatsoever.[14]

Why Not Permit Purchase of Books?

Although the MPLADS programme strictly prohibits the purchase of inventories, the committees of the two Houses are under constant pressure to permit deviation from these guidelines for the purchase of items which are basically inventories and do not under any circumstances fall in the category of durable assets. Initially, the committees resisted the demand by MPs to use their funds to buy computers for educational institutions. Finally, they gave in. Then demands arose for the purchase of audio-visual equipment. In later years it was argued that MPs should have the right to buy books for school libraries. Among those who raised this demand was Mr Vijay Kumar Khandelwal, a member of the Lok Sabha. As a member of the Library Committee of Parliament, he raised this issue at a meeting of that committee on 8 May 2002 and said that while MPs were allowed to fund the construction of libraries, they were not allowed to purchase books. He said the purchase of books should be allowed under MPLADS. The chairman of the committee said the suggestion would be forwarded to the chairman of the MPLADS committee. Mr Pradeep Rawat, another MP, lent his voice to this demand and said the provision of computers to government schools and government-aided schools through MPLADS was a heartening development. However, this in itself is not enough. This left out a large number of non-aided but recognized schools. Further, MPs are not allowed to purchase books and curriculum-based educational software for schools. This he said was a major lacuna because many schools do not buy educational software because of the costs involved. As a result, this impedes the use of computers for educational purposes vis-à-vis administrative purposes.

Another MP who backed this demand was Mr Sahib Singh Verma, the Minister for Labour. He said in a letter on 2 August 2002 that while MPs could buy computers for government schools, they were not permitted to do the same for government libraries.

He also wanted the scheme to permit the purchase of books by libraries. He said the illustrative list of works should permit the purchase of books, computers, furniture and other items of infrastructure development 'in government as well as private libraries'.

Mr Verma's letter was forwarded to the MS&PI, which responded by saying that while the construction of libraries in government/government-aided/government-recognized schools and the purchase of computers by government and government-aided schools were permitted, the purchase of computers for libraries had already been rejected by the committees on MPLADS of both the Houses. As regards books and furniture, the ministry said they were items of inventory for which there is a specific restriction.

Meanwhile, despite this restriction, the Lok Sabha Committee appeared to have been left with little option but to grant ex-post-facto approval for the purchase of books for distribution in schools and public libraries in Sikkim by Mr Bhim Dahal, an MP. The tenth report of the committee dealt with this issue. The member said the books that were purchased for distribution were written by eminent authors like Parijat and dealt with 'women's emancipation and social re-awakening'. Keeping this in mind, the committee said it was giving its approval 'as a one time exemption' for purchase of books worth ₹20 lakh during the years 1997–98 and 1998–99 under MPLADS in Sikkim. The committee made it clear that 'it should be treated as a special case' and was 'not to be quoted as a precedent in future'.

In other words, the tenth report of the Lok Sabha Committee, tabled in the House on 21 November 2002, was belatedly and rather helplessly granting ex-post-facto clearance for the purchase of books by an MP about three to four years ago. The committee, however, did not explain how the nodal district officials allowed the purchase when it was clearly against the guidelines on two counts: (1) purchase of books for schools and (2) purchase of books for libraries. The committee appeared to just gloss over this fact, because no individual was taken to task for such a blatant infringement of the guidelines. From the narration it is clear that the MP sought to explain away the infringement by talking about the purchase of books written by eminent authors but cited the name of just one such author. Also, there was an attempt to rationalize the decision by claiming that the books dealt with 'women's emancipation' and 'social re-awakening', whatever these terms might mean to the MP or the committee that eventually approved it.

In any case, the committee had to revisit this issue following the demands by several other MPs. It did so in its eleventh report while responding to the letters written by Mr Verma and Mr Rawat. It said MPLADS funds are meant for the creation of durable assets and not for the purchase of inventory items. The committee however partially yielded to demand by Mr Verma's and said it would allow the purchase of computers by libraries as well. But all the other demands were rejected. It said books, furniture and curriculum-based educational software are all inventory items on whose purchase there is a specific bar.[15]

Books for Bar Association Libraries

Mr Ravi Shankar Prasad, a member of the Rajya Sabha, submitted a proposal for making an allocation from his MPLADS funds to the Patna Bar Association for the purchase of books for its library. The proposal was discussed by the Rajya Sabha Committee at its meeting on 23 July 2001. Mr Brahmakumar Bhatt, a member of the committee, pointed out that it was not proper to fund Bar Association libraries as they already had enough money.

The chairperson explained that she had made a commitment to the Bar Association, of which Mr Prasad is a member, that the latter could make such a contribution for the purchase of books. Consequently, Mr Prasad had been granted permission to allocate funds for the purchase of books by the library. 'If the committee agreed...then it would be treated as a one time decision and should not be allowed to become a precedent'. The committee finally agreed to treat it as a one-time exception to the rule that prohibits purchase of books, etc.

The MS & PI enclosed an extract of the minutes of this meeting to the Lok Sabha Committee and said the purchase of books is not permitted under MPLADS because of the specific restriction on the purchase of inventories. The guidelines only permit the construction of buildings for public libraries which are open to the general public. While the guidelines prohibit the purchase of books, the ministry said it must be noted that the books are to be purchased for the Patna Bar Association Library, which is not open to the general public.

The Lok Sabha Committee declined approval for Mr Prasad's proposal on the ground that it was against the guidelines and further, it was meant for a particular section of society (the legal fraternity) and not the general public.[16]

How MPs Nudge the Government to Amend the Guidelines

The committees of both the Houses have, over the years, been bombarded with requests for the amendment of the guidelines to suit the needs of individual proposals. More often than not, the committees have succumbed to pressure and suggested amendments, which, in effect, has resulted in nullifying the guidelines. It appears as if the motto is 'if there is a rule, it must be broken'. A case that epitomizes this trend is the violation of the rule that MPLADS funds should not be used to build facilities associated with religious places and that no project which is denominational in character should Neither be proposed

Nor approved.

The Rajya Sabha Committee considered the proposal of Mr Trilochan Kanungo, a member of the Lok Sabha, for construction of a building adjacent to a religious place 'and decided to approve it as a special case'. Though this constituted a gross violation of the rule regarding funding of religious places, the government did not object to it. Following the Rajya Sabha Committee's recommendation, it asked the MP to furnish certain details 'for considering relaxation (of the rule) as a special case'.[17]

The information technology (IT) revolution sweeping the country has touched every field of human endeavour. If that is so, can MPLADS remain untouched? Once people in every constituency realized that funds were available with MPs for development schemes, they began meeting their representatives with a variety of demands. Prominent among them were headmasters of government and government-aided schools in rural areas, who wanted their pupils to catch up with the urban upwardly mobile children who studied in English-medium schools and had access to computers, electronic equipment and audio-visual learning educational tools. They wanted MPs to fund computer laboratories in their schools. MPs, too, were excited to receive such requests because they were as keen as the headmasters to contemporize educational facilities for village kids in their constituencies. Apart from giving them the satisfaction of doing something substantial for these children, they knew they could showcase these achievements and hopefully, convert them to votes in the next elections.

The other thing that the IT revolution did was to encourage government servants with a progressive outlook to dream of computerized government offices at the district, taluk and village levels. Such officials, too, called on their MPs and sought funds for such computerization schemes.

Yet another idea that often cropped up was the setting up of 'Internet Dhabas' in all blocks of all taluks in the country. An 'Internet Dhaba' is basically an Internet kiosk which can be accessed by all citizens. The kiosk would probably have a coffee shop as well and hence the nomenclature. Some of these ideas have taken off and have made things better for a lot of people.

Mr Ram Naik, the Minister of State for Railways, Parliamentary Affairs, Planning and Programme Implementation wrote to the Speaker of the Lok Sabha in May 1999 and suggested an amendment of the guidelines for allocation of MPLADS funds to permit the purchase of (i) audio-visual aids of an educational nature relevant to courses being conducted in government and government-aided schools and (ii) purchase of night soil disposal systems. The minister said the guidelines specifically prohibit the purchase of inventory items/stock of any type. However, an exception has been made in regard to the purchase of computers, ham equipment, and citizen band radio equipment for implementation of electronics projects in government and government-aided schools and institutions. He said he had received requests from MPs for allowing the purchase of audio-visual aids for the benefit of the student community, including colour TV sets, video cassette recorders and players, cassettes, slides and other such material.[18]

The Lok Sabha Committee on MPLADS accepted the proposal of the minister although the guidelines 'specifically prohibit purchase of inventory items/stock of any type . . .' While doing so, it decided to enlarge the scope of this facility by stating that it should be extended to permanently recognized high schools and colleges as well (apart from government and government-aided schools and institutions).[19]

It recommended that the guidelines be amended to read as follows: 'Permitting purchase of audio-visual aids of educational nature in government, government-aided and permanently recognized high schools/colleges'.[20]

Another MP who wanted to utilize these funds for providing equipment to educational institutions was Mr Rupchand Pal of West Bengal. Mr Pal said the guidelines permitted the purchase of computers. He wanted this extended to multimedia projectors, educational CD-Roms, CD writers, scanners, servers and Internet equipment, computer-related furniture and supportive systems like air-conditioners, in order to help educational institutions impart computer education. He also wanted mobile vans with audio-visual arrangements for literacy programmes and for non-formal and family welfare educational programmes.

The government responded by adding the following paragraph as Item 26 in the Illustrative List of Works that can be taken up under the scheme: 'Purchase of Audio-Visual Aids of educational nature for government, government-aided and also unaided but government-recognized educational institutions provided there is proper place and proper provision for safe custody of these aids'.[21]

Among other suggestions made by Mr Pal were: (i) inclusion of audio-visual equipment and such other systems needed to train sportspersons; (ii) chairs, benches, etc., needed in classrooms built under MPLADS; (iii) minimum furniture like beds, etc., for shelters built under this scheme. He said MPs could fund the construction of sports complexes and gymnasiums, but the guidelines do not permit the purchase of supportive systems. Similarly, while shelters can be built for the poor, there is no provision to purchase beds or basic furniture. He wanted these anomalies to be addressed.

Responding to Mr Pal's suggestions, the MS&PI said the purchase of computers was generally disallowed because they are inventory items. However, provision of computers for government and government-aided educational institutions had already been made as 'a special case' for the benefit of the student community. The rest of the items suggested by the MP were inventory items and therefore specifically prohibited, the ministry said.

As regards the suggestion to allow the purchase of mobile vans with audio-visual equipment, the ministry said the objective of the scheme was to take up capital works which are developmental in nature. The guidelines do not permit the purchase of any type of vehicle except ambulances. Further, mobile vans with audio-visual equipment 'does not fit into the basic objective of the Guidelines', it said. Also disallowed is the purchase of beds, benches, furniture, etc., as such inventory items are disallowed. As regards audio-visual equipment for the benefit of the student community, it said it was referring the same to the Lok Sabha and Rajya Sabha Committees.[22]

The Lok Sabha Committee concurred with the ministry and said most of the items listed by the MP 'are of the nature of inventories and not permitted under MPLADS'. In a broad sweep, the committee rejected all these proposals, but the committee's conclusions appeared to be at variance with the recommendation in its first report of May 2000 in which it said the guidelines should be amended to permit the purchase of audio-visual equipment.[23]

Using the Fund for E-Governance and Software Development

Mr C. Kuppuswami wrote to the Lok Sabha Committee in March 2000 suggesting an amendment of the guidelines to permit funding of electronic governance and related software development through this scheme. He said this was the need of the hour 'because E-Governance and software development had assumed great importance in the light of the IT revolution in the country'. Around the same time, Mr Murasoli Maran, Minister of Commerce and Industry and Mr A.K.S. Vijayan wrote to the MS&PI putting across a similar plea. Mr Maran said since e-governance was not included in the illustrative list of works that are permitted under this scheme, district collectors are hesitant to release funds for the same lest they invite audit objections. He suggested MPs should give a thrust to such 'modern tools of development' but the guidelines were not permitting it. Mr Vijayan said he wanted to fund e-governance in government administration in the Thiruvarur district in Tamil Nadu. E-governance, he said, was 'the most felt need of my constituency' and his district had been identified for a pilot project to computerize all government activity from the block to the district level. He said his predecessor had already committed ₹55 lakh for the project between 1998 and 2000 and this needed to be ratified.

The MS&PI responded by saying the basic purpose of this proposal was to computerize government offices, which is not allowed under the scheme. The computer scheme is permitted only in schools.

The Lok Sabha Committee noted the opinion of the ministry and said computerization of government offices 'is not allowed at present'.[24]

Yet another MP who wanted to invest MPLADS funds in a village-level computerization programme in his constituency was Mr Suresh Prabhu. Mr Prabhu, the Minister for Chemicals and Fertilizers wrote to Mr Arun Shourie, the Minister of State for Statistics and Programme Implementation in June 2000 and outlined the project. He said he wished to connect 1,200 villages in the Rajapur parliamentary constituency in Maharashtra through the Internet in a three-phase programme spread over four years. To begin with, he said the ten tehsil headquarters had been connected to a server at the district headquarters. In each of these ten locations there would be kiosks with computer terminals which could be accessed by all persons. He had also identified an NGO that would manage these booths. Since the guidelines permit funding of computer projects in schools, the computerization of the constituency should also be permitted, he said, while pointing out that this is the first project of its kind in the country. Mr Prabhu said the project was held up because of non-clearance by the MS&PI.

Internet Dhabas

The idea of using MPLADS funds for setting up 'Internet Dhabas' came from Dr Bolla Bulli Ramaiah, the chairman of the Lok Sabha Committee. In one of the committee's meetings, Dr Ramaiah suggested that ₹5 lakh be earmarked for setting up these Dhabas in all block headquarters in the country. The committee agreed and said funds should be made available for the same as 'Internet Dhabas' fell in the infrastructure category.[25]

Funding Computer Centres

Mr Arun Shourie, Minister of State in charge of programme implementation wrote to the Speaker of the Lok Sabha in January 2000 and suggested an amendment of the guidelines for utilizing MPLADS funds for establishing computer centres not only in government institutions and government-aided institutions but also in government-recognized institutions. He said he was 'distressed' to report that a project proposed by an honourable member for creating computer centres in educational institutions in Kanpur 'has been buffeted around—with the file going up and down for over six months'. The file kept going 'up and down' because the Uttar Pradesh administration went by a 'literal interpretation' of the guidelines and said the order for the computers could only be placed with UPTRON, a state government undertaking. 'The MP represented, I think quite rightly, that UPTRON was a sick unit, and that better suppliers of the computers—who could be relied on for better after-sales service also, were available.' Further, according to the MP, even in terms of cost, the other companies were quoting less than UPTRON.

The second roadblock that this MP faced was relating to the status of the institutions where the MP wanted to provide this facility. They were private institutions recognized by the government but not aided by the government and, therefore, the guidelines needed to be revised to enable the MP to go ahead with the proposal. The minister therefore urged the Speaker and the Lok Sabha Committee to amend the guidelines.[26]

The committee agreed with the minister and recommended that necessary changes be made in the guidelines to permit establishment of computer centres in government-recognized institutions as well. 'The committee also desire that a specific provision may be made in the guidelines to prevent assets which have been created from being transferred to or by any private body'.[27]

However, this proposal was not approved by the Rajya Sabha Committee. Therefore, the government informed the Lok Sabha Committee in its 'Action-taken Report' that it had hit a roadblock with regard to amending the guidelines to permit funding of computer centres in government-recognized institutions as well. Reacting to the government's response, the Lok Sabha Committee said it 'earnestly desired' that the government implement its recommendation and if necessary, take this up with the Rajya Sabha Committee and get that committee's approval.[28]

Permitting MPs to Fund Unaided Schools

From the very outset MPs were keen to fund projects in schools, but the government was wary of such funds being used by private institutions. It therefore stipulated that MPs should fund projects only in government schools or government-aided schools. Once the scheme got going, MPs stepped up the demand for relaxation of the guidelines with respect to schools. They wanted permission to fund projects in unaided recognized schools and educational institutions, which was actually a euphemism for private schools. Among those who pressed for an amendment of the guidelines in this regard was Mr Ram Naik, the originator of the scheme and Ms Malti Sharma, member of the Rajya Sabha. This was 'strongly' recommended by the Rajya Sabha Committee in its first report. The committee said such schools could be funded provided they fulfilled certain conditions (such as they were registered, government-recognized, followed a syllabus approved by the state government and catered to all sections of society). The committee said the ministry should examine this proposal 'with top priority' and make necessary changes to the guidelines. The ministry responded by saying that the guidelines had already been amended in June 1999 to bring unaided, recognized educational institutions within the ambit of the scheme.[29]

Purchasing Audio-Visual Aids With MPLADS Funds

One of the basic principles guiding MPLADS is that the funds must be used to create durable assets. However, soon after the scheme was launched, MPs started pressing for an amendment of the guidelines to allow the purchase of non-durable material. One of the earliest demands was for permission to fund purchase of audio-visual aids, including television sets, for educational institutions. The Rajya Sabha Committee agreed to this demand in its very first report and said this should be permitted provided there was a provision for safe custody of equipment bought 'under supervision of responsible persons'. The committee said if this recommendation was implemented, it would give 'sufficient flexibility' to the scheme apart from giving a thrust 'to promoting better standards of education', specially in rural areas. It asked the MS&PI to take an active interest in the matter and secure the concurrence of the Speaker of the Lok Sabha to amend the guidelines. The ministry responded by amending the Illustrative List of Works permissible under MPLADS as follows: 'Purchase of audio-visual aids of educational nature for government, government-aided and also unaided but government-recognized educational institutions provided there is proper place and proper provision for safe custody of these aids'.[30]

Relaxing the Upper Limit to Build Cultural Centres

The strange thing about rules is that if one adheres to the letter, one may sometimes miss out on the spirit. That is why those entrusted with the responsibility of implementing rules have to walk the tight rope and ensure that cunning attempts to circumvent them are prevented and a broader pragmatic approach is adopted when rules prevent individuals from giving effect to noble ideas.

One such case is that of Mr Kartar Singh Duggal, a member of the Rajya Sabha, and a noted Punjabi litterateur who wanted to invest MPLADS funds to build cultural centres in Punjab. The only hitch was that the rule put a ceiling of ₹25 lakh per project whereas it would cost a lot more to build these centres. The Rajya Sabha Committee approved the member's proposal and recommended that the the upper limit for spending be relaxed for this project.

The MS&PI, which is generally wary of such proposals, was more than forthcoming in this particular case, specially because of Mr Duggal's standing and the cause (establishment of cultural centres) that he wanted to fund. The district collectors of the Jalandhar, Kapurthala and Amritsar districts were asked 'to take appropriate action in the matter'. It sent yet another communication to the district heads and said the estimated cost of the cultural centres proposed by Mr Duggal might be considered to be ₹110 lakh at Jalandhar, ₹160 lakh at Kapurthala and ₹115 lakh at Amritsar instead of the sums indicated in earlier estimates. The district authorities were asked to get the implementing agencies to prepare exact estimates as per allocations.[31]

Funding Animal Welfare Schemes

Ms Maneka Gandhi, an MP with special concern for animal welfare, raised the issue of spending MPLADS funds for animal welfare programmes. As the Minister of State in the MS&PI, she wrote to the committees of the two Houses on 1 March 2002 suggesting inclusion of works relating to animal care/welfare in the permissible list of works under the guidelines. She said that the government had taken a number of initiatives with regard to animal welfare and with growing awareness, there was a demand for resources to create the necessary infrastructure for animal welfare. Therefore, she wanted works relating to animal care to be included in the guidelines. The Rajya Sabha Committee approved this proposal at its sitting on 7 March 2002. The Lok

Sabha Committee gave its consent on the condition that works relating to animal welfare activities 'should be asset oriented' as per the guidelines.[32]

Health, Sanitation and Amendment of Guidelines

Mr Ram Naik, the Minister of State for Railways, Parliamentary Affairs, Planning and Programme Implementation wrote to the Speaker of the Lok Sabha in May 1999 and suggested the guidelines for allocation of MPLADS funds be amended to permit purchase of 'night soil equipment'. The minister made the suggestion after he received a representation from Mr Francisco C. Sardinha, an MP from Goa. Sardinha said 'disposal of night soil has become a serious health hazard in the port city of Marmagoa and Vasco-da-Gama and its surrounding villages'. He said the municipal authorities had constructed a good number of public toilets for the convenience of tourists and local people. But, 'the disposal of night soil had become a big problem'. He therefore wanted to utilize funds under MPLADS to purchase a 'night soil disposal system', which consisted of a vacuum cleaner, trailer and a tractor 'to dispose of night soil'. If such a system were to be purchased, it would serve 'the useful purpose of carrying of night soil with a modern mechanical system', he said.[33]

The Lok Sabha Committee accepted the proposal put forward by the MP and the government and said the purchase of the night soil disposal system should be permitted 'without any delay'.[34]

The Rajya Sabha Committee endorsed this proposal and said that 'implementation [...] is essential for maintaining high health and sanitation standard...'[35]

The Rajya Sabha Committee was of the view that MPLADS funds could be used for purchase of 'night soil disposal systems' as it was essential to maintain high sanitation standards in rural areas. It urged the ministry to secure the consent of the Speaker of the Lok Sabha. The ministry agreed to the proposal and made the following addition to the Illustrative List of Works permitted under the scheme: 'Purchase of night soil disposal system for local bodies'.[36] The government responded by including this as Item 27 in the Illustrative List of Works given in Appendix I of the guidelines.[37]

NOTES

1. Tenth Report, Committee on MPLADS 2002–2003, presented to the Lok Sabha, 21 November 2002, Lok Sabha Secretariat, New Delhi, pp. 82–83.
2. Ibid., p. 83.
3. Fourth Report, Committee on MPLADS, presented to the Rajya Sabha, 17 December 2002, Rajya Sabha Secretariat, New Delhi, pp. 3–4.
4. Seventh Report, Committee on MPLADS 2000–2001, presented to the Lok Sabha, 31 August 2001, Lok Sabha Secretariat, New Delhi, pp. 3–4.
5. Tenth Report, Committee on MPLADS 2002–2003, presented to the Lok Sabha, 21 November 2002, Lok Sabha Secretariat, New Delhi, pp. 92–93.
6. Fourth Report, Committee on MPLADS, presented to the Rajya Sabha, 17 December 2002, Rajya Sabha Secretariat, New Delhi, p. 51.
7. Ibid., p. 41.
8. Ibid., p. 45.
9. Ibid., p. 7.
10. Ibid., p. 10–11.
11. Seventh Report, Committee on MPLADS 2000–2001, presented to the Lok Sabha, 31 August 2001, Lok Sabha Secretariat, New Delhi, p. 2.
12. Ibid.
13. Eleventh Report, Committee on MPLADS 2003–2004, presented to the Lok Sabha, 9 April 2003, Lok Sabha Secretariat, New Delhi, pp. 49–50.
14. Ibid., pp. 47–48.
15. Ibid., pp. 9–11.
16. Tenth Report, Committee on MPLADS 2002–2003, presented to the Lok Sabha, 21 November 2002, Lok Sabha Secretariat, New Delhi, pp. 80–81.
17. Fourth Report, Committee on MPLADS, presented to the Rajya

Sabha, 17 December 2002, Rajya Sabha Secretariat, New Delhi, p. 11.
18 First Report, Committee on MPLADS 1999–2000, presented to the Lok Sabha, 12 May 2000, Lok Sabha Secretariat, New Delhi, p. 1.
19 Ibid., p. 7.
20 Ibid.
21 Sixth Report, Committee on MPLADS 2000–2001, presented to the Lok Sabha, 31 July 2001, Lok Sabha Secretariat, New Delhi, p. 4.
22 Third Report, Committee on MPLADS 2000–2001, presented to the Lok Sabha on 21 December 2000, Lok Sabha Secretariat, New Delhi, pp. 37–38.
23 Ibid., p. 38.
24 Second Report, Committee on MPLADS 1999–2000, presented to the Lok Sabha, 22 August 2000, Lok Sabha Secretariat, New Delhi, p. 20.
25 Ibid., p. 10.
26 First Report, Committee on MPLADS 1999–2000, presented to the Lok Sabha, 12 May 2000, Lok Sabha Secretariat, New Delhi, p. 12.
27 Ibid., p. 13.
28 Sixth Report, Committee on MPLADS 2000–2001, presented to the Lok Sabha, 31 July 2001, Lok Sabha Secretariat, New Delhi, pp. 2–3.
29 Second Report, Committee on MPLADS, presented to the Rajya Sabha, 11 December 2001, Rajya Sabha Secretariat, New Delhi, p. 37.
30 Ibid., p. 37–38.
31 Fourth Report, Committee on MPLADS, presented to the Rajya Sabha, 17 December 2002, Rajya Sabha Secretariat, New Delhi, p. 25.
32 Tenth Report, Committee on MPLADS 2002–2003, presented to Lok Sabha, 21 November 2002, the Lok Sabha Secretariat, New Delhi, p. 79.
33 First Report, Committee on MPLADS 1999–2000, presented to the Lok Sabha, 12 May 2000, Lok Sabha Secretariat, New Delhi, pp. 1–2.
34 First Report, presented to the Lok Sabha, 12 May 2000, Lok Sabha Secretariat, New Delhi, p. 7.
35 Ibid., p. 6.
36 Second Report, Committee on MPLADS, presented to the Rajya Sabha, 11 December 2001, Rajya Sabha Secretariat, New Delhi, p. 39.
37 Sixth Report, Committee on MPLADS 2000–2001, presented to the Lok Sabha, 31 July 2001, Lok Sabha Secretariat, New Delhi, p. 5.

5

MPLADS and the 'Trust' Deficit

When MPLADS was launched, the government laid down specific injunctions in the guidelines to prevent misuse of these funds. It said the funds should be used only to build durable assets which can be used/accessed by the public at large. Another important injunction was that these funds should not be used to build assets for private entities. Nor should private bodies or agencies be allowed to manage the assets created. It wanted the management of these assets to be in the hands of the district administration or a local body. Initially, this meant utilization of MPLADS for the creation of permanent assets—schools run by government or local bodies, primary health centres run by the local administration, drinking water schemes managed by local bodies, auditoria, community centres, bus stations, bridges, etc.—which would be used by the general public and owned, managed and maintained by the government or elected local bodies. As the programme gained popularity and the corpus was raised from ₹1 crore to ₹2 crore (now ₹5 crore) the pressure from constituents for utilization of these funds mounted. Initially, MPs only proposed projects in government schools, health, centres etc. Later, government-funded or aided schools sought funds for expansion of facilities. Thereafter, unaided but recognized schools (meaning private schools) came into the picture. Most of these schools are run by private trusts and registered societies. Similarly, many trusts and registered societies in the healthcare sector sought help from MPs to augment their services.

The MPs in turn used these instances to mount pressure on the government to relax the rules in regard to allocation of these funds. Because of this pressure, the government's rigidity made way for some flexibility in regard to funding projects by private trusts and societies.

The Rajya Sabha Committee recommended in his first report that MPs should have the right to fund projects related to registered trusts and societies. The MS&PI sought to spike the proposal at the very outset. It said registered societies and trusts are private organizations and any work belonging to them are 'specifically prohibited' under the guidelines. 'If these are included in the scheme, a sizeable amount of MPLAD funds would be bagged by private entrepreneurs which is otherwise meant for projects to be owned by government organizations. Hence the suggestion cannot be agreed to.'

In its second report, the committee agreed with the ministry that societies and trusts 'are private organizations', that if this was allowed a sizeable part of the funds would be 'bagged by private entrepreneurs' and that, in any case, the guidelines prohibit diversion of funds to such entities. However, it wanted the ministry to undertake a survey of societies and trusts 'which are purely under government or semi-government in nature'. Such entities could be funded so that the needs of the people at the grassroots could be met. It wanted the ministry to undertake such a survey and report back to it. The committee's view that there are government and semi-government societies is difficult to comprehend.

Trusts and societies are created by individuals. Sometimes, they fall into government hands because of a conflict among members or because of accusations of misappropriation, etc., but that is rare. In any case, since the committee took this view, the ministry had no option but to respond with its 'Action-taken Report' and it did so by saying that the issue had been referred by it to the committees of the two Houses.[1]

The MS&PI wrote to the secretary general of the Lok Sabha in June 2000 suggesting that the guidelines be amended to include registered societies and trusts in the Illustrative List of Works. It said the guidelines did not permit allocation of funds to such institutions. However, some MPs had put in a request that they be permitted to fund such projects because many of these institutions were doing good work in the area of social service. The Rajya Sabha Committee had considered this question some time ago and said that it was not in favour of such projects. Later on, an exception was made in regard to the construction of buildings of unaided but recognized educational institutions and the guidelines were accordingly amended. Meanwhile, the ministry had received many more representations. It, therefore, suggested that the Lok Sabha Committee approve inclusion of such projects in the guidelines subject to certain conditions. Reputed social service organizations which have been in existence for at least three years could be considered and it should be left to the district head to determine whether the organization is a 'reputed' one or not. The fund should be used to create durable assets available to the people. The assets should vest in the government and there should be a periodical audit and inspection. The beneficiary institution should submit an annual report to the government and agree to comply with these conditions.[2]

The committee concurred with the MS&PI and said the guidelines could be amended to accommodate registered societies and trusts working in the social sector. It also said that the conditions stipulated by the ministry should be incorporated in the guidelines.[3]

Consequent upon these developments, the Rajya Sabha constituted a sub-committee headed by Mr S.R. Bommai to examine the demand for permitting projects within the domain of registered societies and trusts. The committee agreed with the report of the sub-committee that all the seven conditions stipulated by the MS&PI except part of Clause IV was okay and these conditions could be imposed while allocating funds to such organizations.[4]

The guidelines, first formulated by the Ministry of Rural Development and revised many times over because of pressure from MPs, lowered the bar in regard to funding private trusts and societies. Consequently, the guidelines relating to this issue acquired a pragmatic flavour after its revision in November 2005. Following this revision, the guidelines said community infrastructure and public utility building projects proposed by registered societies and trusts could be funded by MPs provided:

> The society/trust is engaged in social service/welfare activity and has been in existence for at least 3 years; it is well established, public spirited, non-profit making entity enjoying a good reputation in the area; it should undertake to operate and maintain the assets created under MPLADS; not more than ₹25 lakh can be spent for one or more works of a particular society; the recommending MP or any of his family members (MP's spouse and the following relations of the MP and the spouse of the MP—parents, brothers, sisters, children, grandchildren and their spouses and their in-laws), should not be President or Chairman or Member of the Managing Committee or Trustee of the Society/Trust.[5]

Thus, while the guidelines allowed funding of private trusts and societies, it said no contributions should be made by MPs to trusts and societies of which they were chairpersons, trustees or members of managing committees. This rule was meant to prevent MPs from using these funds to better their own personal trusts and societies. However, even this rule was waived in the case of Mr Santosh Mohan Dev, MP, Lok Sabha and Mr Karnendu Bhattacharjee, MP, Rajya Sabha. The two MPs argued that this prohibition should not be applicable to MPs from the North-east. Mr Dev wrote to the chairman of the committee and requested that he and Mr Bhattacharjee should be allowed to be president/chairman or member of the managing committee or trustee of the registered society or trust. The Lok Sabha Committee decided to waive the condition that bars MPs who are office-bearers of registered trusts and societies from contributing to their trusts and societies. The committee made the concession 'keeping in view the difficulties faced by them in implementation of the scheme in the North-East Region'.[6]

When the issue came before the Rajya Sabha Committee, the committee loftily declared that it 'agreed with the condition' that MPLADS funds should not be spent on societies and trusts in which the MP had a personal stake. However, it decided to waive this condition in respect of the proposal made by Mr Santosh Mohan Dev and Mr Karnendu Bhattacharjee 'as a special case' and simply reproduced verbatim the reasoning given by the Lok Sabha Committee for agreeing to this proposal.[7]

MPs are never comfortable with restrictions outlined in the guidelines on MPLADS. The general trend is to raise objections, question the rationale behind the restriction imposed, challenge the rules and eventually, if all of this does not work, to seek a waiver of the rule in respect of a particular proposal. This is most apparent in regard to the restrictions in the guidelines in regard to allocation of MPLADS funds for projects taken up by registered trusts and societies of which the MP is a trustee or office-bearer. Mr Sis Ram Ola and Mr Brij Bhushan Sharan Singh, both members of the Lok Sabha, wrote to the Lok Sabha Committee in July and August 2002 respectively, seeking a waiver of the condition that funds cannot be given to a society or trust if the MP making the proposal is the president or chairman or member of the managing committee or trustee.

Mr Ola said this restriction must be removed. He also wanted the ceiling of ₹25 lakh for projects relating to a particular trust or society to be relaxed. In his view, these stipulations were 'impractical' and 'undemocratic' and amounted to a 'black law'. He said that if an MP was running a trust or society efficiently and it was doing good work, how could it be improper to provide a financial institution to such an organization? This amounted to saying that honourable MPs were 'irresponsible' persons, whereas the village sarpanch, members of zila samitis and panchayat samitis, who were called upon to supervise projects under MPLADS, were 'more responsible' than MPs. Mr Ola said such a restriction should not be placed because, in any case, the projects are executed under the supervision of district officials, and the government in any case is empowered to investigate if there are allegations of mala fide actions.

Mr Brij Bhushan Sharan Singh wrote an equally angry letter to the secretariat and said the rule which says an MP cannot allocate funds to an organization if he is an office-bearer in the beneficiary organization 'is a humiliating direction/circular issued by concerned Ministry/Officer'. He wanted this reversed so that MPs could fund institutions with which they are associated.

The MS & PI said that the limit of ₹25 lakh applied to a trust or society as a whole. In other words, it said, this ceiling was not confined to a specific project but to a specific institution.

In its tenth report, the Lok Sabha Committee had said that cost limit of ₹25 lakh was applicable to each work or project of an institution under the scheme and the works 'relating to genuine trusts/societies would be considered by the committee' after having the same verified by the government and in any case, the benefits of MPLADS would not be available to a society or trust if the MP was a member or office-bearer of the institution.

However, this very report waived the rule barring office-bearers and members of trusts and societies from funding projects in their organizations, in the case of Mr Santosh Mohan Dev, member of the Lok Sabha and Mr Karnendu Bhattacharjee, member of the Rajya Sabha, 'as a special case, keeping in view the difficulties faced by them in implementation of the scheme in the North-East region'.

Taking into account all these factors, the Lok Sabha Committee decided to waive all the three conditions it had laid down in its tenth report, in respect of the proposals made by Mr Ola and Mr Singh. These conditions related to the ceiling of ₹25 lakh being applicable to the institution as a whole, verification of proposals pertaining to trusts and societies by the government, and prohibition in regard to a member or an office-bearer of a trust or society allocating funds to such institutions from MPLADS. It only said that registered societies and trusts to which MPs wish to contribute funds 'should have good credentials, sound track record and legal base'.[8]

Yet another issue that has figured at regular intervals is the role of NGOs in executing MPLADS. This is distinct from funding NGOs like trusts and societies to establish facilities in areas such as health, education and rural development. Here, the issue is whether an NGO can be chosen to execute a sanctioned project. The guidelines state that a district authority will identify the agency that will implement a project. It prefers Panchayati Raj institutions in rural areas and urban local bodies in towns and cities. The other options available are government departments or NGOs. However, the entry of NGOs into this area is not to everybody's liking because of the linkages these organizations may have with politicians. When the Lok Sabha Committee sought the views of individuals, organizations and governments on this issue, it got a wide range of responses.

The government of Gujarat said NGOs should be kept away. Only local bodies or government departments must execute projects. The Uttar Pradesh government said it had restricted the role of NGOs in implementing schemes. The government of West Bengal said NGOs could be entrusted with this task provided the district authority and the MP were certain about the credentials of the organization. Several MPs felt that NGOs and charitable trusts with proven integrity should be permitted to execute these projects. They were supportive of the role of NGOs and were not wary of them like some state governments and individuals.

Taking note of the suggestions, the Lok Sabha Committee said that the demand for the exclusion of NGOs from the field of execution of projects 'may seem to be logical so as to do away with the criticism of alleged corruption'. However, it did not favour the idea of banishing this activity because, in its view, the retention of this provision in the guidelines would serve the prime objective of MPLADS. It felt that work should be given only to reputed NGOs and, therefore, suggested that the guidelines be amended to say: 'Provided the district authority shall appoint a reputed NGO as implementing agency in consultation with the MP concerned on the basis of reputation, capability and credentials of the NGO'.[9]

Defining an MP's Family

Thus, to begin with, the committee gave in to such pressures and permitted deviation from the guidelines 'as a special case'. Thereafter, as the pressures mounted for dilution of this rule, the committee asked the government to re-examine the prohibitions it had imposed while redefining the term 'family'. It felt that the definition had enlarged the scope of the family to such an extent that the rule was hurting MPs.

The Lok Sabha Committee noted in its thirteenth report that the definition of family in para 3.21 of the guidelines was 'too broad' and 'no Indian statute encompassed such a wide definition of a family'. The guidelines say that the MP, the MP's spouse and the following relations of the MP and the spouse of the MP—parents, brothers, sisters, children, grandchildren and their spouses and their in-laws—should not be president or chairman or member of the managing committee or trustee of the society or trust to which an MP allocates funds. The committee said that the meaning of 'family', for MPLADS purposes, 'should be restricted to blood relatives only'.

The issue arose when the committee was discussing the draft

of the revised guidelines prepared by the MS & PI. Mr Sadashivrao D. Mandlik, MP and a member of the committee, had given a suggestion for waiving (with some financial limit) the clause which sought to debar a society or trust from receiving MPLADS funds if the MP desirous of making a contribution or his spouse, children and other relatives were associated with the management of the society or trust. Mr Mandlik argued that such public trusts were formed mainly due to the initiative taken by the MPs and the trusts provide most useful services by undertaking activities in the areas of sports, education, etc., which are of value to the community.

The committee examined this issue at its sitting on 20 October 2005. It agreed with Mr Mandlik and said the definition of 'family' was too broad and needed to be changed. It disagreed with the definition of 'family' in the revised guidelines and recommended that it be changed so that the definition is limited to blood relatives only. However, it disagreed with the member on one score. It said it was against a member allocating MPLADS funds to a trust or society where he himself was the trustee, president or member of the managing committee.[10]

Responding to this recommendation, the MS & PI said a broad definition of 'family' had been adopted 'in view of the criticism in the media and elsewhere'. It said this definition 'ensures transparency and accountability of the scheme'. The ministry said that in discussions with the Ministry of Law and Justice, it was found that different laws adopted different definitions of 'family' depending on the context. However, it did not close the issue. It said consultations with the Ministry of Law and Justice were still on. The committee however pressed for a definite response from the government on this issue and asked the nodal ministry to be more specific. The MS & PI responded by saying that 'The Ministry of Law and Justice, Department of Legal Affairs has examined the definition adopted in the guidelines of MPLADS. That department is of the considered view that there may not be any legal objection to continue with the definition of 'family' given in the MPLADS Guidelines.'

This response of the MS&PI provides an example of the clever ways in which the bureaucracy circumvents a question when it does not want to turn down the recommendation of a parliamentary committee. The Lok Sabha Committee was asking the MS&PI as to why the MPLADS guidelines had such a broad definition of 'family' when that was not the case in any other law in the country and why the definition could not be restricted to just blood relatives. The ministry responded by saying the Department of Legal Affairs felt that there might not be any legal objection to continuing with the definition given in the guidelines!

As expected, the Lok Sabha Committee was displeased with the response. It said the MS&PI 'was taking too rigid a stand over a simple but important recommendation of the committee. 'The Committee are of the opinion that it is not fair to stretch the limit of the family to such an extent to cover MP, MP's spouse and their parents, brothers, sisters, children, grandchildren and their spouses and their in-laws, in the name of transparency, accountability and criticism in media and elsewhere.' It said societies, trusts and NGOs were also engaged in developmental work and public welfare activities, and broadening the definition of family only put unnecessary constraints in the smooth functioning of the scheme, thus defeating its laudable objectives. As regards the Department of Legal Affairs, the committee said it had not commented on the appropriateness of the definition of 'family' in the guidelines. Nor had it objected to changing the definition. It, therefore, 'strongly' reiterated its recommendation that the definition of 'family' for MPLADS purposes should be restricted and asked the government to reconsider its decision.[11]

The Lok Sabha Committee reverted to this issue in its fifteenth report. It recalled that at its sitting held on 20 October 2005 the definition of family was too broad and 'no Indian statute encompassed such a wide definition of family'. The committee, therefore, wanted the definition to be confined to the MP's blood relatives only. The committee however said that when it asked the government to reconsider its decision in regard to definition of family, the suggestion 'was agreed to by the Secretaries of the Ministry of Statistics and Programme Implementation and Ministry of Law and Justice' on 14 July 2008.

The committee asked the MS&PI about the source from which the government had drawn the definition of 'family'. The ministry said that it had not relied on any statute or Act.[12]

Thereafter, the MS&PI referred the matter to the Ministry of Law and Justice (Department of Legal Affairs) and while doing so, asked the law officers if some semantic exercise was possible in order to address the issues raised by the MPs. For example, it asked if the term 'family members and relations' could be inserted, instead of including such a large number of relatives in the prohibited list as in the revised guidelines. The Law Department turned down the idea in its response of 15 February 2007. It said the term 'relations' had a wide import and 'could be confusing'. It then referred to the third edition of the *Shorter Oxford English Dictionary* for the definition of 'family'. One of the definitions cited was 'those descended or claiming descent from a common ancestor; a house; kindred; lineage; a race; a people; a group of people'. As can be seen, this definition did not help matters at all. The Law Department also referred to the judgement of the Supreme Court in *K.V. Muthu* v. *Angamuthu Ammal* wherein the apex court defined 'family' as follows:

> In its ordinary and primary sense, the term 'family' signifies the collective body of persons living in one house or under one head or manager or one domestic government. In its restricted sense, 'family' would include only parents and their children. It may include even grandchildren and all the persons of the same blood living together. In its broader sense, it may include persons who are not connected by blood depending upon the context in which the word is used'.

After this rigmarole, the Law Department pronounced its verdict.

It said that in view of the legal position and the context in which the definition of family is proposed to be used, there may not be any objection to continue with the definition of family given in MPLADS. This department also provided a list of statutes where 'family' is defined. The MS&PI promptly quoted this opinion.

At its meeting held on 14 July 2008 the committee returned to this issue when it sought a clarification from the secretary, Department of Legal Affairs. The committee said the present definition of 'family' of an MP included the in-laws of the grandson and granddaughter of the MP. Has such a definition been found in any other statute? The definition varied from statute to statute in any case. The Merchant Shipping Act, the Employees' State Insurance Act, the Payment of Gratuity Act, the Labour Act and the Pension Rules—all of them defined 'family' in different ways. Thereafter, the Supreme Court had come up with a definition which was altogether its own. The chairman of the committee told the secretary, Department of Legal Affairs that the definition of 'family' in MPLADS included even the in-laws of grandchildren. He asked, is there such a definition of family in any statute? The secretary responded by saying, 'Sir, actually the object of the definition is related to the object of the Act.' He went on to explain that examples like the Merchant Shipping Act were not relevant because the description of the family in such a law is for the specific purpose of providing compensation, etc., to a family in case of a tragedy. It also has the purpose of identifying relatives who are not entitled to benefits in such circumstances. In MPLADS, the family is defined is such a way as 'to prevent this scheme to be abused so that there is no favouritism in granting of contracts and other things.' He said there is no 'legality' in choosing a definition. 'It is up to you to decide what level you should stop and proceed. Right now we have a particular definition. If you feel that it should be curtailed we have no problem.' But then, the committee must ensure that it is in consonance with the object of the scheme. 'The object of the scheme is that it should not be abused, there should not be any favouritism'. He said the only concern with diluting the definition and removing some categories mentioned is that it should not lead to 'abuse' of the scheme. It was up to Parliament to take a call on this. Given these circumstances, it was clear that there was no legal issue involved, he said, meaning that it was more a matter of ethics than law.

When the chairman of the committee intervened to say that the definition was so broad that in effect an MP was barred from contributing to a trust in which the in-laws of his grandson or granddaughter were members. This, he felt, was stretching it too far. The secretary responded by saying that it was up to the committee to decide whom to include or exclude in the definition. 'The only object is to ensure that it should not be used as a vehicle for nepotism. So, it is for you to judge and decide the definition of family.'

In his deposition before the committee, the secretary, MS & PI backed up the law secretary. It depends on the purpose for which the definition is used. As the law secretary stated, the purpose was to prevent nepotism.[13]

The committee, however, was adamant. It was in no mood to factor in the issue of nepotism raised by the two secretaries to the government. It said the definition of 'family' in the guidelines was too broad and 'it should be restricted to a reasonable limit'. As it had stated in the thirteenth report, it wanted the definition to be a restriction to blood relatives only. It said many development schemes are undertaken by societies and trusts and the present definition 'restricts the purpose of the scheme'. It said the stand of the MS & PI was 'rigid and predetermined' and therefore strongly recommended that the term 'family' be amended as follows: The family members would include: the MP and his/her spouse; sons and daughters of the MP and their spouses; parents of the MP and the MP's spouse; brothers and sisters of the MP and their spouses; children of brothers and sisters of the MP and their spouses; and grandchildren of the MP.[14]

The committee reiterated its position once again about a year thereafter when it went through the 'Action-taken Reports' of the MS & PI. Responding to the recommendation in the fifteenth report, the ministry said the definition of 'family' in the MPLADS guidelines was an 'inclusive' one and was necessary 'in view of criticism of the scheme'. The committee hit back by once again accusing the MS & PI of taking a 'rigid stance'. It said the revised definition proposed by it 'was quite logical and broad enough to dispel any apprehensions about possible misuse of the scheme'. In fact, it claimed that the 'conservative' approach of the ministry while defining 'family' was 'a hindrance' to the scheme's implementation. It therefore 'strongly' advocated acceptance of its recommendation 'with a view to achieving the objectives of the scheme'.[15]

NOTES

1. Second Report, Committee on MPLADS, presented to the Rajya Sabha, 11 December 2001, Rajya Sabha Secretariat, New Delhi, p. 30.
2. Third Report, Committee on MPLADS 1999–2000, presented to the Lok Sabha, 21 December 2000, Lok Sabha Secretariat, New Delhi, p. 5.
3. Ibid., pp. 8–9.
4. Fourth Report, Committee on MPLADS, presented to the Rajya Sabha, 17 December 2002, Rajya Sabha Secretariat, New Delhi, pp. 13–15.
5. First Report, Member of Parliament Local Area Development Scheme (MPLADS), Ministry of Statistics and Programme Implementation, Government of India, New Delhi, December 2006, p. 6.
6. Tenth Report, Committee on MPLADS 2002–2003, presented to the Lok Sabha, 21 November 2002, Lok Sabha Secretariat, New Delhi, p. 123.
7. Fourth Report, Committee on MPLADS, presented to the Rajya Sabha, 17 December 2002, Rajya Sabha Secretariat, New Delhi, p. 53.
8. Eleventh Report, Committee on MPLADS 2003–2004, presented to the Lok Sabha, 9 April 2003, Lok Sabha Secretariat, New Delhi, pp. 17–19.

9   Fifteenth Report, Committee on MPLADS 2008–2009, presented to the Lok Sabha, 23 March 2001, Lok Sabha Secretariat, New Delhi, pp. 23–25.
10 Thirteenth Report, Committee on MPLADS 2006–2007, presented to the Lok Sabha on 7 December 2006, Lok Sabha Secretariat, New Delhi, p. 25.
11 Fourteenth Report, Committee on MPLADS 2008–2009, presented to the Lok Sabha on 15 December 2008, Lok Sabha Secretariat, New Delhi, pp. 7–8.
12 Fifteenth Report, Committee on MPLADS 2008–2009, presented to the Lok Sabha on 15 December 2008, Lok Sabha Secretariat, New Delhi, p. 33.
13 See ibid., pp. 35–37 for a full narration of the proceedings of that day.
14 Ibid., p. 37.
15 First Report, Committee on MPLADS 2009–2010, Fifteenth Lok Sabha, presented to the Lok Sabha on 24 February 2010, Lok Sabha Secretariat, New Delhi, p. 7.

6

MPLADS Makes Strange Bedfellows— MPs and Bureaucrats

The relationship between MPs and bureaucrats is far from cordial. To put it bluntly, what characterizes this relationship is mutual distrust. Bureaucrats generally feel that MPs, have little respect for norms and that they are always trying to bend the rules to suit their personal and political interests. MPs, on the other hand, see bureaucrats as a bunch of unreasonable and insensitive individuals who are trying to throw their weight around in the districts. The two entities operate in mutually exclusive domains, except for an occasional national day celebration at the district headquarters where the two uneasily and often reluctantly share the dais. In the normal course, the state government draws up the annual budget and determines the allocations under various heads. It also determines the extent to which it will pump in funds to match federal government allocations, specially in the social sector. Further, district-wise plans are drawn up and local governments at the district and village levels are empowered to implement many of these programmes. A substantial part of this activity happens under the direct supervision of the district collector. If an MP wants a certain thing done at the district level, he has to build a rapport with the district collector and get the latter to execute his plans. The arrangement is simple: the MP proposes and the district collector disposes! This is too hurting for the MP and, therefore, he may not make any suggestions at all. Enter MPLADS, and the equation changes: the MP proposes and the district collector disposes as proposed by the MP. This is where the two become strange bedfellows. However, bureaucrats being bureaucrats, they sometimes tend to be too fussy and refuse to consider any proposal that may even marginally deviate from the norms laid down. This leads to a bit of friction, but by and large, MPLADS gives an MP the power to propose and the power to execute development schemes in his constituency. Though the budget at his disposal is not very huge, it is a beginning. He feels he is in control and that gives him a high because most politicians are control freaks.

This is one of the reasons why MPs demand better compliance from district collectors. In a letter to the Lok Sabha Committee in which he made a series of suggestions, Mr Ummareddy Venkateswarlu said the district authorities should send a half-yearly report of the works recommended, works completed and amounts spent to every MP. The government responded by saying that state governments had been requested to issue instructions to all district collectors to furnish monitoring reports to MPs once every two months.[1]

Training Bureaucrats for MPLADS

As stated earlier, MPs often see a bureaucrat as a stumbling block and as an individual who is ever ready to pour cold water on any proposal that they may put forward. This uncomfortable relationship between MPs and bureaucrats often generates much tension and distrust and at times, even animus. Thus, however innovative MPLADS may be from the point of view of parliamentarians and constituents, there is no gainsaying the fact that this programme has often accentuated the conflict between MPs and bureaucrats in general and members of the Indian Administrative Service (IAS) in particular. This conflict was certain to happen because of the very nature of the scheme, which seeks to blur the line between the executive and the legislature by empowering elected representatives to select development schemes for execution and also allocate the funds for the same. A bureaucrat groomed in the traditional mode believes that the separation of powers between legislative and the executive branches should never be breached and his right to execute programmes ought to be absolute. He is, therefore, uncomfortable with the thought that he should share this power with a legislator under this scheme, even if the funds allocated constitute a minuscule part of a district's budget.

As a result, the conflict between the MP and the bureaucrat is the leitmotif of MPLADS, and the bulk of the complaints from MPs to the presiding officers of the two Houses of Parliament and to the respective MPLADS committees relate to the inflexible attitude of district collectors, who turn down many ideas for one reason or the other.

Anticipating such problems, Parliament decided that the areas of conflict can be minimized if MPs and bureaucrats were put through a training programme and the latter were sensitized to MPLADS. It, therefore, incorporated this in the para 5.7 of the guidelines, which says: 'In order to bring about continuous improvement in the implementation of the scheme, the Bureau of Parliamentary Studies and Training (BPST) may arrange training of MPs and district officials in batches, involving, and bringing about interaction with MPs.'

The BPST tried to organize such training workshops twice in December 1997 and May 1999. However, both these attempts had to be aborted because of the premature dissolution of the Lok Sabha. Meanwhile, the two Houses of Parliament decided in February 1999 to constitute committees to monitor the scheme. These committees have the responsibility to: 'Monitor and review periodically the performance and problems in implementation of the MPLAD Scheme' and to consider complaints of MPs in regard to the scheme. Consequent upon the constitution of these committees, the secretariat of the Lok Sabha Committee expressed the view that there was no need to involve BPST in the training of district officials as both the Union government and the governments in the states conducted training and orientation programmes for their officers. The committee reiterated this later and said 'no useful purpose may be served by imparting training to a handful of officers'. Instead, it said it would be better if state governments made arrangements for training district officials in the light of experience gained over the years and also to incorporate 'corrective measures' to attend to the deficiencies observed in the implementation of the scheme. It also said that suggestions and recommendations of the parliamentary committee on MPLADS could be circulated in every department of the state government for the guidance of officials.[2]

However, the matter did not end here. The matter came up before the Lok Sabha Committee once again a few months later when its chairman, Mr B.B. Ramaiah submitted a note saying MPLADS should be included in the training programme for IAS probationers/officers for effective implementation of the scheme. He said this must be part of the curricula at the Lal Bahadur Shastri National Academy of Administration for IAS probationers. Further, all in-service officers should compulsorily be given this orientation-cum-training on MPLADS.

The committee approved the chairman's suggestion and said MPLADS must be part of the curricula at the academy. There should be a comprehensive focus on the scheme, it said. Further, it recommended that there be regular training programmes for IAS officers, management development programmes that also cover MPLADS to enable in-service IAS officers to get updated on the operation of the scheme from time to time, and compulsory training in MPLADS for all officers.[3]

The government's response to these suggestions was that it had forwarded the same to the Rajya Sabha Committee and that further action would be taken after the opinion of the latter committee was known.[4]

Committee Suggests Technical Assistance for MPs

In the initial stages, it appeared as if Rajya Sabha MPs were very keen to ensure that these funds were spent on worthwhile schemes that would bring development to the constituencies they represented. Such was their commitment that they even wanted the MS & PI to 'advise' MPs on the schemes that could be taken up.

As indicated elsewhere in this book, the Rajya Sabha Committee discussed this issue in its very first report when it referred to the need to use the interest generated on MPLADS funds for 'developmental' programmes only. The MS & PI responded by saying that 'the selection of works depends upon the wish of the MP' and it was expected that MPs would suggest schemes that would lead to creation of durable assets. In any case, the utilization of interest that accrued on the funds of each MP would also be done wholly on the advice of the MP concerned.

The ministry's response to the committee's recommendation was considered by the Rajya Sabha Committee in its second report. The committee said it had noted the ministry's view that selection of works depended on the wish of the MP.

> The committee however feels that in order to have a meaningful selection of projects, contributing positively for the economic development of a district implies that ministry should also advise MPs in selecting projects through the help of concerned district collectors in such a manner that it fulfils the requirements of the district given the availability of economic resources in the concerned districts. The committee therefore feels that instead of leaving the entire matter of selecting projects on the wish of the MP, ministry can examine the issue from the aforesaid angle so that the selection of projects could

be made conducive for the economic development of the district'.[5]

Apart from this general observation in regard to governmental assistance, the committee's first report made a specific recommendation that some engineers and officers 'should be made directly responsible to the MPs to assist them in carrying out various projects'. The ministry, however, turned down this recommendation. It said the scheme required MPs to identify a project. It was for the district collector to seek technical advice. It said it would not be possible for the district administration to provide officials exclusively to MPs to prepare estimates or to offer technical advice because there was no provision in the scheme to hire staff or to underwrite contingency expenses.[6]

The committee was, however, disappointed to see the ministry's response. It said the ministry was 'evasive' in its reply when it said it would not be possible for the district administration to provide an official exclusively to an MP. The committee said that if the ministry was keen to help MPs, it could ensure the provision of staff who could offer technical advice. It said the ministry can make suitable changes in the guidelines with the approval of the (Union) Cabinet so that MPs got technical assistance while selecting projects. Such a move would make the projects proposed by MPs 'extremely fruitful'. It, therefore, directed the ministry to reconsider this issue 'more seriously' and give a 'functional twist' to the guidelines.[7]

The committee's persistence forced the MS&PI to give in to the committee's logic, at least partially. It said it had reconsidered this matter and advised all state governments on 5 May 2000 'to take effective steps' to provide technical assistance to MPs.

The Rajya Sabha Committee was pleased to note the ministry's response. It said it was 'happy to note that the matter had been reconsidered by the ministry'. It hoped all state governments would provide technical advice to MPs.[8]

Funding Construction Activity in the Constituency

Members of Parliament are under constant pressure from their constituents to allocate MPLADS funds for a variety of construction proposals. Some of these demands are legitimate, but many are not. Often the proposals violate the guidelines drawn up for the scheme. For example, the guidelines prohibit spending on religious places. Both the constituents and the MPs devise clever methods to circumvent this rule. Since the MP cannot fund construction within the premises of religious places, a site adjacent to the religious place is chosen. Similarly, there is a prohibition on the construction of government buildings, residential quarters, etc. Here too, a way is found to circumvent the rule. Sometimes, the rule is flouted outright.

Spending on Religious Places

One of the first embargoes placed on the utilization of MPLADS funds related to spending on temples, churches, mosques, etc. Even as the programme was launched in 1993, policymakers knew that unless this prohibition was imposed and strictly enforced, Indian MPs would come under a lot of pressure from their constituents to invest these funds to build places of worship. Therefore, since the beginning, MPs are not allowed to divert these funds for religious purposes. But, as always, politicians and their constituents are looking for legitimate ways to beat the rules or to go around them. As a result, many MPs have been suggesting projects which are not strictly 'places of worship' but are connected to such places. For example, Mr Trilochan Kanungo wrote to the Lok Sabha Committee in June 2000 and said that the prohibition that is there in the guidelines relates to the 'sanctum sanctorum' of a place of worship. But the construction of any adjacent room or hall which is used by all sections of the people of the village or locality need not be prohibited. Further, the construction of drinking water facilities or washrooms connected to a place of worship need not be prohibited. The committee referred this to the MS&PI. The ministry said these funds could be spent for creation of drinking water facilities or for building toilets, 'but the above works are not permissible for places of religious worship'.[9]

The committee agreed with the ministry but said that Mr Kanungo's request could be allowed as a special case with the condition that the facilities created should be available to the general public rather than be limited to any religious congregation.[10]

Railways and the Electoral Dividend

There is a constant clamour for expansion of the railway network and railway facilities in every region and in fact in every parliamentary constituency of the country. Constituents often bombard MPs with demands for more and better train services, stoppages of trains passing through a constituency, upgradation of railway stations, railway overbridges or underpasses, and manning of unmanned railway crossings. Consequently, MPs try to shift much of this burden onto the railway minister by frequently raising these demands either through correspondence or through interventions in the two Houses of Parliament. The underdevelopment of the railways is such that the minister in charge is always compelled to juggle around available funds and provide something here and something there, thereby leaving most MPs largely dissatisfied.

Many of these demands relating to the railways are legitimate, but the MPs know that there is only so much that a minister can do, given the constraint of funds. However, impatient constituents do not show any such understanding. When these demands remain unfulfilled, they surmise that their MP is either lazy or ineffective, begin a quiet campaign against the incumbent and get ready to dump him in the next election.

Caught in this no-win situation, MPs begin to scout around

for funds from state governments, local bodies, municipalities, etc. to enhance railway amenities in their areas. MPLADS, therefore, has come as a godsend for them and a large number of MPs seek to push through works relating to railway crossings and overbridges via this scheme. Among those who wanted amendment of the guidelines for this purpose was Mr Kirit Somaiya, MP. He sought permission to use these funds to beautify and clean up railway stations in Mumbai. He said 5.9 million commuters travel in Mumbai suburban trains every day and there is a need to augment facilities at these stations.[11]

However, they run into a roadblock here too, because the guidelines for this scheme clearly prohibits utilization of these funds for projects which have to figure in the central plan or in the central budget.

Given the resource constraints, successive railway ministers have argued that the deployment of MPLADS funds for small works within the railway network would help meet at least some of the demands of the people in different regions of the country. For example, the railway minister, Ms Mamata Banerjee wrote to the MS&PI in January 2000, seeking modification of guidelines to accommodate railway-related works in the guidelines. In that letter she said the 'aspirations of the local populace are sometimes left unsatisfied due to budgetary constraints'. However, some of these demands like building platform shelters, raising of platforms, foot overbridges, construction of waiting rooms, etc. could be met through MPLADS funds. Therefore, she wanted these works to be included in the list of permissible works under this scheme. This letter was referred to by Mr Arun Shourie, the Minister of State in this ministry to the Speaker of the Lok Sabha in which he said that the MPLADS Committee had already permitted construction of railway crossings with these funds. The railway minister had now suggested that 'this aperture be enlarged' so that other assets connected with the railways could be improved. 'I felt that as such assets will be of great use to the general public… The proposal of Ms. Banerjee should be approved'.[12]

The committee, however, disagreed with both the ministers. It said 'no amount should be made available for the MPLADS funds for utilization for plan projects of the Union Government for which budgetary provisions could be made under the Plan allocation'.[13]

Another railway-related proposal that was tossed around from the railways to committees to the government was that of Mr Rupchand Pal, a Lok Sabha member from West Bengal. In his complaint to the Lok Sabha Committee, he said that on the initiative of the Ministry of Railways, one new item was incorporated in the guidelines for MPLADS to permit the construction of level crossings where none exists, within an MP's constituency. Further, the railway minister had also appealed to MPs to utilize MPLADS for such railway projects in their constituencies.

In view of this addition to the guidelines and the railway minister's appeal, Mr Pal wanted to allocate some funds for the construction of a railway level crossing at Chandanpur in the Howrah–Burdwan chord line in the Howrah division of the Eastern Railway. He wrote to the general manager, Eastern Railway, in December 1999 suggesting a level crossing just north of the Chandanpur railway station, which would be funded through MPLADS. He said a level crossing at this point was most necessary because hundreds of people, including school-going children, living in habitations across the line risked their lives every day by crossing the railway line. The general manager of the Railway Division responded positively and sent officials to discuss the project with Mr Pal. It was estimated that the project would cost ₹15.23 lakh. The MP made the recommendation to the district magistrate of Hooghly, who in turn dispatched a cheque for this amount to the railways for executing the project. According to Mr Pal, after a long gap of time, the senior divisional engineer in the Eastern Railway wrote back to the district magistrate to say that the Railways would not be able to execute this project. He also returned the cheque.

In his letter, the senior divisional engineer, Eastern Railway, said that as per the Railway Board's directions, MPLADS funds can be utilized 'only for manning unmanned level crossing'. These funds cannot be accepted for new level crossings like the one suggested by Mr Pal, he said. He further said that as per the Railways rules, the capital cost of construction of the new level crossing gate as well as maintenance charges and the recurring cost of the level crossing gate per year should be borne by the state government and an agreement to this effect should be reached before commencement of the work. Otherwise, it would not be possible to proceed with this proposal, he said.

While doing so, the senior divisional engineer, Railways, said that since the project proposed was a new railway level crossing, it could not be executed. It could be done only if the state government took responsibility for maintenance of the crossing and gave an undertaking to this effect to the Railways. This response of the Railways was making a 'mockery' of the railway minister's appeal to MPs and of the guidelines, he said.

The committee referred this problem to the ministry. The MS&PI said the guidelines had been amended to include 'construction of level crossing at unmanned railway crossings' and that this did not cover new manned level crossings.

The committee noted the ministry's view that the guidelines did not cover new level crossings. However, it approved Mr Pal's proposal because it would result in the creation of a durable asset for use by the general public. It suggested that the MS&PI amend the guidelines once again and include the construction of new railway level crossings.[14]

Railway Overbridges

Most members of the Lok Sabha are under pressure from constituents for speedy implementation of projects relating to the Indian Railways. People in all constituencies keep demanding faster and more passenger trains, stoppages of prestigious trains at stations near them, railway overbridges and underpasses, remodelling of stations and manning of unmanned level crossings. That is why most MPs try to be in the good books of the railway minister and often have a long list of projects which need to be executed. For example, Mr Tanwar Chand Gehlot wanted a railway overbridge to be built on the Ujjain–Bhopal road at Dewas in Madhya Pradesh. He wanted to allocate ₹1 crore from the fund in two instalments of ₹50 lakh over two years. He wrote to Mr Arun Shourie, the Minister of State in the MS&PI, asking for the ministry's clearance in May 2000. In his reply to the MP, Mr Shourie said MPLADS funds cannot be spent on plan projects of the Union government for which a budgetary allocation can be made. 'For this reason, it may be difficult to accommodate the above project under MPLADS.'

However, while rejecting the proposal, Mr Shourie told the MP that his proposal raised a general question, namely, 'if a project is desirable in itself why should MPs be precluded from assigning funds to it—merely on the ground that it could have been taken up through a normal budgetary allocation; after all (i) the project is desirable, and (ii) a budgetary allocation has not been made for it. I feel there is great merit in the question. We will put this matter to the Committees of the two Houses.' The ministry forwarded its opinion to the Lok Sabha Committee.[15]

The committee examined this issue and said the project proposed by the MP is a planned project under the Union government for which funds could be allocated under the five-year plan. It, however, endorsed the view of Mr Shourie and said that 'there was great merit in the proposal' and permission should be granted by the ministry for construction of the overbridge with MPLADS funds.[16]

Community Halls, Mahila Mandals

Ever since the MPLAD Scheme was announced, MPs started getting besieged by people with requests for the construction of community halls in villages and small towns. These halls are primarily used to solemnize weddings and for village-level festivities and cultural programmes. In addition, MPs are under increasing pressure these days to dole out funds to womens' groups. Many states like Andhra Pradesh and Karnataka are actively promoting the formation of womens' self-help groups in the villages. These groups encourage thrift and provide seed capital to members who wish to launch small village-level businesses. This led to greater empowerment of women, and MPs find women voters to be far more vocal and demanding these days. Once they are organized, women want buildings for their Mahila Mandals (women's associations) and for training programmes and workshops organized by the social welfare ministry of the Union government. The demand is so high that MPs want the guidelines to permit funding of such buildings. They also see the value in supporting such initiatives because it can be converted to bulk votes of members of these groups. Mr Ummareddy Venkateswarlu voiced this demand in April 2000 in a letter to the Lok Sabha Committee. The government responded by saying that it had no objection to the construction of community halls and buildings for Mahila Mandals. The committee also gave its consent for the same.[17]

Boundary Walls

Under the guidelines, MPs can fund the construction of schools, classrooms, etc., but not boundary walls of schools. Mr Rasa Singh Rawat drew the attention of the Lok Sabha Committee to this problem and said the district collector of Ajmer, had not accorded sanction to his proposal for building a boundary wall around the playground and other vacant land belonging to a school in his constituency. He wanted this done to prevent trespass of stray cattle, etc., into the school premises and also encroachment of school land. He also wanted to allocate funds for the construction of boundary walls around cremation grounds and graveyards.

They asked the committee to issue a direction to the district collector of Ajmer to sanction this project.

The MS&PI said the list of works permissible do not include construction of boundary walls. 'While...construction of boundary walls around such buildings may be essential for the safety of students, inmates and property, it is felt the clear guidelines for construction of boundary walls may be necessary.' However, since assets created under this scheme should belong to the government or local bodies, aided and unaided educational institutions could be given the benefit 'after they surrender the land in favour of the government as per Para 2.6 of the guidelines'.

The committee agreed with the member's proposal that the guidelines be amended to include the construction of boundary walls under MPLADS. It also hinted at a possible confusion in this regard because some other members had made similar recommendations and such boundary walls were being constructed in their constituencies. In any case, it felt the guidelines should be amended 'to obviate any difficulty being felt by...members'.[18]

Later in this very report, the committee considered the issue of land transfer whenever MPLADS funds were used for projects. It agreed with the suggestions made by MS&PI and said

> The funds from MPLADS may be used for creation of durable assets which shall always be available for public use at large. The ownership of such assets would vest in government. The sale/transfer/disposal of the assets created out of the MPLADS funds shall not be undertaken without the prior approval of the government. The maintenance and upkeep of assets, so created, will also be subject to periodical audit/inspection by the government. The beneficiary organization must enter into a formal agreement in advance with government to comply with the above conditions before the funds from MPLADS are disbursed to the beneficiary organization.[19]

Roads Inside School Grounds

The MS&PI informed the Lok Sabha Committee on 1 December 2000 that it had received a suggestion that construction of roads within the premises of unaided but recognized educational institutions should be permitted. The ministry noted that it had been decided to allow these funds to be used for the construction of buildings within unaided but recognized educational institutions, provided the institution was in existence for not less than two years. Since this was permitted, it felt there was no harm in allowing the construction of roads within such institutional premises. The Lok Sabha Committee agreed with the ministry's suggestion.[20]

Bridge Across the Vaigai

Unlike members of the Lok Sabha, who have to constantly guard their turf and nurse their constituencies, members of the Rajya Sabha can exercise their discretion and utilize the funds at their disposal in more than one region of the state they are elected from. In other words, they need not be obsessed with just one constituency and can be a little more altruistic than their Lok Sabha counterparts. This also enables them to jointly fund a project. One such example was the proposal of five Rajya Sabha members to set apart ₹3.5 crore for construction of a bridge across the Vaigai river between Varusanaadu and Singarajapiram in Andipatti assembly constituency of the Theni district in Tamil Nadu. Four of these MPs—Messrs R. Margabandhu, O.S. Manian, S. Niraikulathan and P. Soundararajan—allocated ₹75 lakh each from their MPLADS funds for the year 2000–01 while Mr N. Thalavaisundaram set apart ₹50 lakh from his fund. The five MPs sought permission to invest these sums jointly on this single project.

This proposal was backed by Mr K. Malaisamy, a member of the Lok Sabha. He drew the attention of the Lok Sabha

Committee to this proposal and argued that no special permission was needed to execute this project in view of the amendments made to para 41 of the guidelines in May 2000 by the ministry. The amended para reads as follows:

> Ideally it would be desirable that the MPs suggest individual works costing not more than ₹25 lakhs per work. However, the amount of ₹25 lakhs per work should not be too rigidly construed. Amounts higher than ₹25 lakhs per work can be spent depending upon the nature of the work. (For example, a single check dam to provide minor irrigation or water supply or a sports stadium may cost more than ₹25 lakhs. In the case of such works higher amount can be legitimately spent)'.

In the light of these changes in the guidelines, no specific exemption was needed to build the bridge, Mr Malaisamy said. He wanted that 'the Collectors and the concerned authorities may be specifically told that they need not obtain specific sanction and exemption from Government of India every time, when the capital works in question could be brought under the guidelines given on 26.5.2006'.[21]

Although the MS & PI brought in the changes to the guidelines as mentioned by Mr Malaisamy, the ministry did not think that this particular project came within the permissible list. It said MPLADS funds could not be utilized for taking major budgeted works and, therefore, declined consent.

The Lok Sabha Committee however disagreed with the ministry and said that since this project would serve the larger public interest, the government must grant it permission 'as a special case'.

Panchayat Offices

The Union government took a major initiative two decades ago to empower democratic bodies like village panchayats at the grassroots. This was done through constitutional amendments to ensure devolution of funds to these bodies. The strengthening of elected bodies at the lowest rung of the democratic ladder has meant more power and more work for elected representatives at the village level. A natural corollary to all this is a suitable panchayat office to meet people and to hold meetings. Panchayat members, therefore, naturally turn to their MPs and MLAs for funds to build these offices. Luckily, MPs now have a fund through which they can dole out sums to construct such buildings. Since the guidelines prohibit construction of government offices, MPs write in to say that panchayat offices should not be classified as government offices. When this issue was raised by Mr Ummareddy Venkateswarlu in April 2000, the MS&PI opined that the ban on the construction of government buildings extended to panchayat offices as well. Panchayat offices were also covered by this restriction' it declared. The Lok Sabha Committee however disagreed. It said the guidelines specifically prohibited construction of government buildings and this included agencies and organizations of the Union and state governments. 'However, panchayat offices should not be covered by this restriction,' it said.[22]

Post Offices

The demands of constituents vary from state to state and from constituency to constituency. In some places, the people want railway overbridges, at others they want bridges across rivers to connect with villages on the other bank. The demands are endless because of the slow pace of development in the first fifty years after independence. In the initial decades, a lot of public money was squandered away on doles and schemes which politicians believed would yield votes. As a result, thousands of crores of public money went down the drain without resulting in creation of durable assets. This resulted in a woeful inadequacy in the physical infrastructure all over the country. The MPs of today bear the burden of this backlog.

Mr Ramesh Chennithala wrote to the Speaker of the Lok Sabha in April 2000 and sought an amendment of the guidelines to enable the construction of post offices. He said the government was spending huge sums of money to rent out private premises to house post offices in villages. This could be obviated if the guidelines permitted MPs to sanction the construction of post offices, which is a public utility service.

The MS & PI responded by saying that allocation of funds for the construction of post offices may not be possible because the Lok Sabha Committee had observed that these funds should not be invested in plan projects for which provision is made in the Union budget.[23]

The Lok Sabha Committee agreed with the ministry's view and took the opportunity to reiterate its earlier opinion that MPLADS funds should not be allocated for plan projects of the Union government.[24]

Gram Pravesh Dwars

Although the purpose of MPLADS is to fund development-oriented schemes in the constituencies of MPs, often MPs come up with proposals which are clearly non-developmental in nature. This creates a tricky situation because the government usually takes a strict view and discourages non-developmental spending whereas the committees of the two Houses tend to take a more lenient view. This leads to differences between the committees and the government on what is permissible and what is not under the scheme. One such case is that of Gram Pravesh Dwars (arches or gateways built at the entrance of villages in many parts of the country in the past). Often, with the passage of time, demographic changes and consequential growth of habitations, these 'dwars' lose their significance, because the villages outgrow them. However, even if this does not happen, village panchayats just do not have the resources to maintain these arches, which have archaeological value. Mr Dilip Gandhi, a member of the Lok Sabha, drew attention to the upkeep of these gateways when he wrote to the MS&PI and said he wanted to allocate funds from MPLADS for the preservation of such 'dwars', which are commonplace in Maharashtra, because of their historical significance, grandeur and architectural value.

Responding to the MP's request, Mr Arun Shourie, Minister of State in the MS&PI, said his department had tried to see how Gram Pravesh Dwars can be deemed to be developmental in nature. 'I am sorry to report that we have not been able to see any way for doing so. For the time being, therefore, there does not seem to be any scope for including such work under MPLADS.'[25]

The Lok Sabha Committee said that in view of 'the historical significance, grandeur and aesthetic architecture of these Pravesh Dwars', it was in favour of spending on their repair and maintenance under this scheme.[26]

Lift Irrigation Schemes

In many states, local governments encourage groups of farmers to lift water from rivers to irrigate their lands whenever these lands are not fed by irrigation canals. Groups of farmers with lands alongside rivers usually get together to raise funds for such minor irrigation schemes. Since elected representatives now have funds at their disposal, such farmers' groups ask MPs and MLAs to underwrite the expenditure of such lift irrigation schemes. In Maharashtra, the state government encourages groups of farmers to get together and form a cooperative society under the Cooperative Societies Act for the purpose of lift irrigation. Mr Ashok N. Mohol wrote to the Lok Sabha Committee in the year 2000 and said he should be permitted to fund such schemes launched by farmers' cooperatives.

The MS&PI, however, rejected the proposal. It said 'any work relating to private enterprise or creation of assets leading to individual benefit has been specifically prohibited'. That is why commercial organizations, registered societies, private institutions and cooperative societies have been put in the prohibited category.[27]

The Lok Sabha Committee agreed with the ministry and said, 'the type of beneficiaries indicated by the Hon'ble MP are a registered society not covered under MPLADS as the benefit would accrue to a group of persons only and not the general public, which will be against the main objective of the scheme'. It, however, asked MS & PI to take up the issue with the government of Maharashtra 'to relax certain restrictions imposed in this regard' and thus obviate the hardships of small and marginal farmers.[28]

Funding Kitchens to Serve Midday Meals

Ms Rita Verma, Minister of State for Human Resource Development, wrote to the Speaker of the Lok Sabha in August 2002 suggesting an amendment to the guidelines to facilitate deployment of MPLADS funds for setting up what she called 'modern kitchens' for efficient implementation of the midday meal scheme through NGOs and other agencies.

In her letter she referred to the National Programme of Nutritional Support to Primary Education, which covers all students from classes I to V in government and government-aided schools and schools run by local bodies. The aim of the programme is to boost enrolment, universalize primary education and enhance the nutritional intake of children attending primary schools. Local bodies are given the responsibility for serving cooked/pre-cooked food with a calorific value equivalent to 100 grams of wheat or rice. The cost of providing cooked meals is to be borne by state governments or implementing agencies but the states complain that they do not have the financial resources to implement the scheme.

Ms Verma referred also to a direction issued by the Supreme

Court in November 2001 that all states must provide cooked meals to children in these schools within six months. When the Union government convened a meeting of states to assess their readiness to implement the court's order, states sought additional financial assistance from the Union government to implement the scheme.

The minister said she was impressed by the work of the ISKCON centre in Bengaluru which is an NGO providing midday meals to 6,000 children in rural areas of the Bengaluru district. ISKCON has a modern kitchen to prepare and pack meals and has transport to send the packets to schools. Having seen the success of this scheme as implemented by ISKCON in Bengaluru, Ms Verma said "it is imperative to involve NGOs in a big way for widening the coverage of the programme'. However, NGOs find it difficult to raise resources for operating mechanized modern kitchens like the one run by ISKCON in Bengaluru. Therefore, she wanted the guidelines for MPLADS to be revised to allow funding of modern kitchens for implementing the midday meal scheme.

The Lok Sabha Secretariat referred the proposal to the MS & PI, which took the oft-repeated view that MPLADS is meant to create durable assets whereas the establishment of modern kitchens would basically involve the purchase of inventory items which are not permitted by the guidelines due to a specific restriction on the purchase of inventory or stock.

Although Ms Verma's proposal dealt with a programme that was intrinsic to universalization of primary education and enhanced nutritional intake for millions of children in these schools across the country, the Lok Sabha Committee rejected it on technical grounds. It said the proposal basically involved the purchase of inventory items, which is not permitted in the guidelines.[29]

NOTES

1. Second Report, Committee on MPLADS 1999–2000, presented to the Lok Sabha, 22 August 2000, Lok Sabha Secretariat, New Delhi, p. 13.
2. First Report, Committee on MPLADS 1999–2000, presented to the Lok Sabha, 12 May 2000, Lok Sabha Secretariat, New Delhi, p. 15.
3. Second Report, Committee on MPLADS 1999–2000, presented to the Lok Sabha, 22 August 2000, Lok Sabha Secretariat, New Delhi, p. 35.
4. Ninth Report, Committee on MPLADS 2000–2001, presented to the Speaker, Lok Sabha, on 12 December 2001, Lok Sabha Secretariat, New Delhi, p. 15,
5. Second Report, Committee on MPLADS, presented to the Rajya Sabha, 11 December 2001, Rajya Sabha Secretariat, New Delhi, pp. 2–3.
6. Ibid., p. 3.
7. Ibid., pp. 3–4.
8. Ibid., p. 4.
9. Third Report, Committee on MPLADS 1999–2000, presented to the Lok Sabha, 21 December 2000, Lok Sabha Secretariat, New Delhi, p. 23.
10. Third Report, Committee on MPLADS 1999–2000, presented to the Lok Sabha, 21 December 2000, Lok Sabha Secretariat, New Delhi, p. 23.
11. First Report, Committee on MPLADS 1999–2000, presented to the Lok Sabha, 12 May 2000, Lok Sabha Secretariat, New Delhi, p. 10.
12. First Report, Committee on MPLADS 1999–2000, presented to the Lok Sabha, 12 May 2000, Lok Sabha Secretariat, New Delhi, pp. 9–10.
13. First Report, Committee on MPLADS 1999–2000, presented to the Lok Sabha, 12 May 2000, Lok Sabha Secretariat, New Delhi, p. 11.
14. Third Report, Committee on MPLADS 2000–2001, presented to the Lok Sabha, on 21 December 2000, Lok Sabha Secretariat, New Delhi, p. 19.
15. Third Report, Committee on MPLADS 1999–2000, presented to the Lok Sabha, 21 December 2000, Lok Sabha Secretariat, New Delhi, p. 25.

16 Third Report, Committee on MPLADS 1999–2000, presented to the Lok Sabha, 21 December 2000, Lok Sabha Secretariat, New Delhi, p. 26.
17 Second Report, Committee on MPLADS 1999–2000, presented to the Lok Sabha, 22 August 2000, Lok Sabha Secretariat, New Delhi, p. 15.
18 Third Report, Committee on MPLADS 1999–2000, presented to the Lok Sabha, 21 December 2000, Lok Sabha Secretariat, New Delhi, pp. 1–3.
19 Ibid., p. 11.
20 Fourth Report, Committee on MPLADS 2000–2001, presented to the Lok Sabha, 23 March 2001, Lok Sabha Secretariat, New Delhi, p. 6.
21 Third Report, Committee on MPLADS 1999–2000, presented to the Lok Sabha, 21 December 2000, Lok Sabha Secretariat, New Delhi, pp. 12–13.
22 Second Report, Committee on MPLADS 1999–2000, presented to the Lok Sabha, 22 August 2000, Lok Sabha Secretariat, New Delhi, p. 15.
23 Third Report, Committee on MPLADS 1999–2000, presented to the Lok Sabha, 21 December 2000, Lok Sabha Secretariat, New Delhi, p. 33.
24 Ibid., p. 34.
25 Fifth Report, Committee on MPLADS 2000–2001, presented to the Lok Sabha, 24 April 2001, Lok Sabha Secretariat, New Delhi, pp. 1–2.
26 Ibid., p. 2.
27 Second Report, Committee on MPLADS 1999–2000, presented to the Lok Sabha, 22 August 2000, Lok Sabha Secretariat, New Delhi, p. 16.
28 Ibid., p. 17.
29 Eleventh Report, Committee on MPLADS 2003–2004, presented to the Lok Sabha, 9 April 2003, Lok Sabha Secretariat, New Delhi, pp. 41–42.

7

In Sickness and Health

The absence of reliable healthcare facilities and hospitals in rural parts of the country puts added pressure on MPs, specially from states like Bihar, Uttar Pradesh, Madhya Pradesh and Orissa, which do not have quality hospitals. As a result, constituents with serious illnesses which require surgeries land up in New Delhi and turn to their MPs for help. First of all, it becomes the responsibility of the MP to provide board and lodging for sick constituents who arrive at his doorstep. If the MP does not show enough concern and if he is not as hospitable as he ought to be, he has had it. Word will go around in the constituency that the MP is insensitive or worse, cruel. Therefore, MPs need to go the extra mile to take care of the sick who seek them out in the national capital.

In India, when voters have such problems, they feel that they have a natural right on the time and resources of elected representatives, specially those whom they supported in the previous election. Therefore, they just land up without notice and with a couple of relatives in tow at the MP's residence in New Delhi. No appointment is sought and none given. Since MPs are allotted spacious apartments or bungalows, constituents consider it their right to seek lodgings in some part of the MP's house.

Once the ailing individual arrives, it becomes the MP's business to provide this person accommodation and, as is often the case, meals. Next, it becomes his job to refer the sick person to one of the prestigious and well-equipped hospitals in the capital like the All-India Institute of Medical Sciences (AIIMS), Safdarjung Hospital or Ram Manohar Lohia Hospital. Since there is a huge waiting list for surgeries in these hospitals, constituents expect their MPs to pull strings, get them to jump the queue and ensure their surgeries and medical treatment at the earliest. The MP is also keen to hasten the process because the presence of this ailing constituent and his or her family members puts a lot of strain on his resources.

The number of sick constituents who knock on the doors of MPs is a barometer of the woefully inadequate medical services in the states they hail from. Sometimes, the number is so huge that a couple of rooms in the houses of these MPs resemble outpatient wards of hospitals. Such MPs often employ a separate secretary to deal with medical cases. These secretaries draft letters of recommendation to directors of these hospitals or heads of departments and follow it up with telephone calls to ensure that patients sent by their boss are attended to. Once the surgery is over, the sick constituent returns to the MP's official residence for post-surgical recuperation and is given extra attention by the MP's staff. Finally, when the patient is fit to return, the MP is called upon to do the final act of munificence—purchasing railway tickets for the patient and his relatives and giving them some pocket money for the journey home.

Those who have an understanding of the role and responsibilities of MPs in democracies in the more advanced nations in Europe and America simply cannot comprehend the pressures that Indian MPs are subjected to. Arranging quality medical care is just one of them. All this puts a great strain on an MP's purse. He has to shell out a lot of money every month to ensure that sick constituents get the best medical care, return home and hopefully sing his praises in the constituency. Such eulogies from constituents however are a double-edged sword—the more the sick praise him, the more will be the pressure on his New Delhi establishment!

MPs just cannot run away from all this. However, while they can do nothing to ward off the pressure this puts on their time, resources and privacy, they look for ways to underwrite the medical expenses of their constituents. With the advent of MPLADS, many of them began to wonder whether these funds could be utilized to pay for surgeries and treatment of major ailments of poor people.

Mr Vinod Khanna set the ball rolling by writing to the chairman of the Lok Sabha Committee in May 2000 suggesting that these funds be made available to pay for the treatment of major ailments of people living below the poverty line. He wrote:

> At times, I personally encounter a number of impoverished people of my constituency who either themselves need to undergo immediate major surgeries or their relatives need major surgeries. Though I have personally tried to help them but feel immensely constrained. The district/state/central relief funds are often inaccessible by these poor people and sometimes in extreme cases a meagre relief is given to them which is never sufficient. In order that immediate and sufficient relief could be given to persons in need of major surgeries or treatment for affliction with major ailments, I request that a sum of ₹10 lakhs may be earmarked from the MPLAD funds for major surgeries and treatment of patients afflicted with major ailments.[1]

The committee sought the opinion of the MS&PI on Mr Khanna's proposal. The ministry responded by quoting the guidelines which says, 'the works under the scheme shall be developmental in nature based on locally felt needs. The emphasis is on creation of durable assets. Funds under the scheme should not be used for incurring revenue expenditure.'

The committee agreed with the views of the ministry and said the basic objective of the scheme is to take up projects which are developmental in nature. Therefore, it declined approval for using these funds for medical treatment of poor people.[2]

Confusion Over Ambulance and Other Issues

Ever since the launch of MPLADS there has been a lot of confusion with regard to funding of services in the healthcare sector. While the guidelines permitted the purchase of ambulances and also indicated, by way of illustration, that X-ray machines could be purchased with these funds, a host of new issues cropped up regularly forcing the MS&PI and the two committees in Parliament to repeatedly draw the attention of MPs to the negative and positive lists. However, since the issue concerned healthcare, there were always grey areas leading to suggestions, complaints and fresh reiteration of guidelines. It was obvious that MPs were keen to utilize these funds to further the basic health needs of their constituents, but often they would be told that rules are rules and they need to be complied with. For example, MPs would ask what purpose would be served by funding the construction of a hospital if the hospital was not adequately equipped. They wanted the rules to be flexible and bent towards the needs of the local populace, but the ministry and the committees would point out that while their intentions were noble, the embargo on the purchase of consumables and inventory items could not be violated.

These controversies and disappointments prompted the director in the MS&PI to send a more detailed list of instructions to district collectors all over the country in October 1999. In that communiqué, the director in the MS&PI said that district authorities were repeatedly seeking clarifications regarding the purchase of ambulances by reputed service organizations like the Red Cross, Ramakrishna Mission, etc. Hence, he was sending out detailed instructions. These instructions said the beneficiary service organization should have been in the health sector for at least three years; the district head must evaluate the organization and decide whether or not it is a reputed one on the basis of its overall performance, reputation, transparency and financial status; the organization should be running a hospital; the ambulance provided would remain the property of the government but its upkeep and maintenance would be the responsibility of the service oganization; ambulances provided to such organizations cannot be equipped with electronic gadgets funded through this scheme; and mobile dispensaries can be funded in rural areas provided they are run by the government or Panchayati Raj institutions. Such mobile dispensaries cannot be provided to non-governmental service organizations.[3]

It has often been seen that some parliamentarians have a knack of circumventing the guidelines and securing clearance of their proposals even when they violate a host of conditions laid down for a grant of MPLADS funds.

Ambulance Okay, Hearse Not Okay

The health minister of Delhi wrote to the minister in-charge of the MS & PI in February 2001 and said Dr Karan Singh, MP, Rajya Sabha, wanted ₹5 lakh to be earmarked from his MPLADS fund for the purchase of a hearse through the Directorate of Health Services, Government of Delhi. The Delhi government wanted the MS & PI to clear the same. The ministry responded by saying that this was not covered under the guidelines.

The Delhi minister wanted the matter to be reconsidered in the light of the fact that the guidelines already permitted the purchase of ambulances and construction of structures in burial and cremation grounds. Logically speaking, 'the purchase of a hearse van should perhaps not be viewed as a significant departure from the Guidelines, as this is only an essential extension or adjunct to the aforesaid facilities already being provided to the community'. This therefore 'calls for relaxation of the Guidelines', he said.[4]

The ministry referred the matter to the MPLADS committees. The committee rejected the proposal and said the purchase of a hearse was not covered under the guidelines. The guidelines only permitted the purchase of ambulances, it said.[5]

Hearse Not Okay, But Garbage Collection Vehicle is Okay

Ms Bijoya Chakravarty, Minister of State for Water Resources, wrote to the committee on 11 March 2002 and sought permission for the purchase of garbage collection vehicles from MPLADS funds. She said she was launching a 'Clean the City Programme' in Guwahati for which these vehicles were needed. The minister's proposal was forwarded to the MS & PI. The ministry responded by saying that earlier Mr Ramakant S. Angle, a member of the Lok Sabha, had sought permission for the purchase of such vehicles with MPLADS funds but his proposal had been turned down by the committees of both Houses. The Lok Sabha Committee, in its seventh report, had said that the guidelines did not permit the purchase of vehicles except ambulances. This had been conveyed by the ministry to the minister's private secretary.[6]

The Lok Sabha Committee, however, upturned its own decision and now allowed the minister to spend MPLADS funds on the purchase of vehicles. While approving the proposal, it imposed the condition that maintenance of the garbage collection vehicles would be guaranteed by the municipal corporation just as an ambulance is maintained by a government hospital.[7]

Buying Hospital Equipment

Mr Rupchand Pal, member, Lok Sabha wrote to the Speaker in February 2000, suggesting an amendment to the guidelines pertaining to hospital equipment. By way of illustration the guidelines said it permitted 'provision of X-Ray Machines to Hospitals/Health Centres run by the State Government/

Local Bodies...'. Mr Pal said that apart from X-ray machines, the guidelines should include ultra sonograph machines, ECG machines, glucose test monitoring machines, audiometers and mobile medical clinic vans.[8]

In its response, the MS&PI said the guidelines permit the purchase of hospital equipment and X-ray machines and this has been mentioned by way of illustration. Since the term 'hospital equipment' already covers all the machines suggested for inclusion under this entry, 'there is no need to include the names of more machines under this entry'. It also made it clear that hospital equipment is allowed only for government hospitals and not for reputed/recognized NGOs.[9]

The Lok Sabha Committee did not disagree with the opinion of the MS&PI.[10]

Buying Hospital Consumables Through MPLADS

Mr Jual Oram, Minister for Tribal Affairs, wrote to the chairman of the Lok Sabha Committee in August 2000, suggesting an amendment of the guidelines to enable MPs to provide funds for the purchase of all kinds of equipment, including hospital beds and consumables by hospitals in the Illustrative List of Works. He said the guidelines provide for the purchase of X-ray machines, ambulances, etc., for government hospitals, but district collectors interpret these guidelines narrowly and disallow purchase of many items needed by hospitals. The committee referred this problem to the MS&PI. The ministry said the guidelines do not permit the purchase of inventory items or stock. Also, consumables like injection syringes, cotton pads, bandages and other medicines are prohibited. However, the ministry said the committee could consider the proposal to permit the purchase of hospital beds as proposed by the minister.

The ministry also heard from another MP, Mr Balram Singh Yadav, a few months later on a similar matter. Mr Yadav wanted the guidelines to permit the purchase of bedsheets and blankets by hospitals. He said he found that blankets and bedsheets provided to patients in hospitals in his constituency were not up to the mark. This was so because they were bought from the open market at cheap rates. On the other hand, if the guidelines were amended, bedsheets and blankets of better quality could be bought from public sector undertakings.

Here again the ministry responded by saying that the guidelines do not permit the purchase of consumables. The committee agreed with the ministry and said it did not approve the purchase of items like bedsheets and blankets as these were all consumables. Further, although the ministry had recommended that Mr Oram's request for the purchase of hospital beds could be considered, the committee rejected this as well.[11]

Funding Blood Banks

An offshoot of the prohibition on funding registered societies and trusts was that MPs could not fund blood banks sponsored by service organizations like the Rotary Club or the Lions Club. Mr Sahib Singh Verma wrote to the Lok Sabha Committee in this regard and said the Rotary Clubs in Delhi were setting up a voluntary blood bank in the city at a cost of ₹5.50 crore. The Union government and the Delhi government had sanctioned ₹28 lakh and ₹25 lakh respectively for this project. Rotary International had committed ₹1.56 crore for the purchase of equipment. The blood bank would be housed in a five-storeyed, centrally air-conditioned building and would be a trail-blazer for similar projects across the country. He wanted to contribute ₹21 lakh towards this project and, therefore, requested the committee to amend the guidelines to make this possible. The commissioner of the MCD referred to Mr Verma's proposal and said his office had sought a clarification from the MS&PI before disbursal of the amount. The ministry's response was that the guidelines only permit construction of government hospital buildings and therefore, the Rotary Blood Bank cannot be funded.

The Lok Sabha Committee overruled the ministry and said the guidelines should be amended to permit funding of registered societies like Rotary Clubs and Lions Clubs when they take up projects like construction of blood banks. The committee said funds could be earmarked for such projects subject to conditions stipulated by the ministry in respect of registered societies and trusts.[12]

The attitude of the ministry changed when the MPs approached Mr Arun Shourie, Minister of State in the MS&PI. The minister responded positively and said the project was of such significance that it warranted approval of the committees of the two Houses of Parliament. Mr Shourie wrote to the chairman of the Lok Sabha Committee on 21 May 2001 that four MPs, three of them from the Upper House and Mr Sahib Singh Verma of the Lok Sabha wanted to contribute ₹20 lakh or more each towards the construction and procurement of equipment for a voluntary blood bank in Delhi.

He said that the Rotary Clubs of Delhi had got together to build a blood bank at a cost of ₹5 crore in the Tughlakabad Institutional Area and four MPs wanted to contribute a total of ₹81 lakh to the project. The minister said, 'Because of the importance of the project; because of the devotion, expertise and integrity of those who are implementing the project; and because of the express desire of the Members of Parliament to support the initiative, we in the ministry strongly recommended the proposal, and do hope that Committees of the Rajya Sabha and the Lok Sabha will be kind enough to approve the contribution.'[13]

Apart from these four MPs, yet another member of the Lok Sabha, Mr Vijay Goel, wrote to the committee and said he should be permitted to contribute ₹10 lakh to this project, even though the blood bank was being built outside his Lok Sabha constituency. He said the mission statement of the blood bank is that 'no one shall die in Delhi for want of blood'. For a project like this, constituency-specific allocation of funds 'is an artificial restriction', more so when it is in a metropolitan city where people living in many neighbouring constituencies benefit from such projects.

The MS&PI wrote to the committee and said there was a need to relax the rule which bars procurement of inventory items as also the rule which imposes a ceiling of ₹25 lakh in regard to equipment purchase.[14]

The proposal made a lot of sense from a humanitarian point of view. Several MPs were coming together to chip in and fund a blood bank. The only hitch was that what they wanted to do did not exactly fit in with the guidelines drawn up for spending MPLADS funds. The Lok Sabha Committee noted that para 4.1 of the guidelines had already been amended to permit expenditure up to ₹25 lakh on a single project. But, there was a restriction on spending on inventory items. The committee said that keeping in view the dire need to have blood banks in Delhi, it would allow the purchase of equipment for a blood bank 'as a special case'. It further recommended that the ceiling of ₹25 lakh be waived if an MP wanted to invest more than this sum for such a project within his constituency. It, however, made it clear that no contribution could be made by an MP outside his constituency except in the case of a natural calamity of rare severity.[15]

The Rajya Sabha Committee considered the proposal of the four MPs, three of whom were from the Rajya Sabha, for the purchase of equipment for the Rotary Blood Bank in Delhi, after it was forwarded to it by the MS&PI. It approved the expenditure and said the import of equipment should be made through the commissioner of the MCD and the equipment purchased should form part of the fixed assets.

Following the committee's decision, the ministry issued instructions to the commissioner of the MCD.[16]

Storage Refrigerators for Blood Banks

Those who initially drafted the guidelines for utilization of MPLADS funds could never have visualized the different and complicated scenarios that may emerge in the future. While they felt, and rightly so, that MPLADS should be used to create durable assets like the construction of school buildings, water supply and sanitation-related works, etc., they did not have any idea of the complex questions that MPs and their constituents would pose as the scheme got going. The originators of this scheme were correct in declaring that inventory items should not be bought with these funds because that would open the floodgates and thousands of crores of rupees would get spent every year via MPLADS, but the spending would not be visible. The purchase of inventory items would also open the doors to corruption with wholesalers and retailers of a variety of goods hovering around the offices of district collectors and MPs and trying every trick in the trade (including bribery) to sell their wares. Soon, the entire scheme would have begun to stink of corruption and there would have been mounting public pressure to dispense with it.

While all this can be said in defence of the guidelines prohibiting the purchase of inventory items, such a blanket ban can also put MPs and the committee monitoring it in a moral dilemma, specially when they get requests related to health or medical care. One such relates to the purchase of storage refrigerators for blood banks. Mr Dinsha J. Patel wrote to the nodal ministry in May 2000 and said his request to fund the purchase of a storage refrigerator for the blood bank of the Indian Red Cross Society at Nadiad had been disallowed because it did not come within the ambit of Item 23 in the Illustrative List. He said the guidelines allow the purchase of an ambulance by the Red Cross Society, but not a refrigerator. Why not a refrigerator? The blood preserved in this refrigerator could save lives, he said, and pleaded with the minister to 'intervene and rectify the item and allow the purchase'.

The ministry saw merit in Mr Patel's request. It said, in another context, it had disallowed the purchase of refrigerators as they were inventory items. However, it wanted the committees of the two Houses to consider Mr Patel's request and reword the guidelines accordingly because they only permit purchase of medical equipment by government hospitals. Item 23, that was blocking the proposal, read as follows:

> Procurement of hospital equipment like X-Ray machines, ambulances for government hospitals and setting up of mobile dispensaries in rural areas by government Panchayati institutions. Ambulance can be provided to reputed service organizations like Red Cross, Ramakrishna Mission etc.

The Lok Sabha Committee noted the comments of the ministry and said that the guidelines could be relaxed 'for allowing purchase of storage refrigerator for blood banks'. It accordingly suggested amendment of the guidelines to read as follows: 'Procurement of hospital equipment like X-Ray machines, ambulances and storage refrigerator for Blood Banks...'[17]

Mr Akbar Ali Khandakar wrote to the chairman of the Lok Sabha Committee in June 2002 and sought permission for funding the purchase of a mobile diagnostic centre-cum-pathological clinic by Bharat Sevashram Sangh, an NGO in Serampore, West Bengal. This mobile diagnostic unit would offer medical services to poor residents of remote villages in the Hooghly district, he said. The mobile unit would be equipped to conduct blood analysis, X-rays, ultrasound tests, ECG tests, and provide patients with on-the-spot results. The MP also cited the guidelines relating to the purchase of hospital equipment and ambulances. He wanted the committee's clearance for the proposal.

The Lok Sabha Committee did not approve the proposal and said the purchase of a mobile diagnostic clinic does not constitute the creation of a durable asset. Also, the proposal involves recurring expenditure, which is against the guidelines of MPLADS, it said. It recalled an earlier decision presented in its seventh report on the request of a Rajya Sabha member to purchase a mobile dental clinic. In that case, the committee had said that keeping in view the instructions issued to district magistrates in October 1999, which stipulated that mobile dispensaries could not be provided to NGOs 'in the name of ambulance or otherwise', the request could not be accepted. The committee, therefore, turned down Mr Khandaker's proposal for similar reasons.[18]

Artificial Limbs for the Disabled

Ever since MPLADS was launched, constituents started approaching MPs for funds for a variety of things. While some works that they want executed—like construction of schools, stadia, water supply lines, etc.—benefit the wider community, they often make requests which sound reasonable but tend to benefit individuals only. For example, when people seek funds from this scheme to provide artificial limbs or bicycles for the disabled, it is not easy for MPs to be simply bureaucratic and say the guidelines do not permit it. Instead what they do is seek amendment of the guidelines to enable them to use these funds for such purposes. Mr R.R. Pramanik made one such request in a letter to the Lok Sabha Committee. The government responded by saying that every scheme had a specific scope and content. 'The MPLAD Scheme specifically aims at construction of assets of durable nature for public use based on locally felt needs. Under the Scheme (Item 8, appendix 2) assets for individual benefits are not permissible. There are already schemes of Ministry of Welfare which should take care of this aspect.'[19]

The Lok Sabha committee, however, disagreed with the government. It said provision should be made for artificial limbs and cycles to 'a fixed number' of needy, disabled persons every year.[20]

NOTES

1. Third Report, Committee on MPLADS 1999–2000, presented to the Lok Sabha, 21 December 2000, Lok Sabha Secretariat, New Delhi,

p. 29.
2. Ibid., p. 30.
3. Ibid., pp. 39–40.
4. Seventh Report, Committee on MPLADS 2000–2001, presented to the Lok Sabha, 31 August 2001, Lok Sabha Secretariat, New Delhi, p. 8.
5. Ibid., p. 9.
6. Tenth Report, Committee on MPLADS 2002–2003, presented to the Lok Sabha, 21 November 2002, Lok Sabha Secretariat, New Delhi, p. 90–91.
7. Ibid., p. 91.
8. Third Report, Committee on MPLADS 1999–2000, presented to the Lok Sabha, 21 December 2000, Lok Sabha Secretariat, New Delhi, p. 35.
9. Ibid., p. 37.
10. Ibid., p. 38.
11. Ibid., p. 22.
12. Ibid., pp. 8–9.
13. Seventh Report, Committee on MPLADS 2000–2001, presented to the Lok Sabha, 31 August 2001, Lok Sabha Secretariat, New Delhi, pp. 5–56.
14. Ibid., pp. 58–59.
15. Ibid., p. 59.
16. Fourth Report, Committee on MPLADS, presented to the Lok Sabha, 17 December 2002, Rajya Sabha Secretariat, New Delhi, p. 30.
17. Second Report, Committee on MPLADS 1999–2000, presented to the Lok Sabha, 22 August 2000, Lok Sabha Secretariat, New Delhi, p. 23.
18. Eleventh Report, Committee on MPLADS 2003–2004, presented to the Lok Sabha, 9 April 2003, Lok Sabha Secretariat, New Delhi, pp. 6–7.
19. Second Report, Committee on MPLADS 1999–2000, presented to the Lok Sabha, 22 August 2000, Lok Sabha Secretariat, New Delhi, p. 9.
20. Ibid., p. 10.

8

Cyclones, Earthquakes, Tsunamis and MPs

Nature has showered many bounteous gifts on India—the mighty Himalayan ranges, the huge rivers that irrigate its semi-arid tracts, the Western and Eastern Ghats, the long coastline and two monsoons that ensure copious rainfall to sustain life and farming. Yet, there is a flip side to all this. Rain storms turn into cyclones that regularly devastate coastal villages and towns and tectonic shifts in the peninsular plate result in seismic episodes that cause large-scale damage in different parts of the country, which are prone to earthquakes. The result is that Indians come face-to-face rather frequently with natural calamities and there is pressure on individual citizens, elected representatives, municipalities and governments to loosen their purse strings and contribute to relief and rehabilitation in a cyclone- or earthquake-hit area.

Such tragedies prick the conscience of MPs, but most of them find it difficult to raise funds for relief and rehabilitation when the disaster in question is not in their backyard, namely, within their parliamentary constituencies or their states. For example, an MP from Karnataka will naturally commiserate with the victims of an earthquake in Gujarat but will hesitate to go on a fundraising mission for the purpose because the demands back home are so pressing. Similarly, MPs from the northern state of Uttar Pradesh will readily offer lip sympathy to victims of a cyclone that hits coastal Andhra Pradesh but will do precious little to garner funds for relief work in the affected areas. This is not because Indian parliamentarians are a heartless lot. They are so overwhelmed by constituency pressures that they simply do not have the time or the resources to attend to the problems in some distant part of the country.

The incapacity to help victims even in such situations when millions are hit by a natural calamity troubles the conscience of many MPs. For such MPs, MPLADS offers a way out. Since they have funds at their disposal, allocation of a small portion of it to victims of a national disaster in some other state would help clear their conscience and build a decent corpus for relief measures. However, as per the guidelines for the scheme, MPLADS funds are to be utilized only in their constituencies by Lok Sabha MPs and only within their states by Rajya Sabha MPs.

Helping Victims of the Orissa Cyclone

Mr Rajesh Pilot, a member of the Lok Sabha, was the first to take the initiative to make some portion of this fund available for relief measures in case of national calamities. Participating in a discussion in the House on 29 November 1999 on the super cyclone that hit Orissa a month earlier, Mr Pilot said a sum of ₹10 lakh should be taken from the MPLADS account of every MP and placed at the disposal of the authorities in Orissa for cyclone relief. The prime minister, Mr Atal Behari Vajpayee, endorsed the proposal and said there ought to be no objection to this suggestion.

In the Rajya Sabha, Dr Najma Heptullah, chairperson of the Committee on MPLADS, raised the issue at a meeting of the committee on 22 December 1999 and suggested that members could contribute ₹10 lakh each towards cyclone relief. The committee authorized her to write to all members with a request that they allocate ₹10 lakh for Orissa cyclone relief. Dr Heptullah wrote to the members the following day. The funds thus collected were to be used for the construction of shelters, houses, schools, roads and bridges. The Rajya Sabha Committee on MPLADS discussed the issue on 18 February 2000 and recommended a 'one-time modification' of the guidelines to enable members to contribute from this fund outside their constituencies and states.[1]

The Rajya Sabha Committee on MPLADS said that a super cyclone accompanied by a severe wind storm at the speed of 250 to 300 kilometres per hour lashed the coastal districts of Orissa on 28 and 29 October 1999 leaving behind an unprecedented trail of devastation and misery The cyclone paralysed life along 300 kilometres of the coast and rains accompanied by cyclonic winds affected habitations as far away as 200 kilometres from the coast. About 8,000 villages in fourteen districts were severely affected of which 2,000 became unapproachable. Nearly 400 villages were destroyed. The crop area affected was 1.5 million hectares of which 50,000 hectares were affected by salinity. The official death toll was 10,000 persons whereas non-official estimates put the death toll at 50,000. As many as 14,800 primary schools were completely destroyed. There was a colossal loss of housing and cattle wealth, scarcity of drinking water, dislocation of telecommunications, loss of power supply, disruption of education and rural industries. It was of the view that the funds from MPLADS could be utilized to provide housing, schools, dispensaries and community centres to the affected people.

Later, the committee decided to utilize the funds for the construction of school-cum-cyclone shelters as private housing was not permitted under the guidelines. The agency chosen to implement the plan was the Housing and Urban Development Corporation (HUDCO), the public sector housing company.[2]

The secretary in the Ministry of Statistics and MP & PI wrote to the secretary general of the Lok Sabha the following month, updated him on all these developments including the assurance given by the prime minister in the Lok Sabha and suggested modification of the guidelines.[3]

The matter was referred to the Lok Sabha Committee on MPLADS, which in turn approved the modification of the guidelines. While doing so, it suggested a general amendment to enable contributions from the fund to attend to relief measures in all such situations in the future. It said the guidelines should be amended to permit contribution by MPs 'not exceeding ₹10 lakh per annum for rehabilitation measures in natural calamity of rare severity in any part of the country'. It also took the opportunity to address another major natural calamity, drought, that occurs regularly in some part of the country or the other.

Since much of agriculture and drinking water sources in India are rain-fed, the failure of the south-west or the north-east monsoons results in drought conditions in rural areas in regions which have scanty rainfall in any given year. This results in lack of potable water and loss of crops, and people living in these areas press for drought relief packages from the state and federal governments. The shortage of drinking water sometimes creates riot-like situations, and MPs representing these areas come under pressure to find remedial measures. Aware of this recurring problem, the Lok Sabha Committee on MPLADS decided to utilize the debate on cyclone relief in Orissa to address this issue. It, therefore, recommended that MPs be permitted to use these funds to provide drinking water tankers and to bore wells in constituencies which face severe drought conditions.[4]

The government implemented the suggestion in regard to natural calamities by adding the following as para 1.3 in the guidelines: 'MPs can recommend works outside their constituencies/sites for an amount not exceeding ₹10 lakh per annum for construction of assets that are permissible in the guidelines, for rehabilitation measures in the event of a natural calamity of rare severity in any part of the country.'[5]

But the matter did not end here. The MS&PI was petitioned

by MPs once again. Some of them felt that the ceiling of ₹10 lakh per natural calamity needlessly tied the hands of MPs who wanted to make a more meaningful contribution from their fund towards relief measures in some situations. The ministry wrote to the Lok Sabha Secretariat on 16 November 2000 and said MPs had pointed out that should there be another natural calamity, those who have contributed to the Orissa Cyclone Relief Fund cannot allocate funds towards any other natural calamity since the guidelines impose a ceiling of ₹10 lakh for such contribution per financial year. It, therefore, wanted that para 1.3 of the guidelines should be amended to enable MPs to contribute up to ₹10 lakh for each natural calamity of rare severity.

However, the ministry suggested a drastic change some months later because even as the country was coping with the ill effects of the Orissa cyclone, several parts of Gujarat were devastated by a major earthquake, and MPs were keen to pump in funds for rehabilitation of the victims. As a result, the MS&PI wrote to district collectors and commissioners of municipal corporations on 31 January 2001 and said the ministry had been getting requests from MPs to be allowed to contribute whatever amount they can from their MPLADS funds for taking up relief and rehabilitation works in the earthquake-affected areas of Gujarat. 'The matter has been considered and it has been decided to relax the provisions contained in para 1.3 of the guidelines allowing MPs to contribute any amount they desire from their MPLADS funds for taking up developmental works that are permissible in the guidelines for rehabilitation in the earthquake-affected areas of Gujarat. The ceiling of ₹10 lakh accordingly stands waived and MPs may assign whatever portion from their balance as they desire to contribute, that they may contribute the entire ₹2 crore accruing to them in a year.'[6]

The ministry's *suo motu* action may have been prompted by the nationwide concern over the calamity that struck Gujarat. This could also have been the reason for the ministry to virtually amend the guidelines without consulting the MPLADS committees of the two Houses of Parliament.

The Lok Sabha Committee on MPLADS however disagreed with the MS & PI. It noted the ministry's decision to amend para 1.3 of the guidelines on MPLADS to allow MPs to contribute any amount they desired up to ₹2 crore for each natural calamity of rare severity in any part of the country. The committee said the MPs 'owe their responsibility towards their constituents' and the MPLAD Scheme was primarily meant to foster development at the constituency level. It, therefore, reiterated its earlier recommendation and said, 'MPs can also recommend works outside their constituencies for an amount not exceeding ₹10 lakhs per annum for construction of assets that are permissible in the Guidelines...'[7]

The committee's final recommendation was as follows: An MP may contribute an amount not exceeding ₹10 lakh for each calamity in a year; if any member wants to contribute more than ₹10 lakh, he should seek permission of the committee; and contribution towards relief work in a year should not exceed ₹10 lakh.

It further said that it would be the responsibility of the government to define the term 'natural calamity of rare severity' to enable MPs to make contributions.[8]

Sadly, despite the enthusiasm of Dr Heptullah, Mr Rajesh Pilot and some others, the response of MPs to the idea of allocating some part of the MPLADS fund to rehabilitation work in states hit by natural calamities was at best lukewarm.

Although Dr Heptullah wrote to all members of the Rajya Sabha in December 1999 requesting them for a contribution, the Rajya Sabha Committee on MPLADS revisited the issue at its meeting held on 28 November 2000 (almost a year later) and authorized her to write once again to all members who had not contributed to cyclone relief in Orissa. The committee said the letter must state that MPs who were not inclined to make the contribution should write to the Rajya Sabha secretariat before 15 December 2000. In case there was no objection from an MP before this date, the secretariat would be authorized to make an automatic deduction of ₹10 lakh from the MP's fund for Orissa relief.[9]

However, even this deadline and virtual ultimatum failed to evoke an adequate response. The committee also realized that it would be inappropriate to consider the non-response to the latest appeal as consent. On 21 March 2001, MPs who had contributed to the fund were invited to an audio-visual presentation by HUDCO on what could be done with the MPLADS funds in Orissa. Thirty-five MPs attended the meeting. As of 18 December 2001 (more than two years after the cyclone hit Orissa) only seventy-eight of 245 members of the Rajya Sabha had contributed to the fund. Their total contribution was ₹7.5 crore.[10]

Meanwhile, in March 2001, the Rajya Sabha Committee on MPLADS took note of the fact that yet another state, Gujarat, had been hit by a natural calamity—a severe earthquake that caused massive destruction in many parts of the state and claimed hundreds of lives. The committee's chairperson reported to the committee that officials from Gujarat had called seeking information on how MPLADS funds had been used for rehabilitation of cyclone victims in Orissa so that they could devise appropriate schemes for using these funds to provide relief to the victims of the earthquake. The officials said they would put across this proposal to MPs from Gujarat.[11]

There are also instances of red tape in regard to transfer of funds from MPs' accounts to the administration of the state where a natural calamity has occurred. These delays may also prompt MPs to have second thoughts on the contribution itself. One such case is that of Mr Moinul Hassan, a member of the Lok Sabha, who wrote to the MS&PI on 16 November 2001 saying that he had withdrawn his consent for a contribution of ₹10 lakh to the Orissa Cyclone Relief Fund. The ministry said the MP had given his consent a year ago and the nodal district collector was requested on 27 November 2000 to transfer the sum to the chief secretary of Orissa. However, despite repeated reminders, the sum was not transferred. Now, Mr Hassan said he had to execute many projects in his constituency and therefore needed the ₹10 lakh, which had in any case not been sent to Orissa. He even promised to make up for this and provide the sum for Orissa cyclone relief 'as early as possible'. The ministry forwarded this request to the Lok Sabha Committee on MPLADS. The latter allowed the MP to go back on his word and said it must be made sure that the ₹10 lakh meant for Orissa is still lying in the account of the MP with the nodal district collector.[12]

The Gujarat Earthquake

The western state of Gujarat was rocked by a devastating earthquake measuring 6.9 on the Richter scale on 26 January 2001 causing massive damage in nine districts of the state. Soon after the earthquake, the presiding officers of the two Houses of Parliament appealed to all members to contribute ₹10 lakh each from their MPLADS funds and also donate a month's salary for rehabilitation of victims of the earthquake.

The Rajya Sabha Committee on MPLADS constituted a subcommittee headed by Dr Najma Heptullah to make a first-hand appraisal of the post-earthquake situation and to suggest what could be done to provide succour to the victims. The members of the subcommittee toured the affected areas of the state in May 2001, met state government officials and considered proposals for rehabilitation programmes.

Though the response of Rajya Sabha members to the appeal for funds for rehabilitation of Orissa cyclone victims was disappointing, there was a substantial improvement in the response of MPs to the appeal made by the chairman of the House for contributions towards earthquake relief in Gujarat. The committee reported that as many as 167 MPs had stepped forward to help and their total contribution was ₹27.15 crore, which meant that many MPs had contributed far more than ₹10 lakh. Among those who decided to transfer a substantial part of their funds at their disposal for rehabilitation of earthquake victims were Pramod Mahajan (₹2.1 crore), Mr Fali S. Nariman (₹2.1 crore), Mr Narendra Mohan (₹2 crore), Mr Gopalsinh G. Solanki (₹2 crore), Dr L.M. Singhvi (₹1 crore), Mr Venkaiah Naidu (₹50 lakh) and Mr Sikander Bhakt (₹50 lakh).[13]

With such a substantial sum in its kitty, the Rajya Sabha Committee on MPLADS held consultations with officials from the state during seven meetings between June 2001 and June 2002 and approved the construction of 474 primary school buildings, 125 community halls, an artisan village, a housing complex, dispensaries and some shelters. Two public sector companies in the housing and construction sector—HUDCO and the National Building Construction Corporation (NBCC)—were entrusted with the task of building the approved schools and other structures.

The committee has reported that matters pertaining to the rehabilitation of Gujarat earthquake victims figured in twenty-two of its meetings between February 2001 and November 2004. In many of these meetings, the committee debated the various options available to undertake rehabilitation work in the state, held extensive discussions with officials from the state and from the public sector undertakings that were to execute the projects.[14]

While funding rehabilitation work in areas hit by natural calamities, the committees have adopted the procedure of collecting donations from members, calling for proposals from MPs hailing from the region and officials from the state governments, and zeroing on some specific projects. Thereafter, the committees meet to get the estimates for each project, allocate funds for the same and identify the agencies to execute the projects.

Sometimes, there are concerns relating to costs and standard of work and the committees are called upon to revisit their decisions in the light of new information. A project relating to the Shri Jain Medical and Educational Trust in Bhuj, Kutch, is one such. It was decided to allocate ₹75 lakh out of the funds collected for rehabilitation of the Gujarat earthquake victims to this institution for construction of buildings. The work was entrusted to HUDCO. The trust, however, wrote to the Lok Sabha secretariat in August, 2002 and said the cost of construction indicated by HUDCO was very high and that it would be far cheaper to entrust the responsibility for the construction to the district collector of Kutch, Bhuj. When quality construction can be assured as per regulations framed by the Kutch Development Authority at a much lower cost, 'why should one spend much more for the same?', the institution asked.

The matter was referred to the MS&PI. The ministry tossed the ball into the court of the Lok Sabha Committee on MPLADS. 'It is for the committee to take a view of the request made by the beneficiary organization,' it said. The committee accepted the opinion of the educational trust that it would be far more economical to entrust the construction to the district collector of Kutch, Bhuj instead of HUDCO.[15]

Relief For Tsunami Victims

On 26 December 2004, a massive earthquake with its epicentre off the coast of Sumatra and measuring nine on the Richter scale triggered a tsunami that caused massive destruction along the coastlines of many countries in the region including Thailand, Indonesia, Sri Lanka and India. In India, the worst-hit areas were the Andaman and Nicobar Islands, Puducherry and the coastal regions of Tamil Nadu, Kerala and Andhra Pradesh on the eastern coastline and even parts of Karnataka on the western coast. Thousands of people lost their lives, many more suffered grievous injuries, and much of the coastal population lost their homes and means of livelihood. The worst affected districts were Nellore, Prakasam, Guntur, East Godavari, West Godavari and Krishna in Andhra Pradesh; Kollam Ernakulam and Alappuzha in Kerala; Kanyakumari, Cuddalore, Nagapattinam, Ramanathapuram, Kanchipuram and Villupuram in Tamil Nadu; Andaman and Nicobar Islands; and Puducherry.

This terrible calamity stirred the conscience of people across the land, and governments, NGOs and a host of national and international organizations rushed in with aid to the victims of the tsunami. As in the past, the presiding officers of the two Houses of Parliament issued a joint appeal to MPs to contribute ₹11 lakh each from their MPLADS funds for the rehabilitation of the victims of the tsunami. On 1 January 2005, the chairman of the Rajya Sabha issued a separate appeal to members. In response to this appeal, 167 members of the Upper House contributed ₹31.36 crore from their MPLADS funds towards rehabilitation projects.[16]

The news of the tsunami and the destruction that it wrought on the eastern coast moved many members of the Rajya Sabha to contribute substantial sums of money towards rehabilitation of the victims. Among those who contributed a huge part of their MPLADS funds were Dr Karan Singh (₹2.20 crore), Dr Bimal Jalan (₹2 crore), Mr Pyarelal Khandelwal (₹2 crore), Mr Santosh Bagrodia (₹1.01 crore), Mr N. Jothi (₹1 crore), Mr T.T.V. Dinakaran (₹1 crore), Mr Lalit Kishore Chaturvedi (₹1 crore), Ms Lata Mangeshkar (₹1.01 crore), Mr Fali S. Nariman (₹1 crore), Mr K. Jana Krishnamurthi (₹60 lakh).[17]

Once members of the House made such a commitment to help the victims, the Rajya Sabha Committee on MPLADS got down to the task of assessing the situation in the affected states and to make proposals for utilization of MPLADS funds. The committee visited the Andaman and Nicobar Islands and many of the coastal areas in the mainland that bore the brunt of the tsunami. It said that the objective of rehabilitation work should be long-term capacity-building by establishing new centres of learning. It said there was a need to create and rebuild the community infrastructure destroyed by the tsunami as well as for building homes for those rendered homeless, specially women, children and the elderly. The committee also visited the tsunami-affected areas in February 2005 to assess the damage. It was of the view that the occupational group that was worst hit was fishermen. It said that the funds should be used to build worksheds-cum-store rooms, net-mending sheds, auction halls and fish-drying platforms. It also favoured the launch of a fishermen's training institute in Puducherry or Karaikal, construction of proper houses at a safe distance from the coast, cyclone shelters and development of a coastal bio-field consisting of mangroves, bamboo, etc. The committee felt that one of the main reasons for the high rate of casualties was the existence of dwellings and commercial activities 'perilously close to the sea'. In most of these areas the enforcement of zoning areas was 'almost negligible'. Had the habitations been away from the seashore, 'the casualties would have been much less'. The committee recommended construction of old-age homes in some coastal areas of Kerala and orphanages in Kancheepuram and Kanyakumari to take care of children who were rendered orphans in the tsunami.[18]

However, the Rajya Sabha Committee on MPLADS was far from satisfied with the attitude of government officials in the affected states. It said that on many occasions it encountered problems in selecting sites for rehabilitation projects and the states were not forthcoming when asked about the status of projects. It felt that rehabilitation would not have the desired effect if it was not done in time. It asked all states to draw up a revised deadline for completion of all pending projects and to do the same within time. The committee was also of the view that local administrators should take a holistic view of rehabilitation. For example, 'a hostel for school children would serve no purpose without a school in the vicinity'.[19] The committee considered tsunami-related issues at sixteen of its meetings from January 2005 to October 2008.[20]

Given the magnitude of the disaster, the guidelines were relaxed to enable members to contribute 'any amount' towards rehabilitation of people hit by the tsunami. Eventually, 207 members of the Lok Sabha and 167 from the Rajya Sabha contributed ₹22.74 crore and ₹31.34 crore respectively for tsunami relief. These funds were used for creation of community infrastructural assets such as schools, hospitals, public health centres, community halls, multipurpose halls for fishermen, cyclone shelters, desalination plants, old-age homes, orphanages, fish-landing centres and ambulances in the affected districts. Of the funds allocated by MPs, ₹34.35 crore had been utilized in rehabilitation works until 31 March 2008. Of this ₹17.85 crore had been spent in Tamil Nadu and ₹9.51 crore in the Andaman and Nicobar Islands and in Kerala, Puducherry and Andhra Pradesh.[21]

The report for the year 2008–09 shows that the spending on tsunami relief projects had risen to ₹38.45 crore up to 31 March 2009. As in the previous year, the bulk of the spending was in Tamil Nadu and the Andaman and Nicobar Islands.[22]

Relief for Victims of Riots

Meanwhile, attempts were made to add a new dimension—riots to the provision that enabled MPs to contribute towards relief and rehabilitation in case of 'natural calamities of rare severity'. Some MPs wrote to the committee in the year 2002 seeking permission to contribute ₹1 crore each from their MPLADS funds towards relief and rehabilitation. Though they made no mention of it, the 'rehabilitation' proposed was obviously that of victims of communal riots that broke out in Gujarat earlier that year.

The request was forwarded by the committee to the MS & PI for comments in June 2002. The ministry referred to para 1.3 of the guidelines and said MPs can recommend works only in the case of natural calamities of rare severity and here again their contribution is not to exceed ₹10 lakh if the calamity occurs outside their constituencies. The ministry said, obviously the MPs wanted to fund rehabilitation of riot victims. 'Riots cannot be considered as a natural calamity' and therefore, is not covered by the guidelines, it said. The ministry also drew the committee's attention to the fact that MPs cannot contribute more than ₹10 lakh for natural calamities outside their constituencies.[23]

The Lok Sabha Committee on MPLADS said it took note of

the desire of some MPs to contribute ₹1 crore each towards relief and rehabilitation in riot-affected areas of Gujarat. The committee said the guidelines should be amended to enable MPs to make such a contribution towards relief measures for riot victims in Gujarat 'as the same was also done in the case of earthquake affected areas of Gujarat'.[24]

NOTES

1. First Report, Committee on MPLADS 1999–2000, presented to the Lok Sabha, 12 May 2000, Lok Sabha Secretariat, New Delhi, p. 20.
2. Third Report, Committee on MPLADS 1999–2000, presented to the Rajya Sabha, 18 December 2001, Rajya Sabha Secretariat, New Delhi, pp. 1–3.
3. First Report, Committee on MPLADS 1999–2000, presented to the Lok Sabha, 12 May 2000, Lok Sabha Secretariat, New Delhi, p. 21.
4. Ibid.
5. Sixth Report, Committee on MPLADS 2000–2001, presented to the Lok Sabha, 31 July 2001, Lok Sabha Secretariat, New Delhi, p. 7.
6. Fourth Report, Committee on MPLADS 2000–2001, presented to the Lok Sabha, 23 March 2001, Lok Sabha Secretariat, New Delhi, p. 2.
7. Ibid.
8. Ibid., p. 3.
9. Third Report, Committee on MPLADS 1999–2000, presented to the Rajya Sabha, 18 December 2001, Rajya Sabha Secretariat, New Delhi, pp. 1–3.
10. Ibid., pp. 5–7.
11. Ibid., p. 4.
12. Tenth Report, Committee on MPLADS 2002–2003, presented to the Lok Sabha, 21 November 2002, Lok Sabha Secretariat, New Delhi, pp. 4–5.
13. Fifth Report, Committee on MPLADS, presented to the Rajya Sabha, 7 December 2004, Rajya Sabha Secretariat, New Delhi, pp. 2–8.
14. See minutes, pp. 25–99, Fifth Report, Committee on MPLADS, presented to the Rajya Sabha, 7 December 2004, Rajya Sabha

Secretariat, New Delhi.
15 Eleventh Report, Committee on MPLADS 2003–2004, presented to the Lok Sabha, 9 April 2003, Lok Sabha Secretariat, New Delhi, pp. 39–40.
16 Sixth Report, Committee on MPLADS, presented to the Rajya Sabha, 23 October 2008, Rajya Sabha Secretariat, New Delhi, p. 1.
17 Ibid., pp. 10–17.
18 Ibid., pp. 2–4.
19 Ibid., pp. 8–9.
20 See minutes, pp. 45–87, Sixth Report, Committee on MPLADS, presented to the Rajya Sabha, 23 October 2008, Rajya Sabha Secretariat, New Delhi.
21 Annual Report, 2007–08, Members of Parliament Local Area Development Scheme, Ministry of Statistics and Programme Implementation, Government of India, New Delhi, p. 18.
22 Annual Report, 2008–09, Members of Parliament Local Area Development Scheme, Ministry of Statistics and Programme Implementation, Government of India, New Delhi, p. 19.
23 Tenth Report, Committee on MPLADS 2002-2003, presented to the Lok Sabha, 21 November 2002, Lok Sabha Secretariat, New Delhi, p. 132.
24 Ibid., pp. 132–33.

9

Lok Sabha Committee vs Rajya Sabha Committee

A request by two MPs, Mr P.H. Pandian and Mr K. Malaisamy for permission to spend some portion of their MPLADS funds to purchase water tankers for the benefit of their constituents placed the MS&PI in a quandary because the committees of the two Houses disagreed with each other on the permissibility of such expenditure.

In his letter, Mr Pandian said there was an acute shortage of drinking water in the Tuticorin and Tirunelveli municipal areas. The two municipalities supplied drinking water by hiring water tankers at great expense. Anxious to cut such public spending on rented tankers, he had allocated ₹70 lakh from his fund for the year 2000–01 for the purchase of eight water tankers—four for each of these municipalities. The district of collector, Tirunelveli, however, had informed him that there was no provision for such spending in the existing guidelines. He wanted the Lok Sabha Committee on MPLADS to permit the purchase of these tankers, meaning thereby that the guidelines be suitably amended.

The MS&PI responded by saying that the Lok Sabha Committee had recommended the use of these funds to purchase water tankers and to dig bore wells. However, when this recommendation was referred to the Rajya Sabha Committee on MPLADS, that committee had not favoured the utilization of these funds to buy water tankers. The ministry said the existing guidelines allowed the construction of water tanks and tubewells, including borewells. The ministry quoted the following extract from the Rajya Sabha Committee's Report: 'The committee considered the proposal regarding utilisation of MPLADS fund for providing drinking water tankers. The committee recommended that water tanks could be provided but not water tankers.'[1]

The Lok Sabha Committee, however, decided to reiterate its earlier recommendation, made in its first report, which said that members could be permitted to utilize MPLADS funds for providing drinking water tankers to mitigate the suffering of people in the constituencies which are in the grip of extreme drought conditions. Further, it said these water tankers must be maintained by local bodies.[2]

The ministry, however, did not implement this recommendation because the Rajya Sabha Committee had opposed it. The ministry stated as much in its 'Action-taken Report'. The Lok Sabha Committee directed the ministry to take this up once again with the Rajya Sabha Committee and get it approved so that funds could be released for the purchase of water tankers. It wanted the ministry to take 'prompt and swift action in this regard'.[3]

Minister Writes, Committees Clash

A missive from the railway minister, Ms Mamata Banerjee, that the guidelines for MPLADS permit members to allocate these funds for small railways-related projects brought the MPLADS committees of the two Houses of Parliament at loggerheads. The railway minister suggested that these funds be spent to augment passenger amenities at railway stations like providing platform shelters, raising of platforms, beautification of stations and building foot overbridges, waiting rooms and booking windows. In its very first report, the Rajya Sabha Committee on MPLADS considered these suggestions and said that it disagreed with the idea of spending MPLADS funds on items of expenditure that are generally covered by the annual budget of the Ministry of Railways. However, it said 'some limited facilities' like the provision of small restaurants and washrooms that could be used by passengers could be considered.

It is difficult to discern the logic of disallowing waiting rooms or renovation of station platforms but permitting the construction of washrooms and restaurants. In any case, this proposal did not find favour with the Lok Sabha Committee on MPLADS. This committee decided that MPLADS funds should not be spent on railway projects, whether big or small, because all these projects had to be financed via the Ministry of Railways' annual plan and budgetary allocations.

Following the Lok Sabha's decision against spending on railway projects, the MS&PI had to perform the unpleasant duty of informing the Rajya Sabha Committee about the other committee's decision and, consequently, about its own opinion that railway-related projects cannot be financed by MPLADS. This was communicated by way of the mandatory 'Action-taken Report' of the MS&PI to the Rajya Sabha Committee. The ministry informed this committee of the Lok Sabha Committee's decision that 'no amount should be made available' for projects for which budgetary provision can be made. 'Keeping in view the decision of the Lok Sabha Committee, even allowing limited facilities at railway stations cannot be considered,' the ministry said.[4]

The Rajya Sabha Committee, however, was not impressed. Parliamentary committees are generally allergic to bureaucratic responses and they place their annoyance on record. The Rajya Sabha Committee on MPLADS was no exception and it told the ministry that it did not like the government merely parroting the opinion of the other committee. It said the ministry had 'simply concurred' with the decision of the Lok Sabha Committee. 'The committee however feels that since such limited facilities like provision of small rest rooms, Sulabh Sauchalayas (wash rooms), at railway stations, which involves small amount of funds for spending could easily be financed from MPLADS funds.'[5]

Committees Clash Over Railway Projects

The demands for spending MPLADS funds on railway projects have been piling up ever since the scheme was introduced, because of the constant pressure from people for manned railway level crossings and overbridges, and passenger amenities at railway stations.

These demands have often compelled the MS&PI and the committees of the two Houses to revisit this issue because, after all, there could be no doubt that the projects proposed would invariably fall in the category of 'development'. However, this has also meant expression of contradictory opinions and conflicting views by the committees of the two Houses on spending on railway projects. While the Lok Sabha Committee felt that some exceptions should be made, the Rajya Sabha Committee took the view that MPLADS funds should not be spent on projects that come within the realm of the Union budget.

For example, the Lok Sabha Committee initially rejected such projects which were proposed and endorsed by two ministers in the Union government heading the Ministry of Railways and the MS&PI. In its first report, it said, 'no amount should be made available for the MPLADS funds for utilization for plan projects of the Union Government for which budgetary provisions could be made under the Plan allocation.'[6]

However, the government and the committee soon took a lenient view when MPs sought permission to spend their funds to construct railway level crossing gates at unmanned level crossings because of the hazards posed by such unmanned crossings. The demand for such spending was so high that the committee was compelled to make an exception in this case.

Then came the case of Mr Rupchand Pal, an MP from West Bengal. He wanted to fund a new railway level crossing near the Chandanpur railway station. Given the density of population in the neighbourhood, Mr Pal said this project needed to be taken up on priority because a large number of people risked their lives crossing the railway lines every day. The Lok Sabha Committee was in two minds and referred this case to the MS&PI. The latter responded by saying that the guidelines only permitted 'construction of level crossing at unmanned railway crossings' and that this did not cover new manned level crossings. The committee, however, approved Mr Pal's proposal and asked the ministry to amend the guidelines yet again.[7]

The committee decided to make yet another exception when Mr Tanwar Chand Gehlot sought permission to fund a railway overbridge to be built on the Ujjain–Bhopal road at Dewas in Madhya Pradesh. It said this was a project that came under the central plan. However, it endorsed the opinion of the MS&PI that 'there was great merit in the proposal' and said the ministry should grant permission for construction of this overbridge.

All this can be viewed either as a flip-flop by the committee or as a pragmatic opening up of the MPLADS programme to address the pressing needs of the people.

The MS&PI forwarded both these recommendations of the Lok Sabha Committee to the Rajya Sabha Committee and sought its views. The latter had already considered this question and rejected the same in June 2000. It considered this issue yet again at its sitting on 26 February 2001 and 'did not agree' to allow construction of passenger amenities on the ground that items covered by the annual budget of the Ministry of Railways were not permissible.[8]

The Lok Sabha Committee said it had noted the decision of the Rajya Sabha Committee 'which has rejected the same on the ground that these items could be covered under the budget allocation of the Ministry of Railways'. However, 'keeping in view the demands of public and requests from hon'ble MPs', the committee recommended that construction of foot overbridges, underbridges and passenger amenities at railway stations might be included in the Illustrative List of Works which can be taken up under MPLADS. [9]

Notes

1. Fifth Report, Committee on MPLADS 2000–2001, presented to the Lok Sabha, 24 April 2001, Lok Sabha Secretariat, New Delhi, p. 4.
2. Ibid.
3. Sixth Report, Committee on MPLADS 2000–2001, presented to the Lok Sabha, 31 July 2001, Lok Sabha Secretariat, New Delhi, pp. 2–3.
4. Second Report, Committee on MPLADS, presented to the Rajya Sabha, 11 December 2001, Rajya Sabha Secretariat, New Delhi, p. 6.
5. Ibid., p. 7.
6. First Report, Committee on MPLADS 1999–2000, presented to the Lok Sabha, 12 May 2000, Lok Sabha Secretariat, New Delhi, p. 11.
7. Third Report, Committee on MPLADS 2000–2001, presented to the Lok Sabha, 21 December 2000, Lok Sabha Secretariat, New Delhi, p. 19.
8. Fifth Report, Committee on MPLADS 2000–2001, presented to the Lok Sabha, 24 April 2001, Lok Sabha Secretariat, New Delhi, p. 7.
9. Ibid., p. 8.

10

MPLADS and Corruption

Corruption has been endemic since independence and has now reached humongous proportions. Yet, the justice system has failed to punish wrongdoers and the most prominent among those who get away are politicians. Despite all the laws and the rigorous anti-corruption campaign in the media, citizens do not see any light at the end of the tunnel. As a result, the image of MPs, which was never very clean, dipped further when word went around that the government had decided to put substantial sums of money in their hands.

One can see two clear reasons for the scepticism about the scheme. The first reason is the trust deficit that MPs have to cope with at all times. This can be traced to the prevailing lack of faith in elected representatives in general. The second reason is that ever since the scheme was launched, people believed that the government had given MPs ₹1 crore a year (something akin to pocket money) and allowed them to spend this amount in any manner they wished. The allocation was soon raised to ₹2 crore and this only reinforced the public perception that MPs were up to no good. Their 'pocket money' had now been doubled and they had huge sums of money to squander. It was not easy to allay the fears of the public because the scheme was unique.

Both the poor and the middle class have reservations, albeit for different reasons, about MPLADS and about how MPs utilize their funds. Poverty, illiteracy and underdevelopment in the rural areas have led to considerable misunderstanding about the role of MPs in general and about the scope and purpose of schemes like MPLADS. The impoverished population thinks that MPLADS is some kind of a purse given to MPs to enable them to dole out money to constituents who are in need. People think they can approach the MP whenever they are pressed for cash for a medical emergency, a wedding or a funeral. They return disappointed when they are told that MPLADS is not meant to be disbursed this way. The middle class on the other hand has a vague understanding of the guidelines of MPLADS and is aware that it is not put into the MP's hands for disbursement to constituents. However, this class is a class of sceptics and is deeply suspicious of the motives of politicians. Therefore, even though district collectors implement the scheme, it believes that MPs manage to get around the rules and find implementing agencies and contractors who will give them 'a cut' in every project.

It is in this background that a Hindi television news channel, Star News (now ABP News), telecast a sting operation done by another media company, Dedicated Investigators Guild (DIG), which showed how MPs were trying to make money on the side while allocating MPLADS funds for projects. DIG's investigators posed as representatives of a fake NGO which wanted MPs to propose projects to be undertaken by them. These 'NGO representatives' realized that MPs wanted commissions to clear projects under this scheme. Once they were assured of a commission, the MPs were willing to issue letters to district authorities in regard to the projects proposed. The ease with which these investigators struck deals with MPs or their secretaries and discussed the percentage of bribes that the companies should pay, showed that systems were already in place to undermine the noble intentions of the scheme and that corruption in the implementation of MPLADS was an established fact.

The Sting Operation

The Dedicated Investigators Guild or DIG is a private company established by like-minded people to investigate public issues. This company did an exposé in May 2005 on the illegal sale of human organs and got on to other investigations which serve a public purpose. Following a tip-off that MPs took commissions to allocate MPLADS funds, DIG began probing this angle. The investigators set up an NGO to facilitate the investigation and to lend the operation credibility. It discussed a possible telecast of its findings with Star News officials and kept the television channel posted on the progress of investigations. It recorded conversations that its representatives had with MPs and their cronies in which the former suggested some projects and the MPs or their representatives readily agreed to allocate funds from MPLADS for these projects provided the MPs got a 'commission' for making the proposal. Once the investigation, carried out via hidden cameras, was complete, DIG sold the investigative film to Star News. The channel telecast the footage recorded on hidden cameras on 19 December 2005 in a programme titled 'Operation Chakravyuh'. This exposé, which came as a shock to viewers and even to MPs who were innocent of the dishonourable ways of some of their colleagues, turned out to be a double whammy, as it came close on the heels of another television sting operation which had exposed the 'Cash for Questions' scandal. In the latter case, another private television channel had shown MPs accepting cash to ask questions in Parliament. The repeated and continuous telecast of 'Operation Chakravyuh' showing MPs and their henchmen negotiating 'commissions' to approve MPLADS projects, ripped apart the claim that MPLADS was a people-friendly programme that had been devised with the sole intention of meeting the local needs of communities at the grassroots level. It provided proof, if proof was needed, that MPLADS had become yet another milch cow for corrupt politicians and showed that the lurking suspicion in the public mind about the sanguinity of the scheme was not misplaced. It put the chattering classes, specially the media and the academia in a 'I told you so' mode.

Parliament Investigates the MPLADS Scandal

Following the exposé by Star News on 19 December, the Speaker announced a parliamentary probe into the conduct of these MPs on 20 December 2005. The Speaker told the Lok Sabha that day that it was a matter of great concern that fresh allegations were being made against MPs in regard to implementation of MPLADS, just when Parliament was in the midst of a probe into another scandal—'Cash for Questions'. 'I have discussed the matter with the leaders of different political parties in the Lok Sabha and there is an agreement that an inquiry should also be held with regard to the new allegation which should be looked into with all the importance that it deserves,' the Speaker said. Meanwhile, pending the inquiry, the Speaker made 'a personal request' to the five MPs named by the television channel—Mr Alemao Churchill, Mr Faggan Singh Kulaste, Mr Ramswaroop Koli, Mr Paras Nath Yadav and Mr Chandra Pratap Singh—not to attend the session until the probe was completed and a decision taken in the matter.

Later that day, the Speaker announced the appointment of a seven-member committee headed by Mr Pawan Kumar Bansal to investigate the allegations made by the television channel and said the five MPs accused of improper conduct could submit their statements or explanations before 2 January 2006. Given the gravity of the allegations, the Speaker wanted a swift and time-bound probe. He directed the committee to complete its work by 31 January 2006. The committee's report, he said, would be presented to the House.[1]

The investigation, however, focused on the conduct of just four members, because one of the five implicated in this scam, Mr Chandra Pratap Singh, was expelled from the membership of the Lok Sabha on 23 December 2005 because of his involvement in the 'Cash for Questions' scandal. This scandal, too, was exposed by a television channel following a sting operation on MPs. The channel's reporters approached MPs with requests to ask questions in Parliament and found that many MPs were willing to oblige them for a price. The remaining four members denied the allegations levelled against them by the channel and alleged that the video footage was edited and doctored.

The committee began its work in right earnest and asked Star News to submit the CDs of the video footage telecast by the channel; the transcripts of the video footage; and the complete unedited video footage of the entire operation. Meanwhile, Mr Pawan Kumar Bansal resigned as chairman of the committee and as a member on 27 January 2006 consequent to his appointment as a minister in the Union Council of Ministers. The Speaker appointed Mr V. Kishore Chandra Deo as chairman following Mr Bansal's resignation. The committee began its work in right earnest soon after its constitution but found that the deadline set by the Speaker for submission of its report was unrealistic. Mr Deo, therefore, urged the Speaker to extend the time granted to the committee until 17 March 2006.

The committee recorded the evidence of Mr Uday Shankar, CEO and Editor, Star News, and several other professionals connected with the sting operation. Among those who tendered evidence were Amitabh Thakur, Mayabhashan Nagvenkar and Jamshed Khan, representatives of DIG, which actually carried out the sting operation and sold the video footage to Star News. Star News representatives gave the committee photocopies of letters dated 7 December 2005 written by Mr Ramswaroop Koli, Mr Faggan Singh Kulaste and Mr Chandra Pratap Singh to the respective district collectors. In these letters, the MPs asked the district collectors to release funds from their MPLADS account to 'Ashray Abhiyan', a fictitious NGO created to carry out the sting operation. They also gave the committee a copy of the agreement between Star News and Mr Amitabh Thakur, the proprietor of DIG, relating to the purchase of the investigative film.

The testimony of these witnesses before the parliamentary committee throws light on the fact that a corrupt politician can turn every idea or scheme into a moneymaking machine. These testimonies, taken from the report of the committee, have been reproduced at length, because they tell us a lot about the corrupt practices that have corroded the MPLAD Scheme.

In his evidence before the parliamentary committee, Mr Amitabh Thakur of DIG said that the investigation was carried out because people said letters from MPs allocating funds from MPLADS could be obtained on payment. His company was keen on exposing this racket and, therefore, went about recording the proceedings of meetings with MPs on hidden cameras. Representatives of Star News corroborated this version and said they entered into a formal contract with DIG after the investigations were complete. The committee asked Mr Thakur to explain the modus operandi. How did they zero in on these MPs from amongst the several hundred MPs in the country? The committee was informed that the media investigators heard from sources that certain MPs could be approached. The investigators narrowed the search to such MPs. Mr Thakur said, 'There are two categories of MPs in this. We met three MPs through middlemen. The other two were contacted through sources as we had a definite information that they do such things. They were known to us journalistically but were not known politically... Sudeep Mishra introduced us to Mr Faggan Singh Kulaste, Mr Koli and Mr C.P. Singh whereas journalistically known sources introduced us to Mr Churchill, Mr Paras Nath Yadav and a member of the Rajya Sabha.'

Mr Jamshed Khan, a member of this investigative team was asked how the team members established contact with the personal assistants of these MPs. The witness said: 'We had met one broker named Shri Sudeep Mishra who took us to these PAs. He was working for these MPs.'

The difference between the two sting operations was noted by the committee. It said that while the 'Cash for Questions' sting operation showed MPs taking money on camera, 'Operation Chakravyuh' was different because there was no exchange of money on camera. Mr Uday Shankar said that in the first case, the channel wanted to show that one could pay an MP and get a question asked. Whereas, in the present case, the purpose of the operation was to show that 'a promise of commission can influence an MP's discretionary powers to issue letters for releasing MPLADS fund.'

The witness said, 'As long as we were able to suggest that that intention was there, we just wanted to bring it in the public domain... We know there is already a significant section within the Indian parliamentary system which felt that there is need for correction. We just wanted to highlight the need for this correction. That was the whole purpose of this operation.'

Mr Shankar's attention was drawn to the fact that there was no offer of money to Mr Paras Nath Yadav. The witness said, 'Actually we offered money to more than one person. In fact, in all cases money had been offered. Cash was offered. We offered money to this particular member. We offered a small sum of money at which he got very much upset. He said the sum offered should be much larger and only then was he willing to talk to us further.'

The committee asked the media investigators whether it was fair to insinuate corruption (via a running commentary) against MPs who had not directly taken any money from DIG representatives. Mr Gagandeo Sethi, Senior Producer, Star News, responded as follows: 'Sir, in the case of one MP, we were not sure because he was not on camera. We said clearly, "whether he took the money or his PA or the middleman, we do not know." We were very clear in the case of one member of Parliament. Out of the six people, we had letters (to the district collectors) from three of them and in case of two, we had letters on camera. Later on, he demanded too much money and for that reason we did not get the letter in our hand. We have five out of the six. For the sixth person, we have applauded him by saying that he is a shining example of honesty.' The sixth person referred to had no intention to make money on the MPLAD Scheme and, therefore, came as a complete surprise to the investigators.

The investigators were asked as to how the media could accuse an MP of being corrupt merely on the evidence of the MP's personal assistant asking and taking money from them. Mr Uday Shankar had this to say: 'Whenever we spoke with the PA and he took money, we have no basis to say that the member had taken the money or money reached the member or was usurped by the PA himself. ... We had only one basis to say this since the PA was sitting in the residence of the member, was talking about money and taking money. Later on, the PA went inside and got the letter signed from the member. It was the same letter, the purpose for which we had gone there. Whether the member took the money or not we have no proof of that.'[2]

The MPs' Submissions in their Defence

The committee headed by Mr Kishore Chandra Deo summoned each of the MPs accused of improper conduct and possible corruption and gave them an opportunity to present their cases. Mr Alemao Churchill denied the allegations and said the tapes had been tampered with. According to him, the transaction shown on television related to a piece of land worth ₹15 lakh which he was offering to the person who had come to see him to build a Konkani library in Goa. He said a lot of things discussed by him with those who approached him had been deleted. 'If I wanted to take money, I could have taken it in the first meeting or in the second meeting or in the third meeting. During the fourth meeting, he offered me ₹1 lakh for the property. He always wanted to give me money. He was forcing me to take money. But I honestly refused to take money. I told him that I am giving the land to him.'

Mr Churchill claimed that an acquaintance from Goa asked him to take the initiative for setting up such a library in Goa.

Later, this person (the investigator) came on the scene and sought his help to get the project funded via MPLADS. 'He came to me four times. I asked him why he was forcing me to accept money. He even entered my bedroom. But all these things have not been shown in the clippings. A lot of things were added and deleted [...] I told him that if he didn't have the land, I would give him some token money, and at that time, he asked me how much the amount would be.' In other words, this is how Mr Churchill explained the references to money on tape. He tried to impress on the committee that far from taking a commission, actually it was he who was offering money to the visitor.[3]

But the committee was not impressed by the explanations offered by Mr Churchill. It noted, on a perusal of the video footage, that the MP 'did talk about commission in lieu of sanctioning ₹15 lakh from his MPLADS fund in favour of the fake NGO. He clearly demanded ₹3 lakh. The footage also showed him taking out his letter pad to write a letter of recommendation.'[4]

Yet, there appeared to be two mitigating factors as far as this MP was concerned. The first was that although the footage showed the MP writing a letter of recommendation, he did not hand this letter over to the media investigators. As a result, the investigators did not have this crucial bit of evidence. The second factor was that the footage did not show him accepting money. After bringing these factors on record, the committee observed that despite this 'it was quite clear that Shri Churchill in unambiguous terms talked about commission in lieu of his recommending release of funds to the fake NGO. The committee find that the defence put forth by Shri Churchill that the negotiations regarding money were in the context of price of land for proposed Konkani Library and not for commission, was not at all convincing. The committee also find it unbelievable that Shri Churchill was offering his land for ₹15 lacs in return for a paltry sum of ₹1 lakh offered by the fake NGO.' It concluded by saying that it was convinced that he was willing to release MPLADS funds for a consideration and that 'he intended to seek monetary consideration by way of a commission.'[5]

Mr Paras Nath Yadav also weaved an interesting story to explain the sequence of events in the video and the references to money caught on tape. The video shows talk of MPLADS, the offer of ₹50,000, the MP handing over a letter to his visitors and taking it back. The media team which did the investigation said the MP was displeased with the amount of commission offered to him and, therefore, took the letter back. But Mr Yadav had a convoluted explanation for each of these situations caught on tape. He said that two persons, who claimed to be running a foreign NGO which undertook welfare works like construction of hospitals and houses for the poor, visited him. The visitors claimed to be doing projects of this kind in Goa and Maharashtra and in some parts of Uttar Pradesh. They offered to undertake such welfare projects in his constituency as well and also offered to provide financial assistance of ₹50 lakh for completion of a school that he was constructing. '... They talked about the modalities of the payment to be made, to which I replied that it is for them to decide....' According to Mr Yadav, on their second visit to his residence, they requested him to release funds from MPLADS for installation of computers in his school. Mr Yadav claims he turned this down because he had already spent the allocated fund for that year. Yet, he wrote a letter to the district magistrate and this was his explanation for writing the letter: 'I merely told them if they were going to do some work, I could write a letter and accordingly I wrote a letter to the DM.'

Even as he gave them a letter to this effect he says, 'I specifically told them that I am not going to give them any funds from my MPLADS and there will be no talk of any commission...I enquired from them what happened to their NGO work and [asked them to] tell me about it...They further told that they had only ₹50,000. I scolded them, asked them to leave my house and snatched the letter from them which I had written for MPLADS... Sir, this is all what happened...I have been trapped under a well-planned conspiracy.'

The committee told Mr Yadav that the video showed him taking back the letter from his visitors 'when it was found that the money which they had brought was less than what he had expected'. Mr Yadav denied this and claimed that the talk of money was in connection with his school for which they had promised ₹50 lakh 'whereas, they were giving only ₹50,000'. 'Hence, I got annoyed and asked them to leave immediately. I was asking the money for the school and not for myself. Had I any such intention, I would have accepted ₹50,000.'

The committee then turned its attention to another problematic situation on the tape where the MP was 'clearly shown asking some percentage as commission'. Mr Yadav denied that any such thing happened. He said, 'Sir, no such thing has happened. This has been morphed and concocted by the electronic media. I only talked about funds for my school...I never talked about MPLAD [s]...The talk about commission in MPLADS is only to damage my reputation and defame me... I have been in politics for the last 25 years very honestly and dedicatedly....'

Mr Yadav told the committee that he did not employ a personal assistant and that he had a regular stream of visitors at his residence and being a peoples' representative, he could not refuse an audience to anyone who came to his residence. He therefore met everyone, offered them tea and listened to them. However, these two visitors were up to no good, he said. The footage on the CD shows that everything had been changed. 'As they were hatching a conspiracy against me, everything has been distorted accordingly in the CD...how and where the CD has been morphed, it is for the committee to decide...'[6]

The committee did not believe Mr Yadav's story as well. It said the footage showed the MP writing a letter in favour of the fake NGO instructing the district magistrate to release ₹10 lakh from his MPLADS fund. Mr Yadav was shown asking for a commission in lieu of the letter. 'As per the...footage, he was offered ₹50,000 which he refused since he expected more. He also appeared annoyed as the amount of commission offered was too less. Finally, he took the letter back from them as there was no agreement with regard to the amount of commission.'

The committee said it had no reason to doubt the genuineness of the visuals, 'according to which, the member was more than willing to recommend release of funds in favour of the fake NGO for an "appropriate" commission without even verifying the credentials of the NGO'. Further, it said there was no letter on record because 'the amount offered as commission was perceived by the member as a "pittance" and peeved by this, he withdrew it (the letter), which he was shown as writing in the video footage'. It also said the MP's claim that the NGO offered ₹50 lakh for the degree college 'does not carry convinction'.[7]

Mr Faggan Singh Kulaste, who signed a letter to the district collector allocating ₹10 lakh to 'Ashray Abhiyan', an NGO set up by the investigators, put the blame entirely on his personal assistant (PA) and even claimed that after the exposé, he had sacked the PA. This is what he had to say: 'Sir, when the incident took place, I was busy with an important tribal conference scheduled to take place in Ranchi. These people came to my house in the morning as has been shown in the tapes and had discussions with my PA and the middleman of which I was neither aware nor it concerned me. After I went to my residence around 1.30 p.m., after attending the sitting of the House, I was told by my PA that some people had come to meet me. Thereafter, I met them. I was told by them that they wanted to install computers in the Madhya Pradesh Small Scale Corporation, a State Government Undertaking. I told them there are certain norms on the basis of which such work is done. I further informed them that I don't speak with the district magistrate again and again on such matters as everything is done according to the due procedure. After talking this much with them, I further told them that I am busy and after saying so, left for my bedroom. Sir, being a people's representative, I meet so many people every day. After watching the tapes, I learnt that my PA must have been hand in glove with them and he could have played mischief against me in connivance with them. I immediately removed him. Sir, I had no ill intention and in no way I was a party to all this. Rest everything is there before you. This is all I have to say in the matter.'

Following his deposition, the committee had some questions for Mr Kulaste. He was asked if he did write a letter to the district collector stating that ₹10 lakh may be released immediately in favour of 'Ashray Abhiyan', an NGO based in Shakarpur, Delhi.

The MP owned up to signing the letter. 'The said letter was brought to me by my PA for signatures, I trusted him, signed it and gave it to him only and not to them. I did not read the contents of the letter and I signed it in good faith because he was my PA for eight years and nothing of this sort had ever happened.' The MP denied that there had ever been any talk of a commission between him and his PA or between him and his visitors.[8]

The committee said that in this case the recorded footage showed that the media investigators were approached by two middlemen—Mr Sudeep Mishra and Mr Yuvraj Singh (the MP's PA). Both these individuals talked about a commission of 20 per cent for releasing ₹10 lakh from MPLADS. Mr Kulaste was also shown talking to these visitors. The visuals also showed him signing a letter addressed to the district collector recommending release of funds. Soon after the MP left the room, the media investigators handed over a packet of money to the member's PA, Mr Yuvraj Singh, 'who clearly referred to this money as commission'.[9]

The committee noted that it had a copy of the letter written by this MP to the district collector for releasing ₹10 lakh to the fake NGO for installing computers at Shakarpur, Delhi. The MP had admitted that he had signed this letter and that Mr Yuvraj Singh was his PA. He, however, claimed that he was not aware of the contents of the letter because he trusted his private secretary. The committee took note of these admissions and denials and said the footage did not show him either negotiating the commission or accepting the money. Only, his PA was seen negotiating the commission. It observed that the guidelines for MPLADS prohibit members of the Lok Sabha from instructing the district collector in their constituency to execute a project in an area that does not fall within the MP's constituency. The committee said the defence offered by the member 'is not wholly convincing'. 'The committee feel that it was highly irresponsible on his part to have signed a letter, handed over to him by his PS, which in fact authorized concerned DC to release money to the tune of ₹10 lakh under his MPLAD Scheme that too for some work to be undertaken outside his constituency.'[10]

Unlike Mr Churchill, Mr Yadav and Mr Kulaste, who admitted to meeting the media investigators who came in the garb of promoters of an NGO, Mr Ramswaroop Koli offered a blanket denial. He told the parliamentary committee that he was never at home when the alleged transaction took place; he never signed the letter which was purported to be in his name; and that he never had a PA named Om Prakash. Mr Koli claimed that representatives of Star News had entered his residence on the pretext of using the washroom and had taken some visuals both inside and outside his house. Then came a flat denial in regard to the documentary evidence that the investigators had, that is, his letter to the district collector. Mr Koli not only denied having written such a letter but also accused the person identified as his PA in the video of having forged his signature. This is what he told the committee: 'As regards the letter in question which is in their possession and purported to have been written by me, I am to submit that I have not signed any such letter nor the signatures on it are mine. If you see all my previous letters written for releasing money from my MPLADS fund, you will find that I write all such letters with my hand only and are never type written (sic). My signatures on the said letter have been forged preferably (sic) by the person named Om Prakash, who has been shown in the video as my PA. I have written to you in my earlier letters dated 23.12.2005 and 17.1.2006 stating that never a person named Om Prakash worked with me as my PA.' When the committee specifically asked him if he had written any letter to the district collector regarding release of MPLADS funds to these media representatives, Mr Koli said, 'I did not give any such letter and signatures on it are also not mine.'

The MP also claimed that he was not at home at the time when the transaction is said to have taken place according to the video. He said he was not at home on 7 December 2005 from 7 to 9.30 p.m. as he was attending a meeting at Rajasthan House along with other MPs from Rajasthan. He even furnished an 'attendance sheet' of that meeting to the committee. Mr Koli had a simple explanation in regard to the use of his letterhead for the official communication to the district collector. He said his letter pads was generally lying around at the typing pool in Parliament House 'and at times are also given to some reliable persons' who used to be hired to do his secretarial work on holidays.[11]

In Mr Koli's case, the committee noted that according to Star News, due to a technical snag the camera got switched off and consequently, there are no visuals showing the interaction of the media investigators with the MP. There is only one clear visual of Mr Om Prakash, said to be the MP's PA and from the audio recording, negotiations regarding a commission could be made out. The journalists procured a letter through Mr Om Prakash for releasing ₹25 lakh from the member's MPLADS fund. The journalists gave the PA ₹25,000 in lieu of that letter. The committee had a copy of this letter, purported to be signed by Mr Koli and addressed to the district collector of Dholpur, for release of ₹25 lakh in favour of the fake NGO for installing computers at Shakarpur, Delhi. In this statement the member denied being present at his residence on the day in question and claimed that he was at Rajasthan House attending a meeting of MPs. He even produced an alibi by way of an attendance register. He also denied that he knew any person by the name of Om Prakash and even showed records from the Lok Sabha Secretariat to establish the fact that no person by that name was his PA. He claimed that the entire episode was a well-planned conspiracy to defame him. He was, however, unable to explain how a complete stranger like Mr Om Prakash was at his residence and was receiving visitors.

The committee said there was no evidence to show that the MP negotiated a commission in lieu of the release of MPLADS funds. It also noted that the signature on the letter to the district collector did not 'exactly tally' with his specimen signatures. But, the letterhead was that of the MP. Nevertheless, the committee said the allegations against the MP could not be established beyond reasonable doubt. However, the committee noted that although the MP claimed that his signature on the letter had been forged, it was 'quite intriguing' that he did not lodge a police complaint in this regard. Further, he made no effort to explain the presence of Mr Om Prakash (a stranger, according to the MP) in his house.[12]

The committee noted that the footage only showed Mr Churchill writing a letter (which he did not hand over to the media investigators). It did not show the MP accepting money. 'The committee, however, noted that the video footage did show negotiations for consideration/commission. The committee also noted that in the cases of Shri Alemao Churchill and Shri Paras Nath Yadav, the negotiations were directly held with the members themselves. On the other hand, in the cases of Shri Faggan Singh Kulaste and Shri Ramswaroop Koli, the negotiations were mainly through middlemen/Private Secretaries of members.'[13]

The Committee's Conclusions

Summing up the evidence, the committee said that in none of the cases was an MP shown actually accepting money in lieu of recommending projects. Mr Churchill and Mr Yadav 'apparently negotiated a cut/commission' in lieu of release of funds. 'Although the deals did not materialize, they cannot be absolved of misconduct in matters relating to release of money from their

MPLADS funds.' In the case of Mr Kulaste, the committee said there was 'no clinching evidence that establishes beyond doubt' that he himself negotiated a commission. However, he did sign the letter to the district collector. The committee did not buy his explanation that he had not read the letter before signing it because he trusted his PA. 'Even if the committee were to go by the member's version, his conduct itself is indicative of indiscretion on his part. The member's PA was shown as accepting money as commission immediately after the member left the room. The member did not state anything about this. The committee took note of the fact that the PA accepted money from the visitors when the MP was on the premises, though not in the same room at the time of the transaction.' The committee felt that the entire episode was of 'deep concern' and the conduct of the member 'is not wholly beyond reproach'.

In Mr Koli's case, the committee said, 'the emphatic denial of everything by Shri Koli appeared to be contrived and unnatural.' The committee wondered how his personal letterhead was used for writing a recommendatory letter without his knowledge or consent. Further, there is no evidence on record to show that this MP made any effort to trace the person who misused his letterhead, something which any MP would have done. 'Shri Koli did nothing of this kind and went on denying everything. His denial was unconvincing. This compels the committee to suspect some degree of complicity of the member in the entire episode.'

In the final analysis, the committee declared that the conduct of Mr Alemao Churchill and Mr Paras Nath Yadav was 'improper and unethical'. The conduct of Mr Faggan Singh Kulaste and Mr Ramswaroop Koli was 'irresponsible and negligent and clearly amounts to an act of impropriety'.

Having arrived at this conclusion in respect of each MP, the committee had to get down to the task of awarding punishment. It noted that in cases of misconduct or contempt committed by members, Parliament had the power to admonish or reprimand a member, direct the member's withdrawal from the House or suspend the member. Parliament also had the power to expel or imprison a member.[14]

The committee said that the conduct of none of the four MPs was above board and therefore, 'they need to be handed outappropriate punishment,' which was proposed as follows: '(i) The period of abstention from the sittings of the House and the committees by all the four members viz. Sarvashri Alemao Churchill, Paras Nath Yadav, Faggan Singh Kulaste and Ramswaroop Koli on a request made by the Speaker, Lok Sabha on 20 December, 2005, may be deemed to be their suspension from the membership of the House. (ii) Shri Alemao Churchill, Shri Paras Nath Yadav, Shri Faggan Singh Kulaste and Shri Ramswaroop Koli may be reprimanded. They may also be suspended from the membership of the House till 22 March, 2006.'

The committee's report indicated that the following two reasons influenced the quantum of punishment: (1) the improper conduct of the members did not strictly relate to their parliamentary duties and (2) none of them was shown actually accepting money.[15]

While disposing of these four cases, the committee took a macro-view of MPLADS, the controversies surrounding the scheme and the measures which Parliament should take to ensure that the scheme was implemented in a proper manner. It said while the scheme was launched with the laudable objective of involving elected representatives in community development, at times doubts have been expressed about effective implementation of the scheme. The committee drew the attention of Parliament to the reports of the Comptroller and Auditor General of India (CAG) in 1998 and 2001 on the working of MPLADS. In those reports the CAG had pointed out certain lacunae with regard to sanctioning of works by district collectors without recommendations from MPs; huge unspent balances accumulating with implementing agencies; non-submission of utilization certificates (UCs); levy of administrative charges by implementing agencies; incomplete and abandoned works; non-maintenance of asset registers;

sanctioning of funds as grants/loans; and inadequate monitoring arrangements.

Taking into account these observations of the CAG, the committee said that 'it was about time the Union Government revised the guidelines governing MPLADS to plug loopholes and lacunae to make it truly effective.' In the light of the scandal that it had investigated, the committee suggested that NGOs and private institutions should be barred from getting any funds under MPLADS. While making this suggestion the committee felt that the truth must be put on record in this matter. It said such a ban must be imposed because 'it is felt that most of such NGOs are merely facades for unscrupulous organisations formed to usurp funds from MPLADS, which are meant for community development works.'[16]

As regards the scheme itself, the committee felt that the role of MPs in recommending works for execution 'cannot strictly be said to relate to their parliamentary duties'. It said every vibrant democracy demands that those who wield power as elected legislators should use it for the public good and not make it an instrument of self-seeking. 'This they can do effectively by personifying the highest standards of personal integrity, probity and rectitude.' It reminded every MP that as an elected representative of the people, a member's status is an exalted one. 'A dignified and ethical conduct by a legislator is one of the primary obligations of a Member of Parliament. Any misconduct by a legislator, whether inside the House or outside it, not only projects a legislator in poor light but also strikes at the very credibility of the democratic institution.'

It reminded members of the general principles laid down in the First Report of the Committee of the House of Commons of the UK on Standards in Public Life, which was headed by Lord Nolan. This committee, popularly known as the Nolan Committee had said: 'It is the personal responsibility of every member of Parliament to maintain those standards of conduct which the House and the electorate are entitled to expect to project the good name of Parliament and to advance the public interest.' Reiterating this principle and advancing a strong argument in favour of punishing legislators who cross the line, the committee headed by Mr Kishore Chandra Deo said: 'Elected representatives have a sacred duty to adhere to the highest norms of conduct. Every act of misconduct by them strikes at the very root of democracy and destroys its credibility. Hence every act of misconduct or misdemeanour, notwithstanding the degree of its gravity, calls for some punitive action or corrective measure.'

The committee went on to say that the strength of any system lies in its capacity to promptly correct aberrations which may creep in from time to time. The committee noted that it was happy 'to discern a firm resolve among the fraternity of legislators to take urgent remedial action whenever the situation so demands, with a view to reclaim the pristine glory of legislative bodies in the country'.[17]

Role of Media

Finally, after asserting the need for strict adherence to ethical norms by legislators and commending 'a sound ethical order' for them, the committee turned its attention to what it described as the bona fides of the sting operation conducted by the DIG team and the role played by Star News in the matter. It said that without having 'full and clinching' evidence with respect to some members, the media team went ahead with the exposé on MPLADS. In other words, the committee was of the view that the 'evidence' aired by the news channel in respect of some MPs was inadequate. The channel told the committee that it had 'clarified' this position while airing the footage but the committee felt that its claim 'does not carry conviction'. Having made this observation, the committee commented on the mad race among news channels to gain popularity and achieve higher TRPs (television rating points). It said in order to gain viewership, television channels were indulging in 'sensationalism'. The committee felt after examining the footage that the television channel had implied that all MPs were susceptible to corruption. If such operations are carried out in an unregulated manner which casts aspersions on MPs, it would erode the credibility of democratic institutions. Therefore, there was a need to regulate 'such motivated trial by the media'. It said the government should lay down guidelines for sting operations 'to ensure that basic journalistic ethics are scrupulously adhered to'.[18]

The report of this parliamentary committee, leading to the suspension of four MPs for three months for 'improper conduct' gave the Lok Sabha Committee on MPLADS the opportunity to claim that 'Parliament had not shied away from taking action against its own members.' As recommended by the committee constituted by the Speaker to inquire into the conduct of some members vis-à-vis MPLADS, four MPs—Messrs Churchill Alemao, Paras Nath Yadav, Faggan Singh Kulaste and Ramswaroop Koli—were suspended from 20 December 2005 to 22 March 2006 because their conduct was not above board. Therefore the committee concluded that as regards the criticism of rampant corruption, a 'proper mechanism' as per the law of the land was available 'and no one, including MPs, is above the law'.[19]

NOTES

1. Report of the Committee to Inquire into Allegations of Improper Conduct on the Part of Some Members in the Matter of Implementation of MPLAD Scheme, tabled in the Lok Sabha on 13 March 2006, Lok Sabha Secretariat, New Delhi, pp. 6–8.
2. Ibid., pp. 11–17.
3. Ibid., p. 18.
4. Ibid., p. 29.
5. Ibid., p. 31.
6. Ibid., pp. 22–24.
7. Ibid., pp. 31–33.
8. Ibid., pp. 9–20.

9   Ibid., pp. 33–34.
10 Ibid., pp. 34–36.
11 Ibid., pp. 21–22.
12 Ibid., pp. 37–39.
13 Ibid., p. 28.
14 Ibid., pp. 40–43.
15 Ibid., p. 50.
16 Ibid., pp. 45–46.
17 Ibid., pp. 46–48.
18 Ibid., pp. 48–49.
19 First Report, Committee on MPLADS 2009–2010, presented to the Lok Sabha, 24 February 2010, Lok Sabha Secretariat, New Delhi, p. 9.

11

The Supreme Court on MPLADS

The MPLAD Scheme is easily one of the most controversial schemes introduced in the country. Ever since its inception in 1993, it has attracted the adverse notice of citizens, the CAG of India, two important commissions appointed by the Government of India to review the working of the Constitution and to consider administrative reforms, several administrators and parliamentarians and the media. In the initial years there was considerable hostility to the scheme because many thought that the government would give every MP a crore of rupees every year as pocket money which he could spend at will in his constituency and that this would merely open up yet another avenue for corruption for politicians. Among parliamentarians who objected to this scheme was Mr Era Sezhiyan, a former MP, who published a book citing innumerable objections. In this environment it was only a matter of time before citizens moved the courts with petitions seeking quashing of the scheme. This did happen with several petitioners knocking at the doors of the Supreme Court and asking the court to declare the scheme unconstitutional. A five-judge Constitution bench of the court comprising the Chief Justice of India K.G. Balakrishnan, Justice R.V. Raveendran, Justice D.K. Jain, Justice. P. Sathasivam and

Justice J.M. Panchal heard all these petitions in *Bhim Singh* v. *Union of India and Ors* and pronounced its judgement in May 2010. In their unanimous judgement, they dismissed all the petitions as 'devoid of merit' and held that MPLADS was a valid scheme within the framework of the Constitution. The judgement came as a disappointment to many citizens who wanted the scheme to be scrapped. However, it put an end to the controversy as to whether the scheme was constitutionally valid. A detailed discussion of the various grounds on which the petitioners challenged the scheme and the opinion of the court on each of these averments is necessary in order to make an assessment of what lies ahead for MPLADS.

The petitioners argued that MPLADS was ultra vires the Constitution and urged the court to scrap the scheme and to order an impartial investigation into the misuse of the scheme. They said the objective of the scheme was to enable MPs to recommend works which were developmental in nature and for the creation of durable assets. Granting MPs the power to spend money for a 'public purpose' violated Article 282 of the Constitution; the scheme was a total abdication of the powers and functions of the Union of India; such wholesale transfer of funds for the benefit of projects cannot be executed under Article 275 as 'grants-in-aid of the revenues of a state' without a proper recommendation of the Finance Commission; and the executive powers of the Union under Article 73 are co-extensive with the legislative powers of the Parliament, hence even executive powers of the Union cannot be exercised contrary to the Seventh Schedule so as to encroach on a subject falling in List II. There were several more objections which were constitutional in nature. The petitioners said the scheme was contrary to the seventy-third and seventy-fourth amendments to the Constitution which entrusted local self-government to panchayats and municipalities. Consequent on these amendments, the decision-making power in regard to development rests with panchayats and municipalities, and MPs cannot encroach upon the powers of these bodies. Also, by enlarging the scope of Article 282, the Centre had infringed the constitutional scheme for flow of finances from the Centre to the states, and this was a clear misuse of the provisions of the Constitution.

The Union government, however, challenged these averments and said MPLADS was intra vires the Constitution, and the source of its power was traceable to certain constitutional provisions. The government said Article 282 had to be given its widest amplitude and should be interpreted widely so that the public purpose enshrined therein could effectively be achieved by the Union and the states to advance the Directive Principles of State Policy. The government said the scheme was implemented based on the sanction of Parliament via the passage of the Appropriation Act every financial year. Appropriation of funds for the scheme is done as per procedure applicable to money bills and the expenditure proposed is laid before both the Houses of Parliament in the form of 'Demands for Grants' and is subject to assent of the House of the People. It said MPLADS was a policy decision which had a parliamentary sanction through Appropriation Acts and therefore, no further legislation was needed. Also, it was not inconsistent with the powers of panchayats and municipalities and did not violate the concept of separation of powers.

After hearing the arguments, the court said seven questions came up for consideration: (i) Whether the scheme is not valid as a grant under Article 282 of the Constitution and whether Article 275 is the only source for a regular and permanent scheme; (ii) whether having regard to Article 266 (3) of the Constitution, apart from the Appropriation Act, an independent substantive enactment is required for MPLADS instead of mere executive guidelines; (iii) whether the scheme falls under Article 280 (3) and exercise of such powers of the Finance Commission by the Planning Commission make the scheme unconstitutional; (iv) whether the scheme obliterates the demarcation between the legislature and the executive by making MPs virtual members of the executive without any accountability; (v) whether the scheme is inconsistent with constitutional provisions which empower local elected bodies; (vi) whether the scheme, even if it is otherwise constitutional, is liable to be quashed for want of adequate safeguards, checks and balances; and (vii) whether the scheme gives an unfair advantage to the MP in contesting elections by violating the provisions of the Constitution. In other words, the court said it would first determine the constitutional scheme regarding allocation of funds and examine whether MPLADS needed special allocation. Next, it would see whether Parliament was empowered under Article 282 to make allocations under MPLADS. Once these issues were out of the way, the court said, it would consider whether a robust accountability was provided under the scheme. Finally, it would consider the question as to whether MPLADS violates the constitutional principle of separation of powers.

The court first dealt with the complex constitutional questions posed by the petitioners. It said after examining the relevant constitutional provisions, it cannot accept the argument that the Appropriation Act by itself does not satisfy the requirements of Article 266 (3) in order to make allocations to the scheme. It said 'it is reasonable to accept' that appropriation of public revenue for the purposes of the MPLAD Scheme has been sanctioned by the Parliament by Appropriation Acts and 'no separate or independent law is necessary' for the purpose. The court also disagreed with the view that the flow of funds to MPLADS violated Article 282. It said the expression 'public purpose' in Article 282 'should be widely construed' and it can be seen that the impugned scheme is designed to promote the purpose underlying the Directive Principles of State Policy. It said no restriction could be placed on the scope and width of the Article as this Article was not subject to any other Article in the Constitution.

Significantly, the court emphasized the principle regarding judicial intervention. It said 'judicial interference is permissible when the action of the government is unconstitutional and not when such action is not wise or that the extent of the expenditure is not for the good of the state. We are of the view that all such questions must be debated and decided in the legislature and not in court.'[1]

No Misuse of Funds

Apart from the constitutionality of MPLADS, the petitioners raised the issue of accountability. They said the scheme had been so devised that the grant is, in effect, made to MPs and is not made to the beneficiaries or the public purpose. It was also contended that the funds were liable to be misused. While considering this question, the court reviewed the guidelines drawn up for the scheme and came to the conclusion that there was 'close coordination' between the Union government, the state government and the district authorities (DA). It said, from the guidelines, it was clear that the role of the MP 'is very limited' to the initial selection of projects subject to the DA finding the project eligible and feasible. The court rejected the contention that there is arbitrary and mala fide use of powers by MPs in allocating work and using the funds. This argument 'does not hold good', it said because there are three levels of accountability (accountability within Parliament, the guidelines and the updates in the annual reports).[2]

The court referred to the work of the Lok Sabha Committee on MPLADS, the review of the scheme in December 2008 and spoke about how the procedure for funds had been streamlined and strengthened. It said now DAs have to submit utilization certificates and audit certificates for early release of funds and fulfil other conditions before the second instalment of funds for an MP is considered in a given year. Among other measures taken are development of software for monitoring the scheme, nomination of seventy-eight officers in the MS&PI as nodal officers for the districts to enter data on projects, and result-oriented reviews of the scheme by the secretary and additional secretary in the ministry.[3]

It was clear from the judgement that the court was impressed by the systems that had been evolved for allocation of funds, for identifying works and for execution of works which are sanctioned. It said the MP only recommended works. The DA had the responsibility to verify the eligibility and technical feasibility of each recommended work. The decision-making power in regard to technical, financial and administrative sanctions accorded under the scheme vested in district-level functionaries, and the state governments monitored the implementation of works. Also, the nodal DA had to coordinate with other districts falling in the same Lok Sabha constituency or other districts where a Rajya Sabha member had recommended the work. 'Thus the nature of the scheme is such that it requires considerable technical, administrative and accounting expertise, highly efficient coordination with various agencies and organizations and a high degree of logistic and managerial support for its successful implementation. Only the District Authorities possess all the above mentioned requisite competence and can effectively implement the scheme at the district level.'[4]

The court dismissed the charge that the funds meant for the scheme were being misused. It also found no merit in the allegation that the scheme was not being monitored properly. It said information furnished to the court showed that the scheme had benefited the local community by meeting various developmental needs such as drinking water schemes, education, electricity, health and family welfare, irrigation, non-conventional energy, roads, bus stands, bridges and sports infrastructure. 'Barring few irregularities, which are taken care of by the State Audit Authorities, the funds allocated under the MPLAD Scheme are being properly monitored for better utilization to achieve the objectives of the Scheme.' The court said 'mere allegation of misuse of the funds under the scheme by some MPs by itself may not be a ground for scrapping of the scheme as checks and safeguards have been provided. Parliament has the power to enquire and take appropriate action against the erring members. Both Lok Sabha and Rajya Sabha have set up Standing Committees to monitor the works under the Scheme.'[5]

The court was also impressed with the guidelines that had been drawn up for the scheme. It said these guidelines have been revised continuously and it is clear that MPLADS funds were for works of a developmental nature and for creation of durable community assets. The guidelines also had a list of prohibited works. It also saw much value in the annual reports which it said 'provide for transparency and accountability in the working of the Scheme'.[6]

Further, information available on the MPLADS website 'clearly show that the Scheme provides various levels of accountability'. It said: 'The argument of the petitioners that MPLADS is inherently arbitrary seems unfounded. No doubt there may be improvements to be made. But this court does not sit in judgement of the veracity of a scheme, but only its legality. When there is evidence that an accountability mechanism is available, there is no reason for us to interfere in the Scheme.'[7]

The court went on to say that the scheme only supplemented the efforts of the state and local authorities and does not seek to interfere either in the functional or financial domain of the local planning authorities of a state. On the other hand, it only strengthens the welfare measures taken by them. The scheme does not override the power of the state government or the local authority. The scheme is subject to supervision and control of the MS & PI. 'We are satisfied that the Government of India is not delegating its power to the Members of Parliament to spend the money contrary to the mandate of the constitutional provisions.'[8]

Does MPLADS Violate the Principle of Separation of Powers?

As regards the contention that MPLADS violates the principle of separation of powers under the Constitution, the court said even though this concept was not found in any particular constitutional provision, it is inherent in the polity adopted by the Constitution. 'The aim of separation of powers is to achieve the maximum extent of accountability of each branch of the government.' While understanding this concept, the court said two aspects must be borne in mind. 'One, that separation of powers is an essential feature of the Constitution. Two, that in modern governance, a strict separation is neither possible, nor desirable. Nevertheless, till this principle of accountability is preserved, there is no violation of separation of powers.'

The court said, 'The Constitution does not prohibit overlap of functions, but in fact provides for some overlap as a parliamentary democracy. But what it prohibits is such exercise of function of the other branch which results in wrestling away of the regime of constitutional accountability.'[9]

The bench cited several judgements of the court to explain the principle of separation of powers. In *Rai Sahib Ram Jawaya Kapur and Ors* v. *The State of Punjab*, the Supreme Court said: 'The Indian Constitution has not indeed recognised the doctrine of separation of powers in its absolute rigidity but the functions of the different parts or branches of the government have been sufficiently differentiated and consequently it can very well be said that our Constitution does not contemplate assumption, by one organ or part of the State, of functions that essentially belong to another. The executive indeed can exercise the powers of departmental or subordinate legislation when such powers are delegated to it by the legislature. It can also, when empowered, exercise judicial functions in a limited way. The executive government, however, can never go against the provisions of the Constitution or of any law.'

In *Keshavananda Bharati* v. *State of Kerala & Another* and later, in *Indira Gandhi* v. *Raj Narain*, the Supreme Court declared separation of powers to be part of the basic structure of the Constitution. In *Keshavananda Bharati*, Justice Shelat and Justice Grover observed that 'there is ample evidence in the Constitution itself to indicate that it creates a system of checks and balances by reason of which powers are so distributed that none of the three organs it sets up can become so predominant as to disable the others from exercising and discharging powers and functions entrusted to them. Though the Constitution does not lay down the principle of separation of powers in all its rigidity as is the case in the United States Constitution but it envisages such a separation to a degree as was found in Ranasinghe's case. The judicial review provided expressly in our Constitution by means of Articles 226 and 32 is one of the features upon which hinges the system of checks of balances.'[10]

In *Indira Nehru Gandhi* v. *Raj Narain*, Justice Ray said, 'The doctrine of separation of powers is carried into effect in countries like America and Australia. In our Constitution there is separation of powers in a broad sense...the doctrine of separation of powers as recognized in America is not applicable in our country.' In the same judgement, the Chief Justice of the court said the American Constitution provided for rigid separation of powers into three basic divisions—the executive, legislature and judicial. The Australian Constitution followed the same pattern. 'Unlike these constitutions, the Indian Constitution does not expressly vest the three kinds of power in three different organs of the State. But the principle of separation of powers is not a magic formula for keeping the three organs of the State within the strict confines of their functions.' He cited the observation of Justice Cardozo of the US Supreme Court in *Panama Refining Company* v. *Ryan* in which the judge said the principle of separation of powers 'is not a doctrinaire concept to be made use of with pedantic rigour'. He said, 'There must be sensible approximation, there must be elasticity of adjustment in response to the practical necessities of Govt which cannot foresee today the developments of tomorrow in their nearly infinite variety.'[11]

The bench sought to clinch the issue vis-à-vis the principle of separation of powers by quoting Justice Chandrachud in *Indira Nehru Gandhi* v. *Raj Narain*. In that case, the judge held: 'A law would be violative of separation of powers not if it results in some overlap of functions of different branches of the State, but if it takes over the essential function of the other branch leading to lapse of constitutional accountability. It is through this test that we must analyse the present scheme.' For these reasons, the court held that MPLADS did not violate the concept of separation of powers. In its view there was no rigid separation of powers in the Constitution and each arm, at times, performed the other functions as well. Also, MPs were 'only seeking to advance public interest and public purpose' through MPLADS and 'it is quite logical for the Member of Parliament to carry out developmental activities in the constituencies.' The court also held that there were adequate safeguards in the guidelines and it had no reason to believe that schemes would not be effectively controlled and implemented.[12]

The court had many good things to say about MPLADS. It said the scheme concentrates on community development and creation of assets at the grassroots level 'and in such circumstances, the same cannot be interfered with by the courts without reasonable grounds.'[13]

Another argument of the petitioners was that the scheme was ultra vires the Constitution because after the passage of the seventy-third and seventy-fourth amendments empowering panchayats and municipal bodies, local development was the exclusive preserve of these bodies. This argument did not impress the court. It said it was not inclined to accept this contention because Panchayati Raj institutions and urban local bodies are the preferred implementing agencies in rural and urban areas.

Finally, the court also rejected the contention that MPLADS gives an unfair advantage to sitting MPs and violates the democratic principle of free and fair elections. The petitioners said sitting MPs had a clear edge over their opponents in an election because they had MPLADS at their disposal. The court rejected this argument on the ground that 'it is not based on any scientific analysis or empirical data.' It said, 'MPLADS makes funds available to sitting MPs for developmental work. If the

MP utilizes the funds properly, it would result in his better performance. If that leads to people voting for the incumbent candidate, it certainly does not violate any principle of free and fair elections.'[14]

Summary of the Judgement

The five-judge bench concluded its judgement as follows:

>*MPLADS falls within the meaning of 'public purpose' under Article 282. Both Articles 275 and 282 are sources of spending funds/monies under the Constitution. The power of Article 282 to sanction grants is not restricted.
>*The constitutional principle of separation of powers will only be violated if an essential function of one branch is taken over by another branch, leading to removal of checks and balances. Even though MPs have been given a seemingly executive function, their role is limited to 'recommending' works and actual implementation is done by local authorities. There is no removal of checks and balances... Therefore, the scheme does not violate separation of powers.
>*Panchayati Raj institutions, municipal as well as local bodies have not been denuded of their role or jurisdiction by the scheme as due place has been accorded to them by the guidelines, in the implementation of the scheme.
>*The court can strike down a law or scheme only on the basis of its vires or unconstitutionality but not on the basis of its viability. When a regime of accountability is available within the scheme, it is not proper for the court to strike it down, unless it violates any constitutional principle. In the present scheme, an accountability regime has been provided. Efforts should be made so that the regime becomes more robust, but in its current form, cannot be struck down as unconstitutional.

*The scheme does not result in an unfair advantage to the sitting members of Parliament and does not amount to a corrupt practice.

*'Accordingly we hold that the impugned MPLAD Scheme is valid and intra vires of the Constitution and all the Writ Petitions as well as transferred cases are liable to be dismissed as devoid of any merit....'[15]

NOTES

1. (2010) 5 Supreme Court Cases, 565
2. Ibid., p. 568.
3. Ibid., p. 562.
4. Ibid.
5. Ibid., p. 570.
6. Ibid., p. 571.
7. Ibid.
8. Ibid.
9. Ibid., p. 572.
10. Ibid., pp. 572–73.
11. Ibid., p. 574.
12. Ibid., p. 578.
13. Ibid., p. 576.
14. Ibid., p. 577.
15. Ibid., p. 578.

12

The Comptroller and Auditor General on MPLADS

The Comptroller and Auditor General (CAG) of India has reviewed the MPLAD Scheme thrice since its inception in 1993. The first review was undertaken in 1998, followed by another in 2001. The CAG had a fresh look at this scheme yet again in 2008. The reports of the CAG after each of these reviews have thrown up a wealth of information on how this scheme is being implemented. Be it the macro-view about the release of funds every year and their utilization or the micro-view of how these funds are deployed by the MPs and the district authorities (DAs) who are responsible for implementing the projects proposed by parliamentarians, what emerges is a rather dismal picture. These reviews clearly establish that there is something seriously wrong in the implementation of this scheme. Even more worrisome is the disinclination of the MS&PI to act on these reports and to ensure better utilization of funds by MPs and DAs.

As stated earlier, the first two reviews of MPLADS took place in 1998 and 2001. These reports, which were tabled in Parliament, had pointed out various lapses in the implementation of the scheme. The MS&PI, however, responded rather casually and submitted Action Taken Notes (ATN) on these reviews in 2009—eleven and eight years after the submission of these reports. The ATN rather casually noted that 'necessary efforts' were being made to complete projects on time, including preparation of model estimates, fixing target dates of completion, etc. The CAG meanwhile decided to conduct a performance audit of MPLADS between April and December 2009 through a test check of records of the nodal departments in the states, district authorities and implementing agencies between 2004–05 and 2008–09. On completion of this exercise, it submitted its report to Parliament and noted that many of the shortcomings pointed out in the two earlier reports 'still persist'.[1]

Before we proceed to the audit of 2009, it would be worthwhile to record the main findings of the CAG after the audit of MPLADS in 2001. In that audit, which relied on a sample survey across the country, the CAG found that DAs had incurred an expenditure of ₹3.97 crore on 570 works not recommended by MPs; as many as 3,397 works costing ₹35.79 crore were taken up for execution without technical sanction; the DAs spent ₹53.74 crore on works which were inadmissible under the scheme; there were delays in completion of 568 works and in some cases, the delay was up to five years; the IAs did not take up 775 sanctioned works estimated to cost ₹10.18 crore; ninety-nine works were abandoned midway for various reasons; 1,688 contracts with an estimated cost of ₹35.74 crore were awarded by the DAs irregularly; in over 70 per cent of the cases DAs did not obtain utilization certificates (UCs) for works costing over ₹161 crore from IAs; the IAs did not refund ₹8.13 crore to DAs, which remained unspent due to cancellation of works or non-commencement of works for some reasons; DAs released funds to IAs for expenditure incurred, without checking utilization; and there were also instances of loss of interest in funds in banks.[2]

The performance audit of 2009 covered 128 DAs of thirty-five states and UTs. Broadly, the audit examined whether the implementation of the scheme was within the MPLADS operational guidelines and instructions and whether it was in compliance with general financial rules, administrative rules and procedures.

The CAG report said the central government released the funds meant for each MP (₹2 crore per annum until 31 March 2011) in two instalments of ₹1 crore each directly to the DA with an intimation sent to the nodal department in each state and to the MP concerned. The DA and the IA deposit the funds in a nationalized bank with separate accounts being opened for each MP. Funds released to the DA are non-lapsable and can be carried forward for utilization in subsequent years. However, funds not released by the Union government before the close of the fiscal year are treated as surrendered/lapsed. The interest generated by the funds parked in nationalized banks is to be used for permissible works recommended by MPs. Since the launch of the scheme in 1993–94, the Union government had spent ₹19,425.75 crore until 2008–09. The total funds available with district authorities was ₹19,845.91 crore, including ₹420.16 crore accrued as interest. The CAG found that of this sum, the DAs had spent ₹18,057.91 (91 per cent).[3] Table 12.1 presents the details of utilization of MPLDS funds from 2004–05 to 2008–09.[4]

The auditors said the performance audit undertaken in 2009 had the following objectives:

To see whether the scheme fulfilled the principal objective of meeting the demands of constituents for basic facilities, community infrastructure, etc; whether the process of selection of works was transparent and guided by merit and relative priority; whether the DAs and IAs complied with guidelines and ensured competitive bids, quality control, etc; whether there was accountability in regard to maintenance and upkeep of assets created; whether the physical and financial performance reports were free from misstatements; whether the list of community assets created was transparently displayed; whether the internal control management and performance monitoring systems and procedures were in order; and whether the MS&PI established a system of corrective action for the scheme as a whole.[5]

Table 12.1: Utilization of MPLADS funds from 2004-05 to 2008-09.

Year	Budget estimates	Funds released	Unspent balance of previous year available with DAs	Interest earned on unspent balance	Total funds available with DAs	Expenditure incurred during the year	Closing balance	Per cent utilization of available funds
(1)	(2)	(3)	(4)	(5)	(6)= (3)+(4)+(5)	(7)	(8)= (6)-(7)	(9)= (7)*100/6)
2004-05	1,580.00	1,310.00	2,404.26	42.35	3,756.61	1,909.11	1,847.50	50.82
2005-06	1,580.00	1,433.90	1,847.50	34.29	3,315.69	1,382.63	1,933.06	41.70
2006-07	1,580.00	1,451.50	1,933.06	31.57	3,416.13	1,278.71	2,137.42	37.43
2007-08	1,580.00	1,470.55	2,137.42	35.12	3,643.09	1,506.45	2,136.64	41.35
2008-09	1,580.00	1,580.00	2,136.64	42.99	3,759.63	1,971.63	1,788.00	52.44

(*Source*: Ministry of Statistics and Programme Implementation)

Lack of Transparency and Objectivity in Selection of Works

The auditors found that the scheme did not specify the mechanism to be adopted by an MP to ensure participation of constituents, local bodies, NGOs, etc. There was no record to indicate that the MP had systematically considered the needs of the local people and prioritized projects. 'The process of selection of works lacked transparency and objectivity to that extent.'

The MS&PI responded to the auditors' objections by stating that MPs recommended works brought to their notice by their constituents and projects were prioritized on the basis of 'suffering' faced by the people. The CAG, however, took this response of the ministry with a pinch of salt. It said that despite the ministry's reply, it should be borne in mind that 'the absence of a monitorable and participatory mechanism to prioritise needs of the MP's constituency opened the scope of utilisation of MPLADS funds in non-priority areas.'[6]

MPs Do Not Adhere to the Ninety-day Deadline

The scheme requires every MP to give a prioritized list of works for execution by the DA during the year, 'preferably within 90 days of the commencement of the financial year'.

Apart from the fact that there was no participatory mechanism within each constituency to guide the MPs in regard to selection and prioritization of projects, the auditors noted that MPs did not recommend projects in time. In the 2009 audit, of the seventy DAs which were examined, the auditors found that in sixty-four DAs, MPs recommended 34,023 works well after the ninety-day deadline set by the guidelines from the commencement of the financial year. This constituted 42.85 per cent of the total recommended works in these districts. They also noticed that MPs recommended works right up to the end of the financial year.

In its response, the ministry advanced the strange argument that 'MPs were not bound by the restriction of the time limit' because the guidelines in this regard were only 'suggestive' in nature. However, this stand of the ministry was contrary to what it said in a letter addressed to all MPs in October 1999. In that letter, the ministry said that if MPs gave recommendations for works under MPLADS at the fag end of the year, it caused 'administrative problems' and also resulted in slow utilization of funds. Citing this contradiction, the auditors said non-compliance with the suggestion that works be recommended within ninety days of the commencement of a financial year had resulted in MPs recommending works throughout the year, resulting in slow utilization of the annual entitlement of MPs.[7]

After examining the issue of delayed recommendations of works by MPs, the CAG has opined that the MS & PI may provide a cut-off date in a financial year for accepting recommendations of works by MPs. Works recommended thereafter can be carried forward to the next financial year.[8] The details of works sanctioned and completed during this period are presented in Table 12.2.

The guidelines stipulate that works recommended by MPs should be completed within one year. The auditors found that of a total of 5,18,243 works sanctioned between 2004–05 and 2008–09, 4,09,662 works were completed, leaving 1,08,581 incomplete works (21 per cent). The percentage of works remaining incomplete ranged from 48.23 in 2004–05 to 59.28 in 2006–07.[9] The details of works sanctioned and completed during this period are presented in Table 12.2.[10]

The audit showed that the delay in execution of works occurred at various stages. The guidelines stipulate that on receipt of the recommendation from the MP, the DA has to verify the 'eligibility' and 'technical feasibility' of each recommended work, get the works technically approved and financial estimates prepared by the IAs. Thereafter, the sanction has to be accorded for each work. All this is to be achieved within forty-five days. However, the auditors found that of the 74,223 sanction orders that were test-checked, delays occurred in respect of 28,135 cases, constituting 38 per cent of the works. Of this, the sanction of

Table 12.2: Works sanctioned and completed during 2004–05 to 2008–09

Year	Opening balance of incomplete works	Works sanctioned during the year	Total works	Works completed during the year	Incomplete works at the end of the year	Percentage of works remaining incomplete out of total works
2004–05	1,15,423	65,356	2,16779	1,12,225	1,04,554	48.23
2005–06	1,04,554	77.045	1,81,599	77,617	1,03,982	57.26
2006–07	1.03.982	66,682	1,70,664	69,486	1,01,178	59.28
2007–08	1,01,178	66,039	1,67,217	69,509	97,708	58.43
2008–09	97,708	91,698	1,89,406	80,825	1,08,581	57.33

(*Source:* Ministry of Statistics and Programme Implementation)

8 per cent of the works came a year after the MPs made the recommendations. The auditors found delays to be high in Bihar, Gujarat, West Bengal and Rajasthan.

The delays occurred mainly because timely action was not taken to secure plans and estimates from the user or implementing agencies. The sanctioning process was 'inefficient' and this delayed the schedule for completion of work. The auditors also found instances where administrative approval and financial sanctions were accorded by the DAs in around 25 per cent of the cases without following the procedure laid down in the guidelines such as obtaining financial estimates from IAs, conducting feasibility studies before commencing the work and obtaining technical clearance from the competent authorities.[11]

MPs Recommend Implementing Agencies

The desire of MPs to identify the IAs is the root cause of much of the adverse publicity that comes their way in regard to this scheme. The guidelines clearly prohibit their involvement in this matter, yet a good percentage of MPs insist on identifying the IAs for the works sanctioned by them. The district authorities often come under pressure and give in to the demands of MPs while appointing the IAs. All this leads to allegations of corruption in MPLADS. Even in the sting operation carried out by a television news channel on some MPs a few years ago, charges of corruption were levelled because the MPs said they would sanction the works for a fee and would ensure that the bribe-givers would be the IAs.

Para 2.11 of the guidelines says DAs must identify the agency that will execute the work. It also says that Panchayati Raj institutions and urban local bodies should be preferred as IAs in rural and urban areas. Further, in December 2006, the MS&PI clarified that the guidelines did not allow MPs to select the executing agency. This was the responsibility of the DAs only. However, auditors found that MPs had recommended the names of IAs along with their recommendations for works in nine states and UTs. Also, in some cases, the recommended IAs were also the user agencies to when the funds were released. Such instances were noticed in 8,746 works with Rajasthan, Uttar Pradesh, Manipur and Meghalaya leading the pack.

The auditors reported that in the test-checked districts, IAs were selected by the recommending MPs themselves in respect of 6,158 works costing ₹187.58 crore sanctioned during 2004–09.

In five selected districts (Hooghly, Kolkata, Paschim Medinipur, Purulia and South 24 Parganas) out of the 6,091 works sanctioned during 2004–09, 1,573 works (25.82 per cent) were executed through private agencies. The auditors also found that when MPs recommended works relating to educational institutions, clubs, NGOs, etc. the very organizations were chosen by them as the agencies to implement the works in these five districts.

The guidelines stipulate that in rural areas, only Panchayati Raj institutions should be the IAs and should execute the works. But, in West Bengal the auditors found that in fourteen cases, the PRIs paid the entire amount (₹1.12 crore) they received from the district authorities to the user agencies, thus violating the scheme's guidelines.

The auditors concluded that 'the DAs failed to apply the necessary checks and balances provided in the scheme guidelines for ensuring transparency and accountability in spending under the scheme.' When all this was brought to the notice of the ministry, it said that under the scheme only the DAs had the sole power to identify the IA. It said it would seek a 'detailed report' from the state and the DAs 'for necessary action'.[12]

MPLADS: The District Administration Throws its Hands Up

Auditors from the CAG's office have looked at MPLADS three times over the last eight years. There is now sufficient evidence to show that there are major deficiencies in the implementation of the scheme. Further, and more importantly, the district administrations are either unwilling or unable to monitor the projects sanctioned under this scheme. Add to this the complaints of misuse of funds, corruption and general disrespect for the guidelines among MPs and we have a recipe for gross misuse of public funds.

The guidelines stipulate that the DAs should follow work estimates and the tendering and administrative procedure of the state or UT government. However, in 2009, auditors found that 703 works in four states involving ₹28.65 crore were not done in accordance with standard tendering procedures. In Nagaland, the auditors found that 209 works were executed by the DAs through IAs 'without inviting any tenders'. In Arunachal Pradesh, 238 works were executed by IAs through private contractors without following competitive bidding. In West Bengal, tendering was not done for 251 works costing ₹20,000 or more as required by the state's financial rules. In Orissa, the auditors found five works executed by IAs through private contractors without following competitive bidding.[13] Table 12.3 presents the details of works awarded in these four states without following tendering procedure.[14]

The CAG reported, 'These instances of award of contract without adopting standard tendering processes and use of private contractors indicated dilution of checks and balances prescribed in the scheme to ensure accountability and the reply indicated complete lack of awareness about implementation details in absence of monitoring by the ministry.'[15]

Government rules require that execution of works should be preceded by financial sanctions and administrative approval from the competent authority. However, in four states the auditors found that 26 per cent of the works amounting to ₹17.80 crore 'were executed either without administrative approval by the DAs or their execution was initiated without obtaining prior financial sanction'. In two sampled districts—Kamrup Metro and Kamrup (Rural)—in Assam, it was found that DAs had released

Table 12.3: Award of works without following tendering procedure

Sr. No.	State	No. of Works	Audit findings	Amount (₹ in crore)
1	Nagaland	209	DAs executed works through IAs without inviting any tenders.	12.03
2	Arunachal Pradesh	238	Execution by IAs through private contractors during 2004–09 without following competitive bidding.	9.97
3	West Bengal	251	Tendering was not done for works costing ₹20,000 or more as required by the West Bengal General Financial Rules. In the case of execution of works by educational institutions, clubs, etc. tendering procedures were not followed and labourers were engaged locally and materials were procured from the local market.	6.15
4	Orissa	5	Execution by IAs through private contractors without following competitive bidding	0.50
Total		703		28.65

(*Source*: Ministry of Statistics and Programme Implementation)

a sum of ₹0.89 crore for works with a sanctioned cost of ₹0.59 crore, resulting in overpayment of ₹0.32 crore. In all these cases the MS&PI said that it would seek detailed reports from the DAs 'for necessary action'.[16]

Delay in execution of works is yet another malaise that afflicts the scheme. The DAs are expected to ensure that every work is eligible and technically feasibile. They are also expected to ensure that all clearances have been obtained from the competent authorities. Thereafter, the sanction letter should stipulate the time-frame for completion of each work. Generally, every project should be completed within one year and the sanction letter should also include a clause for suitable penal action against the IA if the work is not completed in time. However, auditors found that 389 works with an estimated cost of ₹9.17 crore, which was released by the DAs, did not commence at all. This means that the funds released were a complete write-off.

The second category was that of incomplete works. The auditors found that 12,006 works amounting to ₹279.99 crore remained incomplete in sixteen states and UTs for periods ranging from one year to five years and in some cases up to even fifteen years.

The CAG report cited two case studies from Tamil Nadu to highlight the problem of delayed execution of projects under this scheme. The first was a bridge to link ward numbers 72 and 73 in the Chennai Municipal Corporation. It was recommended by the Chennai Central Lok Sabha MP in 2004–05. However, between 2004 and 2009, the alignment of the bridge was changed four times. Meanwhile, the cost of the project had escalated from ₹1.50 crore to ₹5 crore. At the time of audit in August 2009, the work was still at the tendering process. In another case, a road overbridge at Perambur was sanctioned in 2006–07, but the work had not commenced until August 2009 due to frequent revision of estimates. As a result, the estimated cost of the work rose from ₹3.00 crore to ₹8.41 crore in 2009–10. Despite the release of the escalated amount in 2008–09, the work had not begun at the time of audit.[17]

This brings us to a larger issue—the absence of an administrative set-up to implement and monitor MPLADS. There have been many instances where the district magistrates have said that they just do not have the time or the resources to monitor the implementation of this scheme. A test-check conducted by auditors in West Bengal in 2009 highlights this problem. The auditors did a test-check of five districts in that state and found that 1,499 works costing ₹57.01 crore remained incomplete for one to three years. One thousand and four works costing ₹24.14 crore remained incomplete for four to six years. Three hundred and eleven works costing ₹10.29 crore remained incomplete for seven to nine years and 194 works costing ₹2.80 crores remained incomplete for ten to fourteen years. The auditors also found that 305 incomplete works on which a sum of ₹8.50 crore was spent had been abandoned, suspended or were at a standstill, thereby rendering the expenditure incurred on these works unfruitful.[18]

The reasons for delay in the execution of works were varied. They included land disputes, non-availability of land, poor site conditions, lack of technical clearance, inadequate financial estimates, cost escalation, no response to tenders and part completion of works by one agency and refusal by other agencies to take up partially completed works.

These cases of delayed execution or abandonment of works showed that 'the DAs did not always assess the feasibility of the project/work and plan for necessary approvals before according administrative approval and financial sanction. It resulted in idling of funds released to IAs for these works. DAs and IAs also failed to take suitable penal action against the erring agencies as per provisions of the scheme. In many cases the clause outlining penalties or suitable action against the agency concerned in cases of delay was not incorporated in the sanction letter.' [19]

The auditors said: 'The DAs did not maintain records regarding non-commencement of works by IAs after release of funds to them. No action was taken to obtain refund of unutilized funds even though the IAs did not report the status of works for years. DMs of Hooghly and South 24 Parganas stated that they were unable to monitor such large number of works due to lack of adequate infrastructure.'[20]

Now that the funds available to each MP have been raised to ₹5 crore, the absence of an administrative infrastructure at the district level to keep a watchful eye on the scheme is a major lacuna and can result in the misuse of thousands of crores of rupees annually. However, despite the magnitude of the loss that the exchequer can suffer as a result of the enhanced corpus of MPLADS, the government does not appear to have any plan on hand to inject some efficiency into the implementation of the scheme. When the auditors drew the attention of the government to these wastages, the MS&PI promised that it would obtain information on each case from the DAs 'for necessary action'. The works which have not yet been started would be cancelled and in case of irregularities 'necessary instructions would be issued to DAs for fixing the responsibilities and suitable disciplinary action'.[21]

Some Examples of Fraud

Lack of supervision has also led to fraud in the implementation of MPLADS. When auditors test-checked the records at the state and district levels, they came across instances of doubtful expenditure which indicated misappropriation of funds in some districts of West Bengal, Jharkhand, Bihar and Mizoram. The auditors said these instances needed further investigation by the government. Here are a few instances:

The district magistrate of South 24 Paraganas, released a sum of ₹5 lakh in May 2008 to the secretary, Taldi-I Village Education Committee for the construction of a classroom at Rajapur Free Primary School. The DM received the utilization certificate (UC) for the entire amount of ₹5 lakh but the auditors found in July 2009 that the classroom had not been constructed. Following the audit, the district magistrate ordered an investigation by the block development officer, which confirmed the misappropriation. Thereafter a first information report has been lodged with the police.[22]

In Jharkhand, a member of the Rajya Sabha recommended the installation of two solar water-pump sets at an estimated cost of ₹20 lakh. The work was awarded to a firm in Dhanbad. The deputy commissioner of Deoghar, paid the company ₹8 lakh as advance in July 2005 for supply and installation of the pumps. The auditors say that even after a lapse of four years, the firm had not supplied the solar water-pumps as confirmed by the audit team during a joint field verification it conducted along with officials of the district administration. 'However, the DA had taken no action till date.'

In this very district and around the same time, auditors found that the entire sum allocated for the construction of high-yield tubewells sanctioned by a Rajya Sabha MP had not been spent. Scrutiny of measurement books and vouchers showed that some part of the fund had been misappropriated by the IA.

In Bihar, the fraud related to the National Rural Employment Programme (NREP), which was the IA for six works including construction of two *kachcha* roads, two renovation works and construction of two community halls. The auditors found that four of these works were completed on 31 July 2006 and the UCs were submitted to the DA. However, muster rolls showed the engagement of labourers for these works up to 5 December 2006. Two other works were completed by 30 September 2006 but muster rolls were booked up to 26 December 2006. In other words, NREP officials were duping the government by billing MPLADS for works already completed. The auditors said the expenditure of ₹6 lakh was 'doubtful'. They said they were not convinced by the explanations offered by the executive engineer who was in charge of the project.

In Mizoram, the auditors test-checked eighteen works and found that the IAs submitted vouchers on plain paper in support of material worth ₹19 lakh purchased for these works. In many instances, the dates shown for the purchase of material were after the dates shown for completion of works. They concluded that these payments on vouchers were doubtful.[23]

While these are instances of outright fraud, the auditors came across very many cases of substandard work, especially in road construction. However, this is an area where substandard work can mean 100 per cent loss of the funds spent. The auditors found that between during 2004–09, the MCD executed twenty-eight works for improvement/strengthening of roads. In all these cases (without exception!) the contractors used a lower quantity of bitumen (5.86 kg/sq. m as against the required 8.79 kg/sq. m) leading to an excess payment of ₹66 lakh to the contractors.

In the Jalaun district of Uttar Pradesh, four works were sanctioned under this scheme for the construction of cement concrete roads during 2005–07 at a cost of ₹9 lakh. The roads were found substandard 'and their rectification was technically not feasible as the crust thickness of roads was less by one to seven cm of the prescribed 20 cm'. There was yet another instance of the construction of a concrete road where the contractor had violated the technical specifications given for the work. The auditors noted that in this case, the district magistrate had himself detected the substandard quality of the work during inspection, yet no action was taken against the IA. 'This showed lack of supervision and monitoring by the DA,' they said.

In Bihar, when contractors are hired for execution of works, estimates are prepared on the existing schedule of rates in which the contractor's profit of 10 per cent is included. However, when 46 works were executed departmentally, 'contractors' profit was allowed to the concerned officials without deducting it from the estimates' leading to an excess payment of ₹6 lakh. The auditors also found that during 2005–08, an excess payment of ₹55 lakh was made to six executing agencies in Bihar by allowing higher rates than those provided in the estimates.

In Mizoram, a Rajya Sabha member sanctioned the

construction of a playground at an estimated cost of ₹50 lakh. All parts of the work pertained to earth excavation. The auditors found that 'the DA had sanctioned the last two parts of the work without checking the primary records of the parts of the work already done' resulting in an excess expenditure of ₹33 lakh. This means an excess payment of 66 per cent and is indicative of the gross misuse of the scheme by a section of the MPs in connivance with officials in the districts.[24]

Fraud and misuse of MPLADS can be seen in a variety of activities, not just civil works.

For example, on the recommendation of the MP, ten ambulances were purchased for the Andaman and Nicobar Islands in 2008–09. The MP wanted three of these ambulances to be sent to the Salvation Fellowship Trust, Port Blair, the Directorate of Transport Service, Port Blair, and the Primary Health Centre (PHC), Long Islands. However, the ambulances were not issued to the trust and to the directorate because they fell in the prohibited items listed under MPLADS. As regards the PHC in Long Islands, it refused to take the ambulance citing lack of requirement 'as there was no motorable road and garage'. Subsequently, the ambulances were distributed to three different PHCs of the UT without receiving any recommendation from the MP and without assessing the requirement of the PHCs. This showed that the DA did not identify the requirement/ eligibility of the user agencies before according sanction to the MP's recommendation, leading to unplanned purchase and distribution of assets. What a waste of public money! Why did the MP recommend purchase of ten ambulances, when there was no need for it? What was he getting out of it? Why did the district administration in the Andaman and Nicobar Islands act on this recommendation and buy the ambulances without assessing the needs of the PHCs and without checking whether ambulances could be given to agencies like the Salvation Fellowship Trust? How could the MP recommend an ambulance to a PHC located on an island which had no motorable road? Is he so poorly acquainted with his constituency? How could the DA clear this proposal? We may not know who all benefited from this absurd decision other than the company that makes these ambulances, but we do know that a lot of public money went down the drain.[25]

Random checks by the auditors also showed that in one district of Tamil Nadu, eight works which were executed at a cost of ₹69 lakh differed from the recommendations of the MPs. In other words, the work or the site of the work or both differed from what had been recommended by the MP. Here again, payments were made to labourers without maintaining muster rolls; inferior-quality timber which was felled illegally was used and materials were bought in the open market without obtaining competitive rates. Finally, the works were executed in a piecemeal fashion instead of combining them. In this way, the IA avoided obtaining competitive rates.[26]

Consequent upon these findings by its auditors, the CAG said 'suitable action' should be taken against agencies responsible for delayed works, non-completion of works and abandonment of works; in cases where excess or doubtful payments have been made, recoveries should be made from individuals and agencies responsible for overpayment; a penalty should be imposed in case of delayed completion; and the MS&PI should ensure complete documentation at all levels.[27]

Does the MS&PI Have the Will to Do it?

What all these examples show is that many MPs and individuals in the public and private sectors have begun to see MPLADS as a happy grazing ground. The MPs (like the MP from the Andaman and Nicobar Islands who purchased the ambulances which the PHCs did not want) tend to brazen it out in the belief that they enjoy immunity from any kind of civil or criminal proceedings for misuse or misappropriation. Their friends and contacts outside Parliament, who tempt them to misuse the scheme, feel that the long arm of the law is not long enough to catch them because they have the protective shield of the recommending MP before them. There can be no other explanation for such blatant misappropriation of public funds. Can any agency in either the government or private sector purchase ten ambulances without having any plan in regard to their utilization? Such gross misuse of funds is a rarity in either of these sectors. This can happen only when district officials and private players begin to feel that they are not accountable to anybody so long as they mechanically implement an MP's recommendation. One wonders whether a private company like the one in Dhanbad, which deals with solar water-pumps, could have taken ₹8 lakh from any other customer and not supplied the equipment for four years after it received the advance. Similarly, local officials in charge of building a school classroom or managing the rural employment programme could not have committed the fraud they did, if they were not assured of the support of the MPs who suggested those works.

Execution of Works Without MPs' Recommendation

Apart from the delay in the recommendation of projects and non-involvement of constituents in the choice of projects, the auditors found something far more serious—execution of works without the recommendation of MPs. It is difficult to understand how district authorities in various states begin work on MPLADS projects without fulfilment of a primary condition—a recommendation from the MP. As per the guidelines, each MP is required to recommend works on his or her letterhead, duly signed by him or her. Recommendations made by representatives of MPs are not permissible. However, the auditors found that in nine districts in eight states, 700 works costing ₹9.45 crore were executed without a formal recommendation by the MP. In three districts they found that 150 works amounting to ₹2.44 crore were executed on the recommendation of representatives of the MPs such as the personal secretary of the MP, the zonal president of the political party the MP belonged to, etc.

Yet another issue which showed the DAs in poor light was overspending on recommended works. The auditors found 260 works in ten districts had cost ₹2.49 crore more than what was recommended by the MPs. The consent of the MPs was not obtained for the excess expenditure which was incurred from unspent balance of other works and interest accrued on unspent balances. The unauthorized expenditure involved in respect of all these cases which were violative of the guidelines was ₹14.38 crore.

The report of the auditors, however, did not have much of an impact on the MS & PI.

'The ministry states that it was contemplating to investigate the violation of scheme guidelines by the DAs and fix responsibilities for the alleged irregularities.'[28]

The auditors provided two case studies to illustrate the problem. In the West Garo Hills district of Meghalaya, the construction of staff quarters for junior engineers and accountants and renovation of the BDO's office, all of which are prohibited under the scheme, was executed at a cost of ₹7 lakh without receiving any recommendation from the MP.

In Shajapur, Madhya Pradesh, as many as ninety-nine road works costing ₹1.78 crore were sanctioned by the district authorities between 2005 and 2007 on the recommendation of the personal secretary (PS) to the Lok Sabha MP. These recommendations were made on the official letterhead of the MP by his PS who claimed that they were being made 'as per orders of the Hon'ble MP'. These recommendations did not carry the signature of the MP, which was necessary as per the format prescribed for recommending works under this scheme.[29]

In regard to the cost overrun, the CAG reported: 'The ministry should ensure that technical support is provided to MPs for accurately estimating the cost of works recommended by them to allocate funds effectively and judicially to projects.'[30]

MPs Recommend Works in the Prohibited List

As per the guidelines of the scheme, all works which meet the locally felt infrastructure and developmental needs of the community are permissible under MPLADS. However, the auditors found that in a hundred sampled districts an expenditure of ₹73.76 crore was incurred during 2004–09 on 2,340 works which were not permitted as per the guidelines.[31]

The list of prohibited works is provided to every district authority. It is a rather comprehensive list that can be easily understood by persons in charge of districts in the country. It categorically prohibits utilization of MPLADS funds for maintenance works of any type, for renovation and repair works except heritage and archaeological monuments, for residential buildings, for creation of assets for a family or individual, for the purchase of moveable items and for works within religious places. These are some of the main items in the prohibited list. There are several more, but the basic idea is to ensure that the funds are not squandered away for unproductive purposes or to promote individual or family interests of MPs. Instead, they must be used to create durable assets which are of value to the constituency which each MP represents.[32]

The auditors found the district authorities in nineteen states and UTs had permitted the construction of government offices, renovation of government offices and hospitals, the construction of railway stations, jail premises and panchayat bhavans. In seventeen states and UTs, funds were used to build clubs, manufacturing units, bus stations, works relating to cooperative societies and private institutions. In sixteen states and UTs, they found works within the premises of temples, churches, madrasas and construction works for religious places. In twenty-five states and UTs, various renovation, repair and maintenance works for roads, buildings, parks, gardens, ponds, tourist huts and a water supply infrastructure were undertaken. In fourteen states and UTs, funds were used for the purchase of air-conditioners, furniture, etc., for government offices; sports equipment for society/trust-run schools; vehicles for societies/trusts; ambulances for hospitals run by NGOs/trusts; water tankers; audio-visual aids for aided educational institutes, etc. In six states and UTs, buildings were constructed in the name of prominent persons. In eleven states and UTs, funds were given to the Prime Minister's/Chief Minister's Relief Fund, works for individual benefit and for organizing sports competitions.[33]

Nothing establishes the violation of the guidelines and the gross misuse of MPLADS for private rather than public purpose than the following case study from the East district, Sikkim, offered by the auditors after the 2009 audit. They found that forty-three schemes were sanctioned 'for construction of anti-erosion work, protective/retaining wall, jhora training work and drainage system involving ₹2.65 crores. During physical verification of 22 such works in presence of the departmental officers and respective gram panchayats, it was noticed that in 21 cases, works were executed on private individual land at an expenditure of ₹1.39 crore. Further, the contractors engaged in executing 12 cases costing ₹0.59 crore were the land owners themselves or the land belonged to their family members.'

This is possibly the most scandalous instance of misuse of MPLADS funds. When auditors undertook a physical verification of twenty-two works, they found twenty-one cases related to private land. And as if this was not enough, in twelve cases the contractors were themselves the landowners and they had billed the scheme ₹59 lakh![34]

Despite such examples of gross misuse of the scheme, the CAG tended to be diplomatic while summing up the problem. He said, 'The execution of works prohibited under the scheme indicated that MPs had not kept the objectives and guidelines of the scheme in view while recommending works and the DAs had not verified the eligibility of these works before granting administrative approval and financial sanction.' The MS&PI, which is the nodal ministry for disbursement of these funds, did not seem to be scandalized by the report and the case studies offered by the auditors. It employed officialese to the hilt when it said that it would collect details of inadmissible works taken by DAs 'for initiating suitable action'.[35]

Deploying MPLADS Money for Societies and Trusts

The scheme permits utilization of MPLADS for community infrastructure and public utility buildings of societies and trusts, provided the society/trust has been in existence for the preceding three years and engaged in social service/welfare activities. The scheme, however, puts a cap on expenditure on this account and says not more than ₹25 lakh should be spent for one or more works of a particular trust. The CAG found that of the ₹14.40 crore released to societies and trusts in ten states, a sum of ₹5.90 crore was in excess of the prescribed ceiling per society or trust. In seven states, the DAs had sanctioned ₹5.94 crore to 145 societies and trusts which were either ineligible or whose eligibility had not been verified by the DAs.

'This indicated that the DAs had not established an effective mechanism to ensure transfer of funds only to the eligible trusts/societies. Further, it rendered the use of the MPLADS funds for locally felt needs of the constituencies doubtful,' said the auditors. The MS&PI once again came up with a lackadaisical response. It said it had instructed the nodal departments in all states and UTs and the DAs that when an MP recommends funds for a society or trust, the eligibility of the society or trust must be verified. It said it would collect details of cases cited by the auditors from the DAs and initiate 'suitable action'. The auditors were not impressed. They said, 'The reply yet again highlights lack of ownership and helplessness in ensuring compliance to guidelines/instructions.'[36]

The CAG has said that DAs should be held accountable for taking up works that are not permitted under the scheme.[37]

What Becomes of the Assets Created Under the Scheme?

MPLADS is all about creation of durable assets in an MP's constituency. The guidelines drawn up for the scheme emphasize the need for investing public funds earmarked for it in creation of assets that are of value to the community. As the auditors have pointed out, there are many issues in regard to the selection of projects and their execution. However, even if all this is okay and the work sanctioned is completed on time, the story does not end there. The next issue is handing over the assets created to the user agency and its subsequent maintenance. The report of the CAG throws light on these aspects of MPLADS and gives us an insight into the final outcome of the scheme vis-à-vis utilization and maintenance of assets. However, the sample surveys conducted by the auditors in different parts of the country, raise serious questions about the efficacy of MPLADS.

The guidelines state that the district authorities should maintain work registers in regard to each work in progress and also a register of all assets created and transferred to the user agencies. The auditors, however, found that work registers were not being maintained by sixteen DAs whereas among twenty-two other DAs, the registers maintained were incomplete. Similarly, assets registers were not maintained in 115 DAs in thirty-one states and UTs, which amounted to a shocking 90 per cent of the sample! In the absence of assets registers, there was no way of ensuring the custody of the assets or their maintenance.[38]

The scheme envisages that assets created should be put to public use soon after they are ready. In other words, they have to be handed over to the user agency soon after completion. However, the CAG has reported that the auditors examined 15,049 sample works in seven states and UTs undertaken during 2004–09 and found that there was no record of formal handing over of assets to user agencies in respect of 14,828 works worth ₹251.91 crore. In six of these states, there were no documents at all to show the transfer of any work to the user agency. This constituted 98.53 per cent of the projects completed. Nothing can be more scandalous than this![39]

In some other states, the auditors found that the assets could not be used by the user agency because there was no electricity or water connection or proper flooring or the needed furnishings and equipment. The auditors also found that in six districts, the assets created were not being utilized for the purpose for which they were sanctioned. These assets were being used by private trusts and societies running bachelor of computer application (BCA), bachelor of computer science (BCS) courses, English-medium schools or the offices of the societies. The auditors said these instances showed 'complete lack of ownership and monitoring by the ministry'. The MS&PI said it would obtain details of misuse of assets from the DAs.[40]

Under the scheme, the DA is required to obtain a firm commitment from the user agency about the upkeep and maintenance of the proposed asset before the work is sanctioned. This is to ensure that once a public utility is built, there are no issues about maintenance of the utility. This way, the DA knows who will be in charge of the asset once it is ready. However, the auditors found that in 50 per cent of the districts sampled by them in eighteen states and UTs, the district authorities had not taken any commitment for maintenance of assets from the user agencies before permitting execution of the work recommended by the MP. Test-checks of some assets in three states and UTs by the auditors showed that some assets were in a dilapidated condition; there were cases of theft of materials; and assets such as tubewells and water fountains were not working properly due to poor upkeep.[41]

Looking at the cases of misuse of assets, the CAG said the MS&PI should put in place an effective mechanism to monitor and track the assets created from MPLADS funds and their expeditious handing over to the identified agencies; the documentation in respect of handing over MPLADS works and maintenance of assets such as assets registers should be streamlined at the DA level; and the ministry can devise a format for formal agreement between the DA and user agency. The CAG said failure to maintain the asset should invite penal action.[42]

Management of MPLADS Funds and the MS & PI

The CAG examined the availability of MPLADS funds and their utilization on a yearly basis for the years 2004 through 2009 and concluded that during that period, utilization of funds ranged between 37.43 per cent and 52.44 per cent. The auditors found that unutilized funds ranging from ₹1,788 crore to ₹2,137 crore accumulated in various bank accounts opened for MPLADS by the DAs. These funds remained outside the consolidated fund of the Union and the states. The auditors, however, found that the expenditure under the scheme had a propensity to increase at times close to elections. Expenditure peaked in 2004–05 just prior to the Lok Sabha election and at the fag end of the fourteenth Lok Sabha in 2008–09. 'The acceleration of expenditure in the year close to the elections indicated administrative lethargy during the period between two elections due to non-lapsable nature of unspent balances of previous years' the CAG said. What this means is that the DAs and the MPs tend to take it easy in the initial years since they know that the funds do not lapse. The accumulated funds are then utilized in the year prior to the Lok Sabha election, so that the MP can ensure maximum recall of his 'good work' by his constituents and derive maximum electoral mileage out of MPLADS. Obviously, the DAs also collaborate with MPs in this venture.[43]

Apart from the district authorities, the MS & PI is all at sea when it comes to managing MPLADS. The CAG says the ministry has to monitor the receipt of UCs and audit certificates from the DAs and take necessary corrective action in time if the scheme is to be implemented with a degree of accountability. However, the auditors have found that the ministry does not maintain proper registers and records to track the receipt of annual accounts and UCs from the districts. When they did get UCs and audit certificates, these were not analysed by the ministry. Nor did it conduct any review of the records. As a result, auditors could not obtain a comprehensive view of the fund utilization. The auditors also noted that the MS&PI had relaxed the conditions regarding furnishing of UCs and audit certificates by the DAs before the release of the second instalment of funds to each MP's account every year. The ministry said it released the next instalment without UCs in regard to the earlier instalment because it did not want the DAs to be short of funds to implement works recommended by MPs. It also conceded that proper analyses of UCs and audit certificates were not done because of a 'shortage of staff'. Further, the audit certificates sent by the DAs could not be examined 'because officials responsible for examining them did not have expertise in commercial accounting'.

The auditors, however, did not find merit in the explanations offered by the MS&PI. They said the scheme was launched in 1993 and in recent years the unspent balances with DAs ranged from ₹1,788 crore to ₹2,137 crore. The ministry should have been aware of these unspent balances had they been monitoring the UCs and other management information systems (MIS) from the states. The register of UCs and audit certificates maintained by the ministry did not contain information on pending UCs and audit certificates. As a result, it was not an effective tool to monitor the schemes. They also noticed that the rule was not relaxed on the basis of specific requests from the DAs 'but with a view to show expenditure against the amounts budgeted'. The CAG felt that officials in the ministry could have been suitably trained to monitor MPLADS, but 'the ministry failed to do so'. Even seventeen years after implementation, 'no capacity building for effective monitoring was evident' in the MS&PI, the auditors said.[44]

In the absence of strict monitoring by the government, chances of gross misuse of the scheme stand enhanced. As the 2009 review of the scheme by CAG showed, auditors found that the DAs were reporting 'inflated figures of expenditure' to the MS & PI by treating the amount released to the IAs as the final expenditure, without ascertaining the actual expenditure incurred. In twelve districts of six states and UTs the auditors found that ₹100.17 crore was released as an advance to IAs for execution of works during 2004–09, out of which only ₹65.18 crore had been spent. Instead of reporting the actual amount spent, the DAs depicted the entire sum of ₹100.17 crore as having been spent, 'thus inflating the figures of expenditure by ₹35 crore and presenting an incorrect picture of fund utilisation under the scheme'. The auditors also found that in twenty-one constituencies, the DAs had under-reported the interest earned from the MPLADS funds deposited in the accounts of MPs in the banks to the extent of ₹5.60 crore.

A specific case cited by the auditors was that of the West Siang district in Arunachal Pradesh where the DA reported an inflated expenditure of ₹2.48 crore to the Union government and the state government without ascertaining the actual expenditure incurred by the IAs. The DA also asserted that what they had done was correct. In another instance, a Rajya Sabha member from Jammu and Kashmir resigned his seat in April 2006, but the DA released a grant of ₹1 crore in September 2006, five months after his resignation. Further, it was found that this was not backed by any recommendation from the MP till the last day of his membership.

All that the ministry could offer by way of response to these serious charges made by the auditors was that it would obtain information from the DAs on these reported irregularities 'for taking necessary action'.

The auditors also found major discrepancies in the figures cited by DAs in monthly progress reports (MPRs), annual accounts and UCs when they checked the basic records in thirty constituencies in eleven states and UTs pertaining to the period 2004–09. In twenty cases, they found three different expenditure figures of the same financial year were mentioned in the MPR, the annual accounts and the UCs. In twenty-two cases, the MPRs and the closing balance of the annual accounts of the same financial year did not match and in sixteen cases the closing balance of the UCs and the annual accounts of the same financial year did not match.[45]

Among other negative features which have come to the notice of the auditors is diversion of funds, release of funds in excess of prescribed limits, improper maintenance of accounts by the DAs and IAs, use of funds for a contingency far in excess of permitted limits and a glaring discrepancy in accounts maintained by the DAs. Sample tests carried out by the auditors showed that in seven states, ₹4.67 crore of MPLADS funds were not spent for the schemes intended but were diverted to other state and central government programmes. In thirteen states the auditors found that the DAs had released funds to IAs far in excess of what is permitted. Also, while the guidelines require the IAs to refund unspent funds including interest, if any, to the DA within one month of completion of work, there is no provision for refund of funds released by IAs in cases where the works could not be started by them. In some states they found that unspent balances had not been refunded by IAs after completion of work. In twelve states, a sample survey showed that ₹12.14 crore was lying with IAs for 679 works which could not be taken up for implementation. The auditors said this showed deficient monitoring and accounting of funds .This was leading to blocking of funds and misappropriation in some instances. As regards contingency expenses, the guidelines allow the DAs to use 0.5 per cent of the amount for this purpose, but in thirteen states, this provision had been used for purposes which are prohibited by the rules. Yet another problem related to bank accounts. The scheme envisages that DAs and IAs open separate savings accounts for each MP in nationalized banks. In ten states, the auditors found that separate bank accounts were not being maintained for each MP. In four states, they found that DAs and IAs had opened more than one account for each MP.

There were several more problems pertaining to bank

accounts. The guidelines state that the accounts should be maintained MP-wise and the books of accounts should be audited by chartered accountants or other statutory auditors. The auditors found that chartered accountants had not periodically audited the accounts of MPs in forty districts. The accounts of one DA in Jammu and Kashmir and one DA in Lakshadweep had not been audited since the inception of the scheme in 1993. In twelve states, many DAs had not maintained MP-wise cash books. In six Lok Sabha constituencies in the national capital, Delhi, the audit reports of the chartered accountants said vouchers pertaining to the expenditure of ₹1.52 crore were missing. 'The veracity of these audit reports were therefore doubtful,' the CAG said. In the Kamrup (Metro) district in Assam, the DA could not produce vouchers of payments of ₹51 lakh made to a club, an NGO and six registered societies between December 2007 and February 2009.[46]

These discrepancies in three basic accounting records, which should invariably match, 'indicated weak internal controls at the DA's level. In this scenario, the auditors felt that there could be no guarantee of the figures touted by DAs in regard to expenditure incurred, interest earned and the unspent balances lying with them. They concluded that the MS&PI 'had failed to scrutinize these records and take action, as required under the scheme guidelines'.[47]

In the face of such incontrovertible evidence to establish the misuse of MPLADS funds and a host of other irregularities which pointed to lack of supervision by the ministry, the MS&PI began to adopt a 'blow hot, blow cold' attitude. In one response to the CAG, it said it should not be blamed for the incorrect information provided by DAs because despite the shortage of staff in the MPLADS division, the ministry had always tried to verify the main points as per guidelines before releasing the funds 'hoping that information supplied by the DAs were correct'. At another stage, the ministry virtually threw its hands up and said that these discrepancies were not verified because of 'paucity of staff'. However, it promised to ascertain details from DAs 'for taking necessary action'.[48]

The auditors dismissed these explanations as unsatisfactory. They said that according to information provided by the MS&PI, there was no shortage of staff vis-à-vis sanctioned strength in the MPLADS division. Further, it was the responsibility of the ministry to monitor the overall position of funds released and spent; to verify UCs and audit certificates; and to exercise due diligence in processing the proposals from the DAs before sanctioning funds. 'The failure to do so should be viewed as a serious lapse by the officials concerned.'[49]

Under the scheme, the IAs are given funds to execute works and they in turn, are expected to submit UCs in the prescribed format to DAs after the job is done. Auditors examined advances given by eighty DAs to IAs during 2004–09 in respect of 47,533 works. They found that the IAs had not furnished UCs for 19,540 works constituting 41.10 per cent of the works which had cost the exchequer ₹370 crore. In three states—Assam, Jammu and Kashmir and Maharashtra—the IAs did not furnish any UC for the entire amount of money released to them. The MS&PI sought to pass the buck. Though it has the responsibility for overall supervision of MPLADS, it said the DAs had to secure UCs from the IAs. The auditors wondered how the ministry was accounting for funds released and processing fresh proposals in the absence of UCs.[50] The CAG concluded that such lacunae in banking arrangements and accounting procedures showed that internal controls were weak at the IA, DA and ministry levels, thus 'exposing MPLAD funds to the risk of misuse, fraud and corruption'.[51]

Taking an overview of the rather messy financial and accounting procedures, the CAG said the MS&PI should maintain MP-wise grants-in-aid registers with details of funds released, status of receipts of MPRs, UCs and audit certificates in a computerized format with complete data validation and put it on the official website of the ministry. It said the ministry should build capacity for its MPLADS division by strengthening internal controls and financial discipline in release of funds and expenditure. It said the ministry should ensure that DAs forward the UCs regularly and link the funds flow to complete accounting of funds released.[52]

Inadequate Monitoring of MPLADS and its Consequences

Disappointed with the accounting procedures at the IA, DA and ministry levels, the CAG observed that MPRs were not being received by the MS&PI regularly from the DAs. It found that the ministry was unable to ensure timely receipt of MPRs. Nor was it in a position to use the MPRs received for strategic planning. The auditors were also handicapped because the periodical works completion reports were also not being furnished by the DAs. Here is a sample of what the auditors found. In Andhra Pradesh, the auditors test-checked three districts—Hyderabad, Nellore and Srikakulam—and found that while the DAs had reported to the ministry that 3,913 works had been completed between 2004 and 2009, the number of completed works was actually 2,843. In two districts, while the DAs reported that 360 works were incomplete, the actual number was 1,494. Such discrepancies could be seen in the MPRs as well. As against an expenditure of ₹24.90 crore on completed works in two districts, the MPRs showed that the amount spent was ₹54.41 crore. The auditors noted that between 1 January and 31 December 2009, as many as 9,480 MPRs were to be sent by DAs to the ministry on behalf of 790 MPs. However, the register of MPRs with the ministry showed that only 6,665 were received during this period.[53]

In order to ensure transparency, the DAs are required to upload data on work sanction orders issued on the recommendations made by MPs on the MPLADS website or transmit the same to the ministry by uploading these on the website. However, it was found that of the 11,28,573 works sanctioned since the scheme was launched, details of only 4,83,362 works constituting 43 per cent of the total works had been uploaded by the DAs. In eleven states and UTs, as much as 80 per cent of the works executed had not been put on the website. There were also eight DAs who had not uploaded any information on the website. The auditors said the ministry was not in a position to ensure uploading of data in a timely manner. There were also many data entry errors and other mistakes on the website. The work of updating the website had not been completed because of a shortage of staff at the district level, the ministry said.[54]

The MS&PI and the National Informatics Centre developed software for monitoring MPLADS works since November 2004. The software consists of two modules, one at the district level and the other at the IA level. But, on closer examination, the auditors found many discrepancies in entries. In thousands of cases, they found that no dates were entered for work sanction and commencement or the dates entered were wrong. In other instances, different units were used in the cost column that made the data very confusing. There was also a substantial number of omissions in the database, which meant that data validity checks were absent and the information in the system was incapable of providing any reliable monitoring inputs. The MS&PI claimed that it was aware of the infirmities in the system and that it had issued instructions to DAs to update the website and to remove deficiencies. The auditors were not impressed by the ministry's response. They said that even though the ministry was aware of the deficiencies in the website, it had not taken 'any effective measures to rectify the situation'. They said they could not understand how, without identifying and addressing the issues of data validation checks, the ministry could assure itself of updation and validity of data.[55]

In the light of these findings by the CAG, it is clear that the MS&PI has not been able to monitor the scheme effectively. But, the story of unsatisfactory arrangements to oversee the implementation of this scheme continues at the state and district levels. The scheme guidelines stipulate that every state must have a committee under the chairmanship of the chief secretary or development commissioner to review MPLADS implementation at the state level and that this committee should review the working of this scheme along with the DAs and the MPs. However, the auditors found that since the inception of the scheme, such a committee had not been constituted in three states and UTs (Mizoram, Dadra and Nagar Haveli and Daman and Diu). In fourteen states (Andhra Pradesh, Arunachal Pradesh, Chhattisgarh, Gujarat, Haryana, Himachal Pradesh, Jammu and Kashmir, Jharkhand, Karnataka, Manipur, Tamil Nadu, Tripura, Uttar Pradesh and Uttarakhand), though the monitoring committees were set up, they had not met even once since their constitution. In the remaining eighteen states and UTs, the monitoring committees had on an average less than two meetings in recent years. The MS&PI said that it would 'obtain' information from the states and UTs on why they had not adhered to the guidelines in regard to establishing monitoring committees and convening them at regular intervals. Table 12.4 presents the status of meetings of monitoring committees in thirteen states and five UTs during the years from 2006–07 to 2008–09.[56]

The story of improper supervision extends to the district level as well. The guidelines stipulate that the DA must inspect at least 10 per cent of the works sanctioned under this scheme. It also says that to the extent possible the DAs must involve the MPs in inspection of projects. However, the auditors found that 67 per cent of the DAs which were test-checked by them had not inspected a single work between 2004 and 2009. Twenty-six DAs claimed that they had inspected works but had not maintained any records of inspection. In many DAs, inspections were done but MPs were not present. DAs in Kerala claimed that with the existing staff inspection of even completed works was not possible, let alone inspection of works in progress.

Apart from the absence of monitoring, the DAs were violating another stipulation—that they display the list of all completed and ongoing works under MPLADS in the district office. The auditors found that 40 per cent of the test-checked DAs were not

Table 12.4: Status of meetings of monitoring committees in certain states and UTs.

States/UTs	No. of meeting of the Monitoring Committee		
	2006–07	2007–08	2008–09
Assam	1	1	0
Bihar	0	1	0
Goa	1	1	0
Kerala	0	1	1
Madhya Pradesh	0	1	0
Maharashtra	0	0	1
Meghalaya	0	1	0
Nagaland	0	1	0
Orissa	0	3	2
Punjab	0	1	1
Rajasthan	0	2	0
Sikkim	0	3	0
West Bengal	0	1	1
Andaman and Nicobar Islands	1	2	0
Chandigarh	0	0	2
Delhi	0	0	1
Lakshadweep	1	1	0
Puducherry	1	1	0
Total	5	21	9

(*Source*: Ministry of Statistics and Programme Implementation)

displaying the lists of projects. In Kerala the DAs even claimed that such a display of a list of projects was not possible in view of the large number of works.

The CAG said that lack of monitoring by the DAs indicated 'weak internal controls with a possible adverse effect on the timely execution and quality of works'. However, instead of chiding the DAs for being so irresponsible, the MS&PI seemed to gloss over their failure to monitor MPLADS projects. It said DAs might have 'some constraints' like a shortage of staff, which was leading to non-inspection of works. It said it would issue 'further directions' to all DAs to inspect at least 10 per cent of the works. The auditors were also unhappy with the response of the ministry to their observation about the absence of display boards in district offices. The ministry's response only showed 'inadequate monitoring and lack of pro-active role expected from a funding agency'.

Overall, it seemed that the CAG was frustrated by the ministry's response in regard to the lack of monitoring at the district level. It said this 'only confirms lack of ownership and detached role being played by the ministry'.[57]

Among other deficiencies noted by the auditors was the failure of state governments to train district-level officers who are associated with implementation of the schemes. They found that no arrangements were made for such training in fifteen states and UTs. The ministry claimed that as of April 2010, as many as twenty-seven states and UTs had completed training of district-level officials.[58]

The other deficiency was an absence of plaques at the sites of projects indicating the cost of the project, date of commencement, date of completion and name of the sponsoring MP.

The auditors found that plaques were not erected in 4,918 works costing over ₹100 crore in thirty-one DAs test-checked by them. The ministry took the strange view that there might be instances where plaques erected have been damaged or destroyed by vandals.

Yet another deficiency was inadequate spending by MPs in areas inhabited by Scheduled Castes and Scheduled Tribes. The guidelines require them to spend 15 and 7.5 per cent in SC- and ST- inhabited areas in their constituencies. However, the auditors noted that works sanctioned in these areas amounted to only13.69 per cent in eighteen states and UTs in sampled districts. This was because the MS&PI failed to monitor spending in these areas. The CAG also reported the lack of an internal audit in 17 states and UTs. Strangely, the internal audit wing of the MS&PI claimed that an internal audit of the scheme had never been conducted since the inception of the scheme in 1993–94.[59]

After reviewing all this, the CAG said the MS&PI should strengthen internal controls as well as monitoring mechanisms and establish a system that is sensitive to known shortcomings of the scheme. 'Accountability for maintenance of records at various levels should be prescribed and monitored.' Further, the monitoring committee in each state and UT should meet once a year with the participation of MPs 'to enhance accountability of DAs' and DAs should regularly inspect MPLADS works along with the MP concerned. 'All works with an estimated cost of ₹5 lakhs should be inspected by the DA. Failure to do so should be viewed as dereliction of duty and action initiated accordingly against the official.' The auditors also said 'a robust and regular internal audit system should be immediately put in place both at the Ministry and state levels.'[60]

Even as it made these suggestions, the CAG did not hide its disgust in regard to the attitude of the Union government and the governments in the states to the issue of monitoring. It said, 'The facts regarding callous approach to monitoring mechanism and more so to the routine reply indicated lack of governance at both Centre and State levels.' Can there be a greater indictment of the governments than this? Beginning in 2011–12, the spending on MPLADS will more than double and touch nearly ₹4,000 crore annually, but as is obvious in the reports of the CAG, a credible monitoring system is not in place at the district, state and national levels. However, there is no guilt either at the Centre or in the states over the flouting of guidelines. In this scenario, does it make sense to pump in more money into MPLADS?[61]

In conclusion, the CAG said the execution of substantial numbers of DAs on MPs' recommendations indicates inadequate systemic arrangements for ensuring effective use of funds for creation of community-based assets. 'The implementation of works was further characterized by delays, non-adherence to the rules/guidelines, unfruitful expenditure, abandonment of works or non-utilisation, poor maintenance and misuse of assets created.' Further, state governments have a limited role to play in the implementation of the scheme, and the responsibility for monitoring its execution by DAs is primarily with the ministry. The ministry, however, failed to obtain and analyse basic records such as UCs and audited accounts from DAs. The database on the progress of the scheme was 'incomplete, out-of-date and characterized by numerous discrepancies and omissions, making it of little use in monitoring the scheme'. Yet another anomaly was that while the DAs were responsible for implementing the scheme, they were not accountable to an immediate monitoring authority. The MS&PI had the responsibility to monitor the scheme but without the requisite authority to enforce compliance. Accountability of DAs to the state nodal agencies has not been defined in the guidelines. Monitoring of the scheme by the state governments was limited to annual meetings of the Monitoring Committee, 'which too were either not held or not held regularly'. The CAG also noted that to every audit finding, the ministry's response was that it would obtain information from the DAs. 'This indicated not only lack of ownership but also absence of a robust monitoring framework.' In conclusion, the CAG said that many of the systemic weaknesses affecting the implementation of MPLADS had been persisting since its inception seventeen years ago. The lapses were brought to the notice of the ministry in two earlier CAG reports of 1998 and 2001 and the MS&PI took eight years to respond to the observations of the auditors and this 'speaks volumes about the monitoring methods'. Given that many of the weaknesses noted in this audit have been persisting for years, 'any drastic improvement in the implementation of the scheme appears unlikely'. Therefore, the CAG said the ministry should 'carefully review and evaluate the benefits of the scheme' keeping in view the objectives, operational guidelines, actual implementation and the report of the auditors and to take a view regarding continued implementation of the scheme'.[62]

In other words, the CAG was virtually telling the ministry that the time had come to scrap the scheme, since the ministry neither had the wherewithal nor the inclination to implement the scheme as per the guidelines and to ensure full accountability for the expenditure of thousands of crores of public money every year.

How the Government Treats Reports of the CAG

While completing the third major audit of MPLADS in 2009, the CAG was constrained to observe that many of the deficiencies in the execution of this scheme persisted even eleven years after the first audit of the scheme in 1998 and eight years after the second audit in 2001. It was also disappointed to note that the government had not set matters right even though the auditors had drawn its attention to specific areas which needed immediate attention. The CAG said that 'many of the shortcomings, such as execution of various inadmissible/prohibited works, execution of works without recommendation of the MP, incomplete/abandoned works, or regularities in award of contract, delays in sanction of works and completion thereof etc ... pointed out in these two reports persisted (till the current audit)' in 2009.

The auditors noted that the ministry took eight years to send the final Action Taken Note (ATN) on the CAG's report of 2001. As per this ATN, the ministry sent out instructions to the nodal departments in each state and to the DAs and asked them to comply with the audit findings. 'However, the ministry did not mention how it had ensured adherence to its instructions by the DAs. The recurrence of similar shortcomings and lapses on the part of DAs indicated that while the Ministry delayed taking action on these reports, the DAs failed to adhere to the instructions issued by the Ministry.' This was a serious indictment of the ministry by the auditors, and the MS & PI responded with some unconvincing explanations.[63]

The ministry tried to explain away the inordinate delay in submitting its ATNs on the two previous audit reports by claiming that it could not do so because of incomplete replies from the DAs. However, since it is the nodal department that dispenses the funds under MPLADS and since the entire scheme is to be managed and monitored by it, it did not say how it would ensure that in future, it would make DAs comply with the guidelines and its instructions. The replies of the MS & PI to the CAG seemed to indicate that it was just a helpless entity which mechanically disbursed funds every half year without the power to ensure that the DAs spent these funds prudently and as per the guidelines and rules governing the scheme. The ministry's responses also hinted at its reluctance to enforce discipline in the utilization of these funds. It appeared as if the ministry was afraid of acting with clarity and firmness in this regard, lest it annoy the 790 MPs in the country. With such an attitude, which smacks of pusillanimity, one wonders how the Union government can effectively monitor the scheme.

The only silver lining, however, was the ministry's promise, after much prodding by the auditors, that the guidelines would be further amended based on the observations of the CAG to make it more pragmatic. 'The revised guidelines led to the removal of the limit of ₹25 lakhs on individual works to be executed by government departments Agencies, deletion of the illustrative list of permissible items, clear demarcation of the role of the implementing Agency, District Authority, State Government and the Government of India. The guidelines include development of areas inhabited by Scheduled Castes and Scheduled Tribes and special provision for natural calamities, education and cultural development.'[64]

It made bold to claim that in order to avoid a recurrence of lapses and shortcomings in the schemes, it was resorting to the system of inquiry into misappropriation of MPLADS funds; fixing responsibility on the officials concerned found guilty of irregularities; taking disciplinary action against the officials for recouping the funds incurred on inadmissible work including suspected fraud cases.

The ministry also said that it had noted the view of the Supreme Court's judgement in *Bhim Singh* v. *Union of India* in which the court said that efforts must be made to ensure that the accountability regime provided in the scheme becomes robust. The persistence of shortcomings pointed out by the audit underlined the significance of shortcomings pointed out in the observations of the court, it said. The ministry also confessed that the audit findings showed that more than the changes in guidelines, accountability concerns were required to be addressed 'by more useful methods of monitoring'. Given the fact that all the three audit reports constitute a serious indictment of the manner in which the scheme has been implemented and monitored, the MS&PI will have to take urgent steps to set matters right, specially in the light of such confessionals on its part.[65] However, even two years after the latest audit, there was nothing to show that the ministry was ensuring greater diligence in the implementation of the scheme.

How Funds of Former Rajya Sabha MPs are Distributed

The CAG examined the issue of leftover funds of former Rajya Sabha MPs in its 2009 report. The scheme says unspent balances of former members of the Rajya Sabha from a state should be equally distributed among the successor MPs from that state. However, auditors found that unspent balances of ₹82.54 crore left by predecessor MPs in ten states had not been distributed among the successor MPs of the states.

The non-distribution was highest in Maharashtra (₹39.67 crore), followed by Jammu and Kashmir, Gujarat, West Bengal and Haryana, where the unspent balances per state ranged from ₹8 crore to ₹10 crore.

Also, there were aberrations in distribution of unspent balances like in Chhattisgarh. The DA, Bilaspur, distributed the unspent balance of ₹0.62 crore between two members of the Rajya Sabha from that state, though all five members of that state were entitled to it.[66]

Natural Calamities

The guidelines permit MPs to contribute towards rehabilitation work in the event of a calamity of a severe nature in any part of the country. The auditors of the CAG have reported in 2009 that twelve DAs from different states released ₹6.61 crore to the Andaman and Nicobar Islands, Puducherry and Tamil Nadu during 2005–07 for tsunami relief. However, the DAs who had received these funds, which were donations from MPs hailing from other states, had not sent the UCs regarding utilization of these sums to the DAs which had sent them the funds. The auditors saw this as yet another instance of 'absence of internal control mechanism'.[67]

What the CAG Had to Say About Implementation of MPLADS

Some of the major findings of this audit of MPLADS conducted in 2009 by the CAG are as follows: The scheme does not ensure participation of constituents such as resident fora, local bodies, NGOs, etc., in determining works responsive to locally felt needs; there are several loopholes in the sanctioning process; funds are misused for the construction of offices, residential buildings, etc.; funds are misused for augmenting the infrastructure of societies and trusts in violation of guidelines; and although they are prohibited from doing so, some MPs choose the IAs.

There were weaknesses in the sanction process. For example, the auditors found 700 works costing ₹9.45 crore without receiving any recommendations from the MPs concerned. In three states, the district authorities executed works costing ₹2.44 crore on the recommendation of representatives of the MPs rather than the MPs themselves. In seven states, auditors found 260 works which had cost ₹2.49 crore more than the cost sanctioned by the MP.

The scheme does not permit expenditure on the construction of offices, residential buildings of government departments and cooperative societies, works which benefit commercial organizations, individuals or a family and works within the premises of religious institutions. Yet, in a hundred sampled districts of twenty-nine states and UTs, the auditors found that an expenditure of ₹73.76 crore was incurred on 2,340 such works between 2004 and 2009.

In ten states, a sum of ₹14.40 crore was sanctioned for works pertaining to thirty-four trusts and societies which exceeded the ceiling of ₹25 lakh per trust/society fixed under the scheme, by ₹5.90 crore. In seven states the district authorities sanctioned a sum of ₹5.94 crore to 145 trusts and societies which were either ineligible as per the scheme guidelines or whose eligibility had not been verified by the DAs.

MPs have not been assigned any role in the selection of IAs as per the guidelines. Yet, in nine states and UTs, the MPs had given the names of the IAs along with their recommendations and recommended the release of funds directly to the user agency in respect of 8,746 works.

In eleven states and UTs, the auditors found that 305 incomplete works costing ₹8.50 crore had been abandoned or suspended, thereby rendering the expenditure incurred on these works unfruitful.

Basic internal control records such as assets registers and works registers which ensure accountability structures within the scheme were missing in a number of instances with 90 per cent of the audited district authorities not maintaining assets/works registers. In five states and UTs, works costing approximately ₹3 crore were not put to intended use or were not being used for the purpose for which they were sanctioned.

The utilization of funds every year ranged between 37.43 per cent and 52.44 per cent of the funds made available to the DAs, thereby leaving substantial closing balances (₹1,788 crore to 2,137 crore) in various bank accounts outside the consolidated fund of the Union and the states. The expenditure under the scheme had a propensity to increase at the times closer to elections, while during the intervening period, funds tended to accumulate.

The release of funds to DAs by the MS&PI was not always in accordance with the conditions laid down in the guidelines. Funds were released to many DAs despite substantial unspent balances in their accounts, resulting in excess release of funds. The auditors also noticed cases of diversion of funds, release of advances to IAs in excess of the prescribed limit and non-refund of unspent balances by the IAs.

The unspent balances of 82.54 crore left by predecessor Rajya Sabha MPs in ten states had not been distributed among the successor Rajya Sabha MPs of those states, rendering them idle.

The MS&PI could not ensure proper and timely receipt of MPRs, which were required to be used for strategic planning and to prepare the details of fund release and expenditure. About 58 per cent of the MPRs available with the ministry were more than two months old.

The scheme guidelines stipulated e-monitoring, using the MPLADS web portal. However, as on 31 March 2009, details of only 43 per cent of completed works were uploaded on the website of MPLADS by the district authorities. The database, too, was characterized by a number of omissions and errors rendering it unreliable.

The auditors also found that in three states and UTs, the monitoring committees to review MPLADS had not been constituted. In fourteen states, the committees had been constituted but they had never met. In the remaining eighteen states and UTs, they did not meet annually.

While the DAs were required to inspect at least 10 per cent of the sanctioned works, eighty-six DAs in twenty-three states and UTs that were audited had not inspected any work during 2004–09.[68]

What the Auditors Recommend

Following the fairly exhaustive audit of MPLADS across 128 districts in thirty-five states and UTs by the Comptroller and Auditor General, the CAG made the following recommendations:

The MS&PI should maintain an MP-wise grants-in-aid register with details of funds released, the status of receipt of MPRs, UCs and audit certificates in a computerized format with complete data validation and place it on the official website of the ministry for monitoring the fund utilization under the scheme.

The ministry should build the capacity of its MPLADS division by strengthening internal controls and financial discipline in release and expenditure under the scheme for timely remedial action.

The ministry should ensure complete documentation at all levels. Maintenance of records such as works registers, muster rolls, measurement books, works completion reports, cash books, etc., at the DA/IA level as required under PWD manuals should be monitored closely.

The ministry should ensure that DAs forward UCs regularly. Fund flow should be linked to complete accounting of the funds released.

The cases of excess/avoidable/doubtful payments pointed out in this report may be examined and recoveries made from individuals/agencies responsible for overpayment. In the cases of delayed completion of works, where the scheme guidelines stipulate the levy of penalty, it should be imposed.

DAs should be held accountable for taking up works that are not permitted under the scheme.

Suitable action may be taken against agencies responsible for incomplete or delayed works, especially in cases where non-completion has resulted in abandonment of works.[69]

Findings of the CAG

As can be seen from the performance audit report of the CAG, the conclusions arrived at by the auditors constituted a comprehensive indictment of those who are responsible for the management of this scheme. One must wait and see what the MS&PI has to say in response to these findings. Going by the lackadaisical response of the ministry to the two previous audits, one is well advised to keep the threshold of expectations rather low.

The MS&PI submitted ATNs on the CAG's report of 1998 only in November 2009, after a good eleven years. The ATNs for the CAG's report of 2001 were submitted in December 2009, after a lapse of eight years. But even this belated 'Action-taken Report' fell far short of the expectation of the auditors. The CAG said the ATNs submitted by the government 'reveals that even this response was based on compiled data received from the states' meaning that the ministry had just done a cut-and-paste job of responses sent in by the states. The CAG said the ministry did not furnish any reply to the conclusion drawn in the audit report presented in 2001 to the effect that 'in its present form, the scheme, which was in operation since December 1993 had hardly served its main objective and the Central Government needed to have a thorough review of the arrangements for the implementation of the scheme.'[70]

However, since the Union government has decided to raise the corpus for MPLADS by 150 per cent, one hopes the ministry realizes that it will be disbursing close to one billion US dollars every year towards MPLADS. By any standard, this is a lot of money and it certainly warrants far greater diligence in utilization of funds and management of the scheme itself. This will mean strict measures to correct the anomalies found by the auditors in 2009, failing which there could be a 150 per cent jump in the amount of MPLADS funds that is squandered away each year.

This can be averted if the MS&PI pays heed to the recommendations of the CAG in regard to strengthening financial discipline, better control of funds, improved documentation at all levels, maintenance of records in respect of each work under the scheme, imposition of penalties on IAs that violate the guidelines, suitable action against agencies responsible for delays or incomplete work, and making the DAs accountable for taking up works under this scheme.

The MPs have succeeded in securing a spectacular hike in the corpus. The people, therefore, have a right to demand that there be a corresponding improvement in the commitment of MPs to spend these sums judiciously, keeping in mind the guidelines and the larger public good in their constituencies.

NOTES

1. Report number 31 of 2010–11, Comptroller and Auditor General of India, p. vii.
2. Ibid., p. 7.
3. Ibid., p. 3.
4. Ibid.
5. Ibid., p. 5.
6. Ibid., p. 9.
7. Ibid., pp. 9–10.
8. Ibid., p. 15.
9. Ibid., p. 17.
10. Ibid., Table 4.1, p. 15.
11. Ibid., pp. 18–19.
12. Ibid.
13. Ibid., p. 20.
14. Ibid., p. 20.

15 Ibid., p. 21.
16 Ibid., p. 21.
17 Ibid., pp. 21–22.
18 Ibid., p. 23.
19 Ibid., p. 25.
20 Ibid., p. 23.
21 Ibid., p. 25.
22 Ibid., p. 26.
23 Ibid., pp. 26–27.
24 Ibid., pp. 27–28.
25 Ibid., p. 29.
26 Ibid., p. 29.
27 Ibid., p. 30.
28 Ibid., pp. 9–11.
29 Ibid., p. 10.
30 Ibid., p. 15.
31 Ibid., p. 11.
32 Ibid., Annexure 3.3, p. 71.
33 Ibid., pp. 11–12.
34 Ibid., p. 13.
35 Ibid., pp. 12–13.
36 Ibid., pp. 13–14.
37 Ibid., p. 15.
38 Ibid., p. 31.
39 Ibid.
40 Ibid., pp. 32–33.
41 Ibid., p. 34.
42 Ibid., p. 34.
43 Ibid., p. 36.
44 Ibid., pp. 36–37.
45 Ibid., pp. 37–39.
46 Ibid., pp. 42–45.
47 Ibid., p. 39.
48 Ibid., pp. 39–40.
49 Ibid., p. 40.
50 Ibid., pp. 40–41.
51 Ibid., p. 45.

52 Ibid., p. 46.
53 Ibid., p. 48.
54 Ibid., p. 49.
55 Ibid., p. 51.
56 Ibid., pp. 52–53.
57 Ibid., p. 54.
58 Ibid., p. 53.
59 Ibid., pp. 55–56.
60 Ibid., p. 57.
61 Ibid., pp. 52–53.
62 Ibid., pp. 59–60.
63 Ibid., pp. 51–52.
64 Ibid., p. 51.
65 Ibid., p. 52.
66 Ibid., p. 41.
67 Ibid., p. 40.
68 Ibid., pp. ix–xi.
69 Ibid., pp. xi–xii.
70 Ibid., p. 7.

13

What Independent Surveys Say About MPLADS

The MS&PI presented the first comprehensive report on MPLADS in 2006, thirteen years after the programme was launched. This became possible only after the software for monitoring MPLADS works at the district level was developed and launched in November 2004. Prior to this, only macro-level information was available on the physical and financial aspects of the scheme. The launch of the software not only ensured e-governance but also transparency and accountability at the district level because it enabled the people to get information on works sanctioned, costs, implementation status, etc.

The report presented a year-wise distribution of funds since the launch of the scheme in 1993–94. The analysis of various aspects of the scheme and the tabulation of data on a variety of issues including sanction of funds, utilization, nature of works recommended by MPs, and sector-wise and state-wise implementation of the programme enabled the media, civil society and parliamentarians themselves to get an idea of where this scheme was headed.

Since then, the MS&PI has been submitting annual reports

on the status of the programme. The report for the year 2008–09 provides the latest information on allocation of funds for MPLADS since its inception. This table shows that the scheme took off with a modest allocation of ₹37.80 crores in 1993–94 and this had risen to ₹1,580 crore in 2008–09. Overall, in the sixteen years since inception, the total outgo from the Union government's coffers towards MPLADS stood at ₹19,425.75 crore, which at current foreign exchange rates works out to about US$3.6 billion.

The year-wise and cumulative release of funds right from the beginning till the close of the financial year 2008–2009 is presented in Table 13.1 [1]

Table 13.1: Year–wise release of MPLADS funds

MPLADS Funds Released (₹/in Crore)		
Year	Funds Released	Cumulative Release
1993–94	37.80	37.80
1994–95	771.00	808.80
1995–96	763.00	1571.80
1996–97	778.00	2349.80
1997–98	488.00	2837.80
1998–99	789.50	3627.30
1999–2000	1390.50	5017.80
2000–01	2080.00	7097.80
2001–02	1800.00	8897.80
2002–03	1600.00	10497.80
2003–04	1682.00	12179.80
2004–05	1310.00	13489.80
2005–06	1433.90	14923.70
2006–07	1451.50	16375.20
2007–08	1470.55	17845.75
2008–09	**1580.00**	**19425.75**

The government has reported that the utilization of funds under MPLADS has risen since the commencement of the fiscal year 2004–05. In the five-year period since then, the government released ₹7,245.95 crores whereas ₹8,318.02 crore had been spent on various works. The expenditure is higher because of the spillover of funds from the previous years. Since these funds do not lapse and since the gestation period for many programmes is long, expenditure in a particular fiscal year is always higher than the allocation. In 2008–09, utilization was 114.80 per cent of the fund released.

During this five-year period, 4.36 lakh works were recommended by MPs. Of these 3.87 lakh works were sanctioned and 4.29 lakh works were completed. Here again, the works completed exceed the works sanctioned because of the carry-over of projects from previous years.

In the fiscal year 2008–09, the government released the entire allocation of ₹1,580 crore. Reports from the districts showed that the expenditure during this year was ₹1,724.01 crore, which meant utilization of 109.11 per cent.[2]

These reports provide extensive information in regard to guidelines, changes in rules, the national implementation status and state-wise data on the working of the scheme. For example, the analysis done by the ministry in its first report shows that in the first thirteen years, 39 per cent of the funds were utilized for building roads, pathways and bridges, 18 per cent were spent on improving educational facilities and 8 per cent towards drinking water schemes. 'Other public facilities' took up 20 per cent. The ministry arrived at this estimate on the basis of information it obtained from 369 of the 428 nodal districts in the country for 1.34 lakh works costing ₹2,380.71 crore. In order to step up monitoring, the MS&PI has been urging state governments to utilize the software and upload data from all districts. These reminders have resulted in better compliance and data entry for 4.85 lakh works based on 1,732 recommendations by MPs which have been uploaded by DAs from 420 of the 430 nodal districts by the end of the year 2008–09.[3]

The sector-wise distribution of works under MPLADS until 2005–06 is presented in Table 13.2.[4]

Table 13.2: Sector-wise distribution of works under MPLADS till 2005–06

Sectors	Cost of works sanctioned (₹ in crore)	Percentage Distribution of cost of works sanctioned	Number of works sanctioned
Drinking Water Facility	195.10	0.08	20,163
Education	422.19	0.18	20,310
Electricity Facility	69.66	0.03	5,734
Health and Family Welfare	72.96	0.03	1,952
Irrigation	79.90	0.03	2,991
Non-Conventional Energy Sources	1.33	0.001	74
Other Public Facilities	474.54	0.20	30,023
Road, Pathways and Bridges	916.70	0.39	45,828
Sanitation and Public Health	64.26	0.03	3,916
Sports	37.18	0.02	1,532
Total	**2,380.71**	**1.00**	**1,34,090**

This sector-wise distribution of works has undergone a change over the years, because of changing priorities at the constituency level and changes in guidelines permitting items of expenditure which were hitherto prohibited. By the end of the financial year 2008–09, the allocation for roads, pathways and bridges had declined to 31.97 per cent, whereas 'other public facilities' took up 28.32 per cent. Education and drinking water facilities were allocated 16.29 per cent and 10.85 per cent respectively. This changed sector-wise distribution of works on all-India basis till the end of the financial year 2008–09 is presented in Figure 13.1.[5]

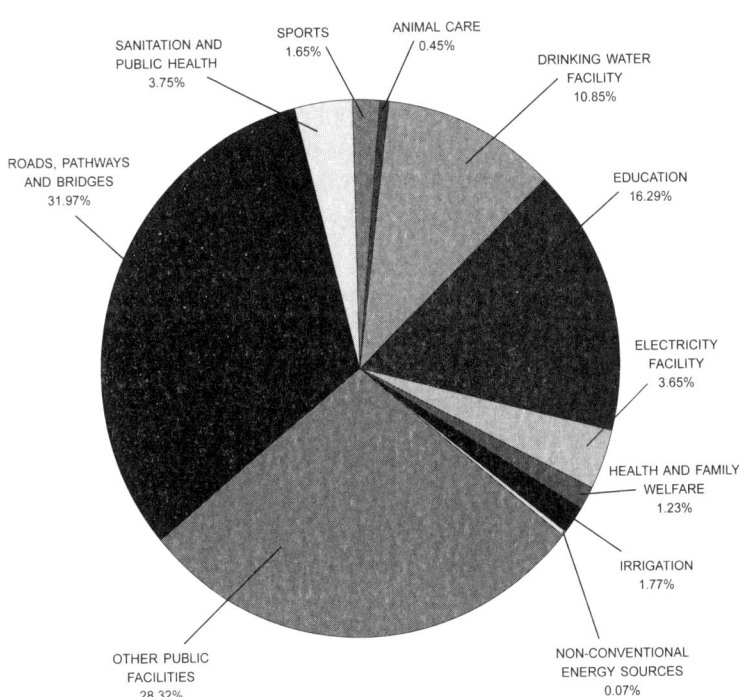

Figure 13.1 Sector-wise distribution of works (all-India) till 2008–09.

Monitoring MPLADS

Since the inception of MPLADS, the two Houses of Parliament and the MS&PI have been resorting to ad hoc monitoring of the scheme via committee meetings, annual review meetings and occasional field visits. For example, the Minister of State in the MS&PI visited West Bengal and Bihar along with senior officials of the ministry to assess the implementation of the scheme in

2008–09. During the year, ministry officials reviewed the scheme in Jharkhand and Arunachal Pradesh. The year also saw two review meetings taken by the minister of state in the MS & PI with secretaries in charge of nodal departments for MPLADS in states and UTs.[6]

However, although thousands of crores of rupees are spent on MPLADS, the MS & PI had no mechanism to regularly monitor the works executed all over the country. It also did not have a mechanism to get a feedback from the constituencies. This was seen as a major lacuna by the Planning Commission and the CAG. In order to address this problem, at least partially, the government felt that it should ensure physical monitoring and verification of at least a sample of MPLADS projects in selected districts by an independent agency. This process was set in motion during the fiscal year 2007–08 with the government hiring the NABARD Consultancy Services (NABCONS) to monitor the works and 'to have a fairly comprehensive assessment 'of the scheme and 'to have a feedback mechanism for course corrections' in implementation. NABCONS was asked to see whether MPLADS funds were being utilized for works for which they are meant; to check the general quality of works created; and to check whether all parameters have been taken into account while sanctioning and executing MPLADS.[7]

NABCONS was asked to send out teams 'to check the general quality of assets (created), nature of ownership, maintenance and upkeep of assets, whether all requisite clearances have been obtained, the impact of the works from social, environmental and other angles, time of sanctioning and completion of the assets, furnishing of utilization and completion certificates, present usage etc.'. This organization was asked to sample fifty completed works in each selected district with the sample including works launched in different years, works involving low and high budgets, works pertaining to trusts and societies and works in different sectors such as drinking water, education, electricity, health and family welfare, and irrigation, etc. The sample was also to include works proposed by both Lok Sabha and Rajya Sabha members.[8]

According to the MS&PI, the monitoring agency covered thirty districts in the country in 2007–08 and forty-three districts in 2008–09. NABCONS has reported on the best practices followed by some DAs in implementing the scheme as also on the shortcomings it has observed. It has reported on the sanction of non-eligible works, delays, grant of funds to NGOs which do not qualify for MPLADS funds, non-availability of works-related data, lack of maintenance of assets, etc. In their overall assessment of the implementation of the scheme in forty-three districts covered in the second phase of the appraisal, NABCONS have said:

> Field studies revealed a mix of positive and negative aspects in implementation, with the positive aspects outweighing the negative aspects; good response from people to continuance of MPLADS; quality of works generally observed to be 'good' or 'satisfactory'; overwhelming perception of local community (90 to 100 per cent) was that MPLADS has had 'a very positive impact'; the scheme has fulfilled the objective of meeting the expectations of the people 'in a decentralized, participatory manner'; the benefits have generally accrued to all sections of the society; conflicts in regard to sharing the benefits of the scheme and access to facilities created were 'insignificant'. As general social participation is ensured from the conceptual stage itself for each project and it has become 'a characteristic feature of the scheme in all the districts'.[9]

Assessing the impact of MPLADS, the government is of the view that since inception, the scheme has 'immensely benefited the local community through the creation of durable assets'. It said that NABCONS' overall assessment was that there had been a 'generally good response' to the scheme and the overwhelming perception of local communities (90–100 per cent) was that the scheme had had 'a very positive impact'.

NABCONS has also reported that at the macro-level, the achievement of MPLADS appears incomparable with other schemes, in that it is the only scheme at the all-India level which focuses on a decentralized approach to scheme implementation based on involvement of local communities, groups and individuals right from the stage of identification of works/facilities as per the felt needs of the people. With about 10.40 lakh works completed by utilizing the funds worth about ₹19,000 crore since inception, the impact of the scheme on the local economy and social dynamics of the communities in rural and urban areas 'is perceived to be substantial', it reported.

However, even as it hailed the scheme, NABCONS chose to hedge its bets when it said that the scheme had left 'a mix of largely positive and few negative aspects in the process of implementation'. The MS&PI is of the view that the best feature of the scheme is the involvement of people in identification of schemes. This decentralized approach and the funding of minor works crucial to communities make this scheme 'incomparable' to other schemes. Yet, 'maintenance (of completed projects) was an area of concern to a great level.'[10]

NOTES

1. Annual Report, 2008–09, Members of Parliament Local Area Development Scheme (MPLADS), Ministry of Statistics and Programme Implementation, Government of India, New Delhi, p. 15.
2. Ibid., p. 18.
3. Ibid., p. 22.
4. Table 2.4.1, p. 28, First Report, Members of Parliament Local Area Development Scheme (MPLADS), Ministry of Statistics and Programme Implementation, Government of India, New Delhi, December 2006.

5   Annual Report, 2008–09, Members of Parliament Local Area Development Scheme (MPLADS), Ministry of Statistics and Programme Implementation, Government of India, New Delhi, p. 23.
6   Annual Report, 2008-09, Members of Parliament Local Area Development Scheme (MPLADS), Ministry of Statistics and Programme Implementation, Government of India, New Delhi, p.23.
7   Ibid., p. 24.
8   Ibid., p. 25.
9   Ibid., p. 26.
10 Ibid., p. 210.

14

MPLADS and Accountability

This broad survey of the working of MPLADS over the last eighteen years has thrown up a host of issues. While many of them will be dealt with in the concluding chapter, the issue of ethics and privileges will need to be touched upon separately, in view of the widening role of MPs, the increase in the corpus for MPLADS and the substantial body of evidence regarding infringement of rules and guidelines vis-à-vis this scheme.

Over the years, Indian MPs have become a pampered lot. Although the need for an enforceable code of conduct for MPs was felt six decades ago, Parliament never got down to drafting and enforcing such a code and to lay down an ethical framework for the conduct of parliamentarians. However, there was no such lethargy when it came to expanding the privileges of MPs. Anxious to keep MPs happy, every government has done its bit to widen their perks and privileges. The launch of MPLADS and the increase in the annual allocation per MP from ₹1 crore to ₹5 crore is probably the most obvious example of how MPs are pampered. However, there would be less criticism of schemes of this kind if only there was even a quarter of this enthusiasm to enforce ethics. Parliamentarians fail to realize that the credibility of Parliament remains intact only when privileges and ethics are seen as two sides of the same coin. While they clamour for more privileges, their hackles are raised when people demand that the concept of accountability ought to keep pace with the burgeoning privileges of MPs.

Two developments in the second half of 2011 throw light on this problem and also alerts citizens to the dangers that lie ahead if a proper regime of accountability is not put in place and if there is no credible arrangement for an effective oversight of the conduct of MPs.

The first of these events, which should raise the red flag in the public mind, is the report of the Lok Sabha Committee on MPLADS, which was tabled in the House in August 2011, some months after the finance minister, Mr Pranab Mukherjee, announced the government's decision to enhance the allocation under the scheme to ₹5 crore per annum per MP. However, anyone hoping for some correlation between higher spending and better accountability will be sorely disappointed. What emerges from this report is that while the committee takes umbrage at the Union government's opinion that the role of the two parliamentary committees overseeing the scheme is only 'advisory', all this indignation dissipates in the face of evidence of a gross violation of the scheme's guidelines by MPs. This report of the committee on 'Effective Monitoring of MPLAD Scheme to Avoid Delays in Execution of MPLADS Works', is, therefore, a study in contrast.[1]

The other development, which should put citizens on alert, is the angry reactions of MPs to the statement of the rural development minister, Mr Jairam Ramesh, on the social audit of MPLADS. Responding to complaints from MPs about corruption in the implementation of the Mahatma Gandhi National Rural Employment Generation Scheme (MGNREGS)—the flagship social sector programme launched by the United Progressive Alliance (UPA) government at the Centre—the minister said those who bandied such allegations were not open to the idea of subjecting MPLADS spending to a social audit. 'Whenever there is criticism of MGNREGS in Parliament, I say if the same social audit was there for MPLADS then it would be good for the country. But they (MPs) are not ready for social audit of MPLADS,' Mr Ramesh said at a public function in New Delhi. He also hinted that the complaints about the rural employment scheme had something to do with the desire of MPs to have control over spending under this head in their constituencies. 'MPs want that all the works are conducted with their consent... Their intention is different'.[2]

While MPs reacted angrily to the minister's comments, the idea of a social audit of MPLADS was welcomed by just one political party—the Communist Party of India (Marxist). It is also the only political party which has consistently demanded that MPLADS be scrapped.

The Press Trust of India quoted the party's leader Mr Sitaram Yechury as saying, 'The money that has been spent by the MPs must be subjected to a social audit. This is public money and it needs to be under public scrutiny.' The communist leader said such an audit would be in national interest. However, whenever he had mooted the idea in Parliament, the MPs were not ready for it. Referring to his party's stand, he said, 'CPM is the only party, which has maintained that MPLADS must be scrapped. The job of the MPs actually is to keep vigilance on the executive. That is what a legislature is supposed to do apart from making laws and drawing attention of the country and the government to the issues of public importance.'[3]

But, such support for the idea of a social audit of the scheme was the exception, rather than the rule. The general mood of MPs is always lukewarm when it comes to a proper audit of privileges, facilities and schemes that are tailored for them. 'How dare you?' would be their instinctive response to such proposals but they do not say so in so many words. They prefer to lend lip service to the idea of scrutiny but quietly and diplomatically quash the idea before it ever takes off. This view of MPs was angrily articulated by Mr Shivanand Tiwari, member of the Rajya Sabha and a leader of the Janata Dal (United). He demanded a 'public apology' from the minister and claimed that the government had never proposed to conduct a social audit of the expenditure under MPLADS. 'I am curious to know as to when the government proposed to conduct a social audit of expenditure under the MPLAD scheme. More than that, when did MPs reject this demand? MPs are not opposed to any audit of MPLAD scheme', the MP told *The Indian Express*. The newspaper reported that he even threatened to move a privilege motion against Mr Ramesh if he failed to substantiate his remarks. He accused the minister of being in the habit of making statements 'to project himself holier than other MPs'.[4]

While this episode provides citizens a glimpse of how MPs respond when the people ask them to be accountable, the report of the Lok Sabha Committee on MPLADS referred to earlier provides evidence of another kind, which is equally troubling. It tells us how inadequate the oversight arrangements are when it comes to spending MPLADS funds. More importantly, it tells us how disinterested committees of Parliament can be when faced with evidence of misuse of these funds and gross violation of guidelines by MPs.

The chairman and members of the Lok Sabha Committee on MPLADs seem to get all worked up about what they perceive to be a downgrading of their role by the government. However they become tongue-tied when presented with data which shows their colleagues in poor light. This attitude of the committee is truly worrisome now that around ₹4,000 crore will be allocated to this scheme annually from the fiscal year 2011–12.

The committee, which was examining the issue of effective monitoring of the scheme, summoned officials in the MS & PI to understand how the government monitored the scheme. It also had before it a sample of field reports from several states by an agency (NABCONS) hired by the ministry to sample some of the works executed under the scheme. How it deals with these two issues is at once revealing and disturbing.

The report begins with the committee expressing its anger

over the wording of para 6.1 of the guidelines which says the committee's role is to advise the nodal ministry at the Centre and the opinion of the secretary, MS&PI, that the two parliamentary committees overseeing MPLADS are only 'advisory committees'. The members of this committee, who obviously perceive themselves more as monitors than advisors, are so livid about the description of their role in the guidelines that they say this provision is 'derogatory and uncalled for' and that it has been incorporated 'in utter disregard of the status of Parliament in our polity'. The committee accuses the MS&PI of having incorporated this in the guidelines 'for its own convenience' and says it deprecates 'the callous attitude and approach of the ministry in the matter'. The committee, therefore, directs the ministry to reword para 6.1 of the guidelines as follows: 'There are two separate committees of Parliament (Rajya Sabha and Lok Sabha) on Members of Parliament Local Area Development Scheme to review periodically the performance and problems in the implementation of MPLAD Scheme, to consider complaints of Members of Lok Sabha/Rajya Sabha (as the case may be) in regard to the implementation of the Scheme and to perform such other functions in respect of effective and efficient functioning of the MPLAD Scheme as may be assigned to it by the Speaker/Chairman (as the case may be) from time to time.'[5]

As regards monitoring, the committee had a long list of complaints about the manner in which the MS&PI was supervising the implementation of the scheme. Some of them are: The ministry does not analyse the MPRs submitted by the DAs and take action against those who delay projects; perusal of the minutes of the biannual review meetings held by the ministry shows a 'lack of seriousness'. 'It appears that these meetings are being held more as a bi-annual ritual rather than as a serious business for effective implementation of the scheme,' it says, adding that visits by senior officers of the ministry to the states every quarter to review the working of the scheme and to visit sites were not 'result oriented'.[6]

In fact, the report constitutes a damning indictment of the MS & PI for its failure to monitor the scheme at various levels. The committee was equally disappointed with the attitude of state governments vis-à-vis the scheme. The committee toured five states during 2010–11. Four of these states had not furnished any information on inspections conducted by state-level officers. Further, none of the states visited by the committee provided details of reviews of MPLADS projects by district officials. The report of NABCONS after a sample survey shows that in 60 per cent of the cases, no structured and specific inspection is carried out by district officials, nor are there proper records of inspections. It has, therefore, recommended that a provision be made in the guidelines that the implementing agencies must maintain a works register giving details of the physical and financial progress of the works undertaken. These registers should also provide details of spot inspections made by the IAs.[7]

This committee also considered the report of NABCONS, which had done a sample survey in 133 districts of the country in three phases of monitoring. The committee was thrilled to note the agency's opinion that the scheme had 'resulted in creation of fairly good quality assets towards economic and social infrastructure'. The sample survey showed that 86 per cent of the works monitored by it had a 'positive impact' on the local community.[8]

The sample survey also listed a wide range of violations of the scheme's guidelines, but the committee chose to ignore evidence that directly implicated MPs. Instead, it sought to highlight aspects of the report which showed the IAs or monitoring agencies in poor light. For example, it referred to delays in the sanction and execution of works, poor maintenance of MPLADS assets, non-erection of plaques at work sites, etc., and said a separate cell must be created in the MPLADS division in the ministry 'to monitor such violations'. Similarly, there must be a separate cell with dedicated staff at the district level to monitor the projects. In other words, it wanted effective macro-level monitoring by the Union government and micro-level monitoring in the states.[9]

While all this is legitimate given the opinion of NABCONS surveyors on these matters, the silence of the committee on other aspects of the sample survey report is indeed deafening and is indicative of the obsession of the committee members with their privileges and their reluctance to acknowledge, let alone set right, issues touching upon violation of guidelines and unethical practices by MPs. Here are some examples of violation of guidelines by MPs (and the kind of projects they sanctioned), about which the committee makes no observation although its report lists them all: 'Assets' allegedly created under the scheme which 'could not be traced' by the surveyors; construction of community halls etc., within religious places in gross violation of guidelines; construction of shopping complexes to promote private enterprise; diversion of computers bought for schools to commercial enterprises; supply of computers to private educational institutions; community centres built with MPLADS funds being commercially let out by the beneficiary agencies; and repeat expenditure on a length of road via MPLADS after the very same contract has been 'executed' under MLALADS—a similar constituency development scheme for state legislators.[10]

Here are the details: NABCONS reports that a sum of ₹25 lakh was sanctioned from the MPLADS fund for the construction of a 'women maternity shed' at Thongkhong, Lakshmi Bazaar in Imphal West district, Manipur. A library costing ₹5 lakh was sanctioned in the same district at Langol as also a road branching off from National Highway 39 for ₹4 lakh. The surveyors could not trace any of these assets![11]

Similarly in Sikkim (East district), two sanctioned projects—improvement of the link road at Lingdum and the construction of a playground and fencing at Cheda School, Deorali—'could not be located by the study team as also by the official of the rural, management and development department'.[12]

In the 1960s and '70s, the Union government offered assistance to states which launched employment guarantee schemes in drought-hit regions. Severe drought conditions often prevailed in many states, leading to loss of jobs for the rural poor and loss of lives from starvation. Several schemes were thought of to alleviate the suffering of millions of people in these states. One such was a food-for-work programme which gave rural workers employment during a drought year. The workers would get a substantial part of their wages in the form of foodgrains. They were to be assigned tasks that would result in the creation of durable assets in the villages. The idea was that the monies spent on drought relief would result in communities having something tangible, like a freshwater tank, a primary school, a healthcare centre or a road. However, like many other great ideas that have floundered, this too, failed to yield the required results because in most cases corrupt politicians and bureaucrats ganged up with contractors and used these funds to build roads and tank bunds that would be washed away in the first showers after the drought. The muster rolls of workers were fudged, substandard materials were used and the government was billed for a project that was worthless. A couple of years later, the region would once again be afflicted with drought and the politician-bureaucrat-contractor mafia would draw huge sums of money to build the very same roads or tank bunds. That is why, although billions of rupees were spent over the last fifty years in the name of drought relief, there are no durable assets worth the name in India's villages.

One is reminded of this ugly nexus between the politician, the bureaucrat and the contractor in implementing drought-relief programmes when one sees the report of the NABCONS surveyors from Manipur, Sikkim and the Agra district of Uttar Pradesh. The surveyors inspected a 2.60 kilometre road from Gadi Ramsukh to the house of the village's 'pramukhji' (headman). The first question that arises is why public money is being spent to build a road right up to the house of the village headman. But, this is a minor infringement compared to the more serious issue—possibly one of fraud—which is at hand. The surveyors found that this road had already been constructed with the MPLADS fund. Now, it was being taken up once again for 'upgradation' under MPLADS. The surveyors also inspected a 1.15 kilometre road from Nagla Badli towards Dayalbagh in the same district. During 2001-02, a sum of ₹9.03 lakh was spent from MPLADS for upgradation of the road from earth work to soiling. However, the very next year, in 2002–03, the same road was further 'upgraded' at a cost of ₹9.32 lakh with MPLADS funds.

Reports from the Murshidabad district in West Bengal indicate that MPLADS funds were ploughed into eleven road-building works which fell into the 'repair and renovation' category, prohibited by the guidelines. 'Repair and renovation' is obviously barred because of the terrible experience of 'renovating' roads under rural development and drought-relief programmes in the past. Yet, MPs flagrantly violate the rules and sanction such projects which are seen to be dubious in nature. The other disturbing aspect of this road 'renovation' exercise is that the DA released the full sanctioned amount in a single instalment for all these works to the agency which got these contracts.[13]

Similar instances of road 'improvement' were reported from Karnataka. In Bangalore rural districts, the surveyors found that twenty-six of the thirty road works sanctioned related to 'road improvement'. In the Bijapur district, the surveyors found six such works which are barred by the guidelines.[14] The Lok Sabha Committee on MPLADS, however, has nothing to say about any of these cases.

Equally serious is the finding by surveyors that in the Haridwar district, Uttarakhand, the Rohtak district, Haryana, and the Ranchi district, Jharkhand, several crores of rupees have been spent from MPLADS funds to promote the interests of private trusts and societies or NGOs. The most shocking case detected by surveyors relates to the Haridwar district where eighteen works costing ₹2.40 crore were allocated to a single NGO called Delta Development Agency.[15] This constitutes a gross violation of the guidelines, which clearly prohibits repeated grant of contracts to private agencies.

The report from Rohtak is that as many as nine projects have been funded via MPLADS for just one organization—the Aurobindo Institute of Indian Culture—which is a trust. These nine projects involved a financial sanction of ₹1.29 crore between March 1999 and July 2003. This is extraordinary because the guidelines at that time did not permit allocation of MPLADS funds to societies, trusts and NGOs. Further, even though such allocations were permitted later, the guidelines stipulated that the investment in a trust or society can be done only for a single project, not exceeding ₹25 lakh. Finally, even more shocking was the report of the surveyors that although a sum of ₹1.29 crore had been invested in a single institution obviously run by individuals, 'no inspection had been done by the district authority'.[16]

Another case of a similar nature was reported by the surveyors from the Ranchi district of Jharkhand where they found that a sum of ₹53.89 lakh had been spent on four works for a single trust called the Purshree Trust.[17]

Spending MPLADS funds—which is public money—on religious places is a complete taboo as far as the guidelines are concerned. But, going by the sample survey, this is observed more in the breach. The surveyors found a number of cases of violation of guidelines in regard to non-investment of funds in religious places in the state of Goa. In the South Goa district they found seven MPLADS schemes—construction of community halls—within or near religious places. Most of these violations related to religious places in Quepem, Gogal and Ponda.[18]

Similar violations were noticed in the Aurangabad district, Maharashtra. The surveyors found four cases wherein these funds were used to build what are described as 'cultural halls' in lands belonging to temple trusts. In the Ahmednagar district in the same state, the surveyors said they found cultural halls being constructed near temples 'or temples were constructed inside community halls'.[19]

Another category of misuse of MPLADS is misrepresentation of the purpose of the proposed work or encroachment of the constructed property once it is ready. For example, in the Ahmednagar district of Maharashtra, a sabhamandap was constructed near a mosque. The surveyors found that 'scrap dealer Mr Hussain Banemia (was) using it for storing scrap and it was used as animal shed'. Similarly, in the same state a 'Samskruthik Bhavan' (cultural centre) at Sangamner 'was locked for all time' and the milk society had the key to the hall whereas the key to the cultural hall at Hatgaon 'was with a private doctor'.

In the same state, in the Chandrapur district, Gandhi Chowk was beautified at Warora Tal but the asset is being used by small transport operators 'in blatant change of the usage'. In another instance, a stage has been constructed in a high school and has now become the home of a homeless family.[20]

Misuse of MPLADS money to promote private enterprise or commercial activity of organizations is an equally serious violation of the guidelines, but it appears to be happening on a scale that should cause worry for all those who hold public money in trust. Here are some disturbing examples, apart from the glaring misuse of these funds to promote privately owned trusts. In the Jorhat district of Assam, these funds are used to renovate a college hostel and a principal's room and to provide marble flooring in a building; community halls are constructed in two religious places; some works meant for public use remain locked up and a public facility is being used for a commercial purpose; in the Gaya district, Bihar, these funds are used to build a hall for a Bar Association (which is prohibited by the guidelines).[21]

In Goa, the surveyors found private coaching classes being conducted in a gymnasium built with these funds. Similarly, a public health centre built for the Lions Club in Marmagoa has been rented out to a medical general practitioner.[22]

In the Rewa district, Madhya Pradesh, a sum of ₹6.1 lakh was spent on an X-ray machine given to the president of a privately owned medical facility. In the Bhopal district in the same state, a sum of ₹7 lakh each was spent on the creation of two buildings in hospitals, but the surveyors doubted whether these buildings were available to people free of charge. In one instance, they found the hospital staff were staying in the building.[23]

In the Shimla district, Himachal Pradesh, a multipurpose complex was constructed at a cost of ₹3 lakh and handed over to some private business people for profit. This complex now works as a business hub.[24]

The surveyors found that the computers purchased with MPLADS funds for two private schools had been diverted for commercial use by the managements of these institutions.[25]

In the Aurangabad district of Maharashtra, a concrete road was constructed at Pratapnagar exclusively for the benefit of a private housing colony. Also, the road was built on privately owned land, the ownership of which is under dispute.[26]

The police forces do not have adequate accommodation for rest and recuperation between duty schedules. This is a reality across the country and so, it is quite common for policemen—especially in the lower rungs of the force—to beseech MPs for help. Often, MPs respond to these entreaties purely out of humanitarian considerations and offer MPLADS funds to build something or the other for these policemen. The only problem is that the guidelines do not permit such spending. Any item of expenditure that falls within the standard budgeted spending of the state or the Union government is not permitted. But, MPs recommend such works and the district authorities execute them. For example, in the Ranchi district, Jharkhand, a sum of ₹35 lakhs has been spent on an auditorium and six rooms to serve as a 'police building' and a guest house for the Jharkhand Armed Police.[27]

In Bijapur district, Karnataka, an MP has sanctioned a cultural building at a police ground, which is being used by the Police Welfare Association.[28]

The report from the Raigarh district, Chhattisgarh, is that a sum of ₹5.62 lakh has been spent on a mango nursery and to grow horticultural crops, but the surveyors were clueless about who or which agency owned and managed this nursery. In the Chittoor district of Andhra Pradesh, the premises of a 'godown' in the Mandal Parishad, Punganur, and a community hall at V. Kota are used as commercial shopping arcades and rented out by the Mandal Parishad; a building has been constructed for the Prohibition and Excise Employees Welfare and Computerization Centre making it an asset for an association of employees and not for the general public; MPLADS funds are invested to complete work on a mutton and fish market, although these funds are not to be invested on incomplete works or on commercial ventures like shops.[29]

Surveyors found that a huge sum of money—₹63 lakh—was spent to construct a commercial market complex at Khumbong in the Imphal West district of Manipur and another sum of ₹24 lakh was sanctioned for a working women's hostel, which is actually a commercial establishment.[30]

Instances of investment in shopping complexes were also found in Kilchettipattu and three other villages in the Thiruvannamalai district of Tamil Nadu.[31]

MPLADS funds were used to build what is called a mathemathical lab in a private school in the Kurukshetra district, Haryana and to construct a room for the Kashyap Rajput Sabha, which is obviously a caste association.[32]

There are also instances of district officials using MPLADS for ineligible construction within or around the district collector's office. In the Chandrapur district of Maharashtra, a waiting hall was built at the collector's office as also 'a multipurpose hall'. There are also 'Kisan Bhavans' built with this money but the exact purpose of these buildings is not known.[33]

Lawyers seem to have considerable influence on MPs and often get parliamentarians to put in MPLADS money to build their association premises. This happens in many parts of the country and results in regular violation of the guidelines, which clearly state that these funds should not be used to benefit organizations of professionals or such closed groups or to build assets that are not open to the general public. Field reports from Ghaziabad in Uttar Pradesh indicate that a 600-square-foot hall has been built using these funds for the Bar Association of Ghaziabad to accommodate lawyers, who use the premises for their offices. In the same state, in Bareilly, a Bar Association building has been constructed with MPLADS funds and the same is used by lawyers to set up their offices.[34]

Likewise, the lawyers of Bijapur coaxed their MP to part with some funds to build the Lawyers' Association building, which is meant for lawyers only.[35]

There are also many instances of the assets created under this scheme being idle for long periods of time. The surveyors of NABCONS found that a Primary Health Centre at Ulandai in Vandavasi block in the Thiruvannamalai district, Tamil Nadu, was constructed in 2006, but was yet to be put to use, four years after it got ready.[36]

Two more such appalling instances came to light when the surveyors went around Puducherry. A community hall was built in Vadukuppam in Ariakuppam block. The project was completed on 28 August 2006, but it had not been opened to the public because it was 'awaiting inauguration by the MP'. Similarly, a community hall in Ramji Nagar in the same block was of 'no use' to the people, because 'it had not been formally inaugurated'. Is there no limit to the self-importance of public representatives?[37]

The random sampling of MPLADS works by NABCONS shows that there is a gross violation of the guidelines in many cases. If MPs and bureaucrats are allowed to get away with this, the loss to the public exchequer is certain to be substantial since the annual allocation for the scheme has been raised by 150 per cent.

NOTES

1. Fourth Report, Committee on MPLADS, Fifteenth Lok Sabha, Lok Sabha Secretariat, presented to the Lok Sabha on 11 August 2011.
2. *The Indian Express*, New Delhi, Friday, 16 September 2011.
3. Press Trust of India, posted online Monday, 19 September 2011.
4. *The Indian Express*, New Delhi, 17 September 2011.
5. Fourth Report, Committee on MPLADS, Fifteenth Lok Sabha, Lok Sabha Secretariat, presented to the Lok Sabha on 11 August 2011, p. 40.
6. Ibid., pp. 41–44.
7. Ibid., pp. 50–53.
8. Ibid., p. 44.
9. Ibid., pp. 44–48.
10. Ibid., pp. 55–71.
11. Ibid., p. 64.
12. Ibid., p. 66.
13. Ibid., p. 70.
14. Ibid., p. 60.
15. Ibid., p. 69.
16. Ibid., p. 58.
17. Ibid., p. 59.
18. Ibid., p. 57.
19. Ibid., pp. 62–63.
20. Ibid., p. 63.
21. Ibid., p. 55–56.
22. Ibid., p. 57.
23. Ibid., pp. 61–62.
24. Ibid., p. 59.
25. Ibid., p. 68.
26. Ibid., p. 62.
27. Ibid., p. 59.
28. Ibid., p. 60.
29. Ibid., p. 55.
30. Ibid., p. 64.
31. Ibid., p. 66.
32. Ibid., p. 58.

33. Ibid., p. 63.
34. Ibid., p. 68.
35. Ibid., p. 60.
36. Ibid., p. 66.
37. Ibid., p. 71.

Conclusion

Should MPs be Bogged Down With Local Development

Even before the launch of MPLADS in India, there has been a debate in the country on the role of parliamentarians. Since MPs are peoples' representatives who are elected to a legislature at the federal level, where much of the deliberations have a national and even international perspective, it is often asked as to whether MPs should get bogged down in village-level development in their constituencies. MPs are essentially lawmakers with a national responsibility and, therefore, ought to be focused on this larger responsibility, according to academics. But the ground reality is quite different, especially in developing societies like India. Over the years, electors in India have begun to value their vote a great deal and have stepped up their demands on elected representatives. They expect their MPs and MLAs to be on call 24x7, which is not easy because of the size of the constituencies both in demographic and geographic terms. A Lok Sabha MP currently represents over 2 million people, of whom about 1.5 million are electors. Many rural constituencies stretch to over 200–300 kilometres end to end and have hundreds of villages and dozens of small towns. Barring those who have no desire to return to Parliament, all other MPs are perpetually on tour. The three sessions of Parliament are spread over five months.

During these sessions, most Lok Sabha MPs fly back to their constituencies over the weekend to attend to constituency-level programmes and return to Delhi on Monday morning. In the seven months when Parliament is not in session, much of the time is spent in the constituency, except when an MP has to attend a meeting of a parliamentary committee in the capital or travel with it to other parts of the country.

It is simply not possible for an MP to even meet his constituents once during a five-year term. But, the people are unrelenting in their demand that the MP show up in their village or town as and when they want him. Since most MPs fail this test, barbs are flung at them at every stop when they launch their campaign for a second term. 'So, now that elections have been announced, you are back! Where were you the last five years?' is a common refrain across constituencies all over the country. Most Indian MPs treat this as a professional hazard and brazen it out for a fortnight. They know that once the election is over, public anger over their so-called absenteeism will subside. Meanwhile, MPLADS has come as a godsend for all MPs who sincerely believe that they must be seen as doing something worthwhile and specific within their constituencies and that they must 'give' something tangible to their constituents. Also, it must be something that is visible and that which reminds the people of the MP's commitment to them and advertises his good intentions and deeds—like bus shelters, water tanks, bridges and buildings which loudly proclaim that they are built out of MPLADS funds by the particular MP. Such MPs sincerely believe that their primary loyalty is to their constituencies and not to Parliament.

There are many reasons why MPLADS is popular with MPs. For diligent Lok Sabha MPs who feel that they owe a duty to their constituents, the scheme enables them to earmark some funds for projects that will alleviate hardship for people living in a village or in some part of a town in the constituency. Given the terrible living conditions in large parts of the country, electors are grateful if an MP can set apart some funds for construction of toilets or to draw a pipeline to bring drinking water to a village. This will end the drudgery of hundreds of women who have to trudge many miles to a water source and back. Once MPLADS got rolling, MPs have begun to see a change in the way their constituents treat them. Instead of hurling insults at them for not being around, electors meet MPs these days with demands for projects that will make life a little better for them. When these projects are executed, the results are obvious and visible to everyone. Plaques announcing the good work of MPs are now strewn all across constituencies. In a sense, they also announce the presence of the MP and his commitment to the people who have elected him. So, MPs who fully and wisely utilize MPLADS funds over a five- or ten-year period are bound to have good visibility in their constituencies and are unlikely to face jibes from their constituents when they set out yet again to seek a fresh mandate. Since a majority of MPs want to come back to Parliament, MPLADS is the panacea to the problem of convincing electors that they are around and that they have the constituency's best interests in mind much of the time.

All this however does not apply to members of the Rajya Sabha, because unlike the Lok Sabha MPs, they have no constituency that is geographically demarcated. They are not elected directly by the people. Instead, most of them are elected by members of the legislative assembly of each state. A few are nominated by the president. Broadly speaking, Rajya Sabha MPs treat the state they are elected from, as their constituency. Since they do not come to Parliament through direct election, they do not have pressures like their counterparts in the Lok Sabha. Therefore, they have far greater flexibility to spend their MPLADS funds. There is also no fear of people taunting them for not being around.

There is another reason why MPLADS is popular with MPs—it offers some of them great scope for corruption. While a majority of MPs utilize the scheme to choose projects that would help their constituents and allow the DAs to execute them in the best way possible, there are many MPs who see MPLADS as a milch cow. Until 2011, they had ₹2 crore at their disposal every year and used some part of it for non-productive schemes because they were assured of 'a cut' by the IA. Now, they have ₹5 crore a year to squander on projects that are not on their constituents' priority list. The scope for corruption is much higher among Rajya Sabha members because they are not as accountable to the people as their Lok Sabha counterparts. The three reports of the CAG on the working of this scheme and several other sample surveys done by the government and other agencies have thrown up a host of anomalies in the working of MPLADS, the most important of which is the contempt that MPs show for the guidelines.[1]

Impact of MPLADS on Quality of Work in Parliament

With the increase in the corpus of MPLADS, parliamentarians will be called upon to devote much more time to their constituencies and to the infrastructural needs of their electors. This will mean sanction of many more works, their supervision, monitoring of complaints, etc. and thereafter, the formal inauguration of each of these projects. This will keep MPs much more engaged in their constituencies. Consequently, this is bound to diminish the time MPs have for their parliamentary duties. It is a safe bet to conclude that this will have a negative impact on the quality of debates in Parliament; the quality of questions that come up during Question Hour; attendance levels in the two Houses and in parliamentary committees; and on the quality of work MPs do in these committees.

Yet, since the Supreme Court has declared the scheme to be constitutionally valid, one is inclined to give it a fair trial, provided Parliament ensures strict adherence to guidelines.

The CAG has audited MPLADS on three occasions in the past eighteen years and in each of these audits, the auditors have expressed concern over the lack of supervision of this scheme at the district level. It is generally noticed that the district administration neither has the inclination nor the time to monitor the scheme. The general impression is that the district administration does not have the resources to handle this responsibility.

Now that the funds available to each MP has been raised to ₹5 crore, the absence of an administrative infrastructure at the district level to keep a watchful eye on the scheme is a major lacuna and can result in the misuse of thousands of crores of rupees annually. However, despite the magnitude of the loss that the exchequer can suffer as a result of the enhanced corpus of MPLADS, the government does not appear to have any plan on hand to inject some efficiency into the implementation of the scheme. When the auditors drew the attention of the government to these wastages, the MS&PI promised that it would obtain information on each case from the DAs 'for necessary action'. The works which have not yet been started would be cancelled and in case of irregularities 'necessary instructions would be issued to DAs for fixing the responsibilities and suitable disciplinary action'.

Should MPLADS be Scrapped?

Members of Parliament in other democracies do not have funds at their disposal to spend on local area development and please their constituents. That is why in India, the media and civil society wonder whether it is in public interest to allow parliamentarians to cross the Lakshman rekha and intrude into the space of the executive via MPLADS. Such a development, it is often argued, is antithetical to the principle of separation of powers. The introduction of the scheme has also raised legitimate concerns about accountability and transparency in regard to the manner in which these sums are spent. Scholars wonder whether it is in public interest to put so much money in the hands of MPs and allow them to spend on projects that are outside the scheme of the planned development of districts.

Since there is no scheme like MPLADS in other democracies, the public perception is that as always, the Indian politician had strayed outside the field of best democratic practices. It is said that MPs have taken the excuse of underdevelopment and bureaucratic apathy towards the felt needs of India's poor and cunningly devised a scheme that in effect has created a new grazing ground for the corrupt. When the scheme was launched, the people had no idea of the MPLADS guidelines or about how the scheme worked. They were, and still are, unaware of the fact that the scheme works on the 'MP proposes, bureaucrat disposes' principle. They believe that every MP has ₹5 crore every year in his kitty and can spend this amount according to his whim. They are unaware of the fact that the projects proposed by MPs cannot be implemented unless they are approved and sanctioned by the district collector. Nor are they aware that the district collector has to choose the IA and that schemes that figure in the negative list cannot be funded by MPs. While there are instances of these rules being broken, the basic premise on which the scheme is built holds good in a majority of cases. In all such instances, when an MP and a district collector work in consonance with the guidelines, the scheme is hailed by constituents as a harbinger of speedy development.

Despite all the criticism that has been heaped on the scheme, the committees of the two Houses of Parliament offer a stout defence of MPLADS. The Lok Sabha Committee on MPLADS has argued that the scheme was not started 'as an incentive or facility' for an MP but 'to provide scope for a more pro-active role in the need-based development of the local areas'. It said MPs derive their legitimacy from the fact that they are peoples' representatives and they possess an intuitive understanding of their needs. 'This is the very axiomatic edifice on which MPLAD Scheme is based and the scheme envisages, through a recommendatory role, for a more direct involvement of the Members of Parliament in the betterment of people. In fact, the scheme attempts to foster a symbiotic relationship between the people and their representatives in an innovative manner. The MPLADS is basically a constituency development fund in which the MP plays a catalytic role.'[2]

As regards the constitutional validity of the scheme, the Lok Sabha Committee appreciatively quotes the MS&PI's opinion that the scheme 'has the authority of law as prescribed in the Constitution and is implemented in accordance with the constitutional provisions'. The committee's assertion that the scheme is within the framework of the Constitution stands reinforced by the unanimous verdict of a constitutional bench of the Supreme Court in May 2010.

Further, the Lok Sabha Committee chose to address the issue of constitutionality and the argument on separation of powers in a different way. It claimed that the idea of MPLADS was 'in consonance with the current global thinking on development and the demands of the civil society, particularly in the context of under-developed and developing countries'. The scheme, it said, made provision 'for a more interventionist and pro-active role for parliamentarians at the ground level and in local community development'.[3]

The committee fully endorsed the view of the MS&PI that the scheme 'attempts to foster a symbiotic relationship between the people and their representatives in an innovative manner'. The Lok Sabha Committee also cited the responses it got when it solicited public opinion and suggestions on MPLADS. The committee secretariat received 200 responses and most of the respondents have favoured the scheme's continuance.[4]

This is a strong defence of the scheme and it seems to be posited on the argument that democratic practices in developing societies must be in harmony with the ground situation in these countries. It also touches on the vibrancy of India's democracy and the scope offered by the Constitution for minor intrusions by one organ of the state into the domain of the other.

The Lok Sabha Committee that probed the improper conduct of MPs vis-à-vis MPLADS had a different take on the way the scheme was being used and misused. It was categorical that unscrupulous organizations had sprung up to usurp MPLADS funds.

Taking into account these observations of the CAG, the committee said, 'it was about time the Union Government revised the guidelines governing MPLADS to plug loopholes and lacunae to make it truly effective.' In the light of the scandal that it had investigated, the committee suggested that NGOs and private institutions should be barred from getting any funds under MPLADS. While making this suggestion the committee felt that the truth must be put on record in this matter. It said such a ban must be imposed because 'it is felt that most of such NGOs are merely facades for unscrupulous organisations formed to usurp funds from MPLADS, which are meant for community development works'.[5]

The committee also raised doubts as to whether MPLADS fell within the domain known as 'parliamentary duties'. It felt that the role of MPs in recommending works for execution 'cannot strictly be said to relate to their parliamentary duties'. It said every vibrant democracy demands that those who wield power as elected legislators should use it for the public good and not make it an instrument of self-seeking. 'This they can do effectively by personifying the highest standards of personal integrity, probity and rectitude.' It reminded every MP that as an elected representative of the people, a member's status is an exalted one. 'A dignified and ethical conduct by a legislator is one of the primary obligations of a Member of Parliament. Any misconduct by a legislator, whether inside the House or outside it, not only projects a legislator in poor light but also strikes at the very credibility of the democratic institution.'[6]

Despite the Supreme Court judgement certifying to the constitutional validity of the scheme, some scepticism in regard to its working would be in order, especially in view of the opinion of the Lok Sabha Committee that probed the MPLADS scandal, the opinion of the CAG of India, the legitimate concerns expressed by Mr Era Sezhiyan and Mr J.M. Lyngdoh and the available evidence about the misuse of the scheme by many MPs and the cases of corruption.

The NABCONS survey has thrown up disturbing facts. These have been discussed in detail in the earlier chapters, but a brief recall of some of these cases would be in order.

The guidelines prohibit MPs from identifying the IA because this is seen as the root cause of corruption. Yet, DAs often come under pressure to appoint an IA of the MP's choice. The auditors found evidence of MPs recommending IAs in nine states and UTs. In five selected districts, the auditors found that over 25 per cent of the works sanctioned were executed by private agencies, and strangely, when MPs recommended works for NGOs, clubs and educational institutions, the beneficiary institutions were themselves appointed as the IAs for the projects. The CAG also found that contracts were awarded without adopting standard tendering processes. Another irregularity was the absence of financial sanction and administrative approval. Auditors found that 26 per cent of the works were executed without sanction in four states that were surveyed by them.

The auditors have also come up with evidence which establishes fraud. Some samples of state- and district-level records showed misappropriation of funds in some states, including West Bengal, Jharkhand, Bihar and Mizoram. School classrooms which were 'constructed' by village education committees were nowhere to be found. An FIR had to be lodged with the police about the missing classroom! In Jharkhand a company took an advance of ₹8 lakh for installing solar water-pumps and vanished. In Bihar, officials of the National Rural Employment Programme (NREP) were duping the government by claiming MPLADS funds for roads already constructed. In Sikkim, funds from this scheme were used to construct anti-erosion bunds and walls to protect the private property of the MP and his relatives. Of twenty-two works sanctioned, all but one related to private property and in a dozen cases the contractors were also the beneficiaries. But, the biggest area of misuse is allocation of these funds to trusts and societies, often controlled by the MPs themselves. In ten states, the CAG found that funds in excess of the prescribed ceiling per society or trust had been released. In seven states, auditors found that 145 ineligible societies and trusts were given funds. Finally, the accounts are not audited regularly. The auditors found forty such districts. Strangely, the accounts of one DA in Jammu and Kashmir and another DA in Lakshadweep had not been audited since the inception of the scheme in 1993!

Actually, some of the cases discussed by the surveyors, which show blatant misuse of the scheme, warrant criminal investigation. Field reports which speak about public money having gone down the drain on works which were never executed are too serious for any agency or institution to gloss over. Similarly, diversion of crores of rupees from this fund to the coffers of private trusts, societies and NGOs, or to effect improvements in private property or to further the business interests of individuals, are infringements that warrant severest action. Each of these instances constitute a betrayal of trust by the MPs who recommended these works and in effect amount to gross misuse of public funds. The response of the parliamentary committee on MPLADS to all the evidence that was placed before it is disturbing. It had nothing to say on these aspects of the NABCONS survey. This raises the question as to whether people can rely on parliamentary committees to discipline members and protect public interest. If these instances do not stir the conscience of parliamentarians, what will? Further, if such apathy is the standard response of Parliament, can we continue with a scheme that puts so much money in the hands of MPs?

It must also be noted that the government has not taken any initiative to create the administrative infrastructure to monitor the scheme at the district level. Instead, it has raised the fund per MP per year to ₹5 crore. Since the outgo from the fiscal year 2011–12 will be close to ₹4,000 crore per annum, stricter enforcement of accountability norms both at the level of the MP and the district administration is an imperative. Side by side, Parliament will have to ensure greater vigilance to prevent MPLADS from becoming a moneymaking machine for unscrupulous public representatives.

MPLADS, therefore, deserves only a qualified thumbs-up. Since the Supreme Court has categorically and unequivocally declared that the scheme is constitutionally valid, it would be inappropriate to challenge the vires of the scheme all over again at this juncture. Instead, there is a need to mount pressure on Parliament to ensure that MPs adhere to the guidelines. The Union government must have the gumption to withhold funds to all MPs who fail to comply with the guidelines. There is also a need for 100 per cent transparency in the allocation of these funds and accountability in regard to implementation of the projects recommended by members. Finally, it must be said that even though the scheme is constitutionally valid, there will be no moral sanctity for its continuance if MPs do not adhere to the scheme's guidelines. Often, MPs tend to be rather brazen in violating the guidelines. It is as if they are throwing a challenge to the government and asking it to do whatever it wants. Now that the government has announced a humongous increase in the annual allocation for the scheme, it cannot shirk the responsibility of ensuring strict compliance with the guidelines. As everyone knows and as successive audit reports establish, non-compliance with guidelines is the starting point of corruption. Therefore, if MPs lack the discipline to conform to the guidelines, MPLADS must be scrapped.

NOTES

1. Report No. 31 of 2010–11, Comptroller and Auditor General of India, p. 25.
2. Fifteenth Report, Committee on MPLADS 2008–2009, presented to the Lok Sabha, 23 March 2010, Lok Sabha Secretariat, New Delhi, p. 12.
3. Ibid.

4. Ibid. p. 13.
5. Report of the Committee to Inquire into Allegations of Improper Conduct on the Part of Some Members in the Matter of Implementation of MPLAD Scheme, tabled in the Lok Sabha on 13 March 2006, Lok Sabha Secretariat, New Delhi, pp. 45–46.
6. Ibid.